Marketing Essentials

Student Activity Workbook with Academic Integration

Lois Schneider Farese

Grady Kimbrell

Carl A. Woloszyk, Ph.D.

McGraw Hill Glencoe

 **Glencoe**

The *McGraw Hill* Companies

Printed in the United States of America.

Send all inquiries to:
Glencoe/McGraw-Hill
21600 Oxnard St., Suite 500
Woodland Hills, CA 91367-4908

ISBN 978-0-07-878038-7 (Student Edition)
MHID 0-07-878038-1 (Student Edition)

ISBN 978-0-07-878039-4 (Teacher Annotated Edition)
MHID 0-07-878039-X (Teacher Annotated Edition)

1 2 3 4 5 6 7 8 9   079   12 11 10 09 08

CONTENTS

Chapter 1 Marketing Is All Around Us

Note Taking
Main Ideas and Supporting Details

Directions As you read, write key words and short phrases in the Cues column. Write notes, facts, and main ideas in the Note Taking column. Then summarize the section in the Summary box.

Cues	Note Taking
• Marketing and the Marketing Concept	• Marketing and the Marketing Concept
• The Importance of Marketing	• The Importance of Marketing
• Fundamentals of Marketing	• Fundamentals of Marketing

Summary

Chapter 1 Chapter 1

Chapter 1 Marketing Is All Around Us

 ## Academic Integration: Mathematics
Creating a Spreadsheet

Production Costs and Profit The price a manufacturer can obtain for its product is determined by the market. So the lower the production cost, the higher the manufacturer's profit. For example, if a product costs $7 per unit when 10,000 are produced and $6 per unit when 20,000 are produced, the profit will be $1 more per unit for the production quantity of 20,000 units.

	A	B	C	D	E
1	# of Units	Price	Unit Cost	Profit	
2	5,000	$9.00	$6.00	$3.00	
3	10,000	$9.00			
4	15,000	$9.00			
5	20,000	$9.00			
6	25,000	$9.00			
7	30,000	$9.00			
8	35,000	$9.00			

Directions Follow these steps to create a spreadsheet to determine how profit changes when the production cost varies. Then answer the questions below.
- Turn on your computer and open your spreadsheet software program.
- Create a spreadsheet like the one above using your spreadsheet software program.
- Assume that a product costs $6 to produce in a quantity of 5,000. For each additional 5,000 produced, the cost decreases by $0.10 up to 30,000 units. Thereafter, the cost increases again by $0.10. In column C of the spreadsheet, input the fixed unit cost for each level of production.
- Enter a formula in cell D3 to determine the profit for each quantity produced. To determine the profit, subtract cell C from cell B (subtract unit cost from price).
- Print out a copy of your work if your teacher has instructed you to do so.

1. At which level of production will the manufacturer have the highest profit per unit?

   _____

2. Why do you think a manufacturer's fixed cost of producing a product would not just continue to decrease as a larger quantity is produced, regardless of the amount?

   _____

   _____

   _____

Chapter 1 Marketing Is All Around Us

 ## Real-World Application
Functions and Utilities of Marketing

Directions For each of the examples noted below, write the function of marketing that it describes. Select from the following seven marketing core functions: channel management, market planning, marketing information management, pricing, product/service management, promotion, and selling.

Function	Example
_____	**1.** A retail store employee puts a pair of shoes on a customer and asks how they feel.
_____	**2.** A retailer decides to mark down all swimsuits in August.
_____	**3.** A team of workers approach customers in a mall to ask them their opinion about the upcoming political election and the candidates running for office.
_____	
_____	**4.** A television commercial stresses the benefits of buying a new protein bar.
_____	**5.** A company develops specific marketing strategies to target a select audience.
_____	**6.** A small manufacturer applies for a bank loan in order to upgrade its computer network.
	7. A manufacturer of apparel signs a contract with a company that specializes in trucking and warehousing of imported goods.

Directions For each of the following examples, write the economic utility that it describes. Economic utilities include: form, place, possession, time, and information.

Utility	Example
_____	**8.** Adding aloe to hand soap.
_____	**9.** Offering installment credit in the sale of appliances.
_____	**10.** Including a link on a company Web site that explains how to return used laser printer ink cartridges.
_____	**11.** Offering overnight delivery of candy and fresh flowers on February 13.
_____	**12.** A company Web site offering the sale of its products directly to consumers.

Chapter 1 Marketing Is All Around Us

Real-World Application
Key Marketing Concepts

Directions Read the following scenario, keeping in mind these key concepts: the four Ps of the marketing mix, industrial market, consumer market, customer profile, and market share. Below, note the details of this scenario related to each concept.

Scenario An apparel manufacturer makes garments for sports-related activities. A major portion of its business is selling sports-related garments to high schools, colleges, and professional sports teams. The other portion of its business focuses on young males and females who buy sports-related apparel for their personal use. These young adults are between the ages of 20 and 35 with household incomes of more than $50,000. They are active and fashion conscious. The garments are designed to be comfortable. They use fabrics that are currently in fashion and are priced a little higher than those of most competitors. The company has 40 percent of the athletic apparel market. Some of the reasons for its popularity are the use of professional athletes to endorse this brand and the extensive advertising done in broadcast and print media. Sports-related magazines like *Sports Illustrated*, *Golf*, *Tennis*, and *Health & Fitness* are used to promote the brand. Consumers can purchase these products in specialty sports shops and major department stores.

1. The Four Ps of the Marketing Mix

   _____

   _____

   _____

2. Industrial Market

   _____

   _____

3. Consumer Market

   _____

4. Customer Profile

   _____

   _____

5. Market Share

   _____

Chapter 1 Marketing Is All Around Us

 DECA Connection
Marketing Consultant

Role Play Imagine that you are a marketing consultant. A craftsman (judge) is trying to decide if he wants to expand his business and invest in marketing activities. The craftsman has little formal business experience. He has been selling his wares in local craft shows for the past five years. He has hired you to advise him on the marketing core functions involved with this possible expansion. His customer base includes a few people who have hired him to make unique crafts for their homes and as gifts. He has the customers' e-mail addresses in a database but he has never used it.

Directions Role-play a meeting with the craftsman (judge) during which you share your ideas. Use your knowledge of marketing to explain the benefits of marketing, and how the functions of marketing can help him grow his business. Organize your thoughts around the performance indicators noted below. Use them to jot down your ideas during the preparation period. Time your preparation to last 15 minutes and your role play to last a maximum of ten minutes.

Assessment You will be evaluated on how well you meet the following performance indicators:

Score:

_____ Distinguish between economic goods and services.

_____ Determine forms of economic utility created by marketing activities.

_____ Describe marketing functions and related activities.

_____ Describe current business trends.

_____ Explain the concept of marketing strategies.

Scoring Assume each performance indicator is worth 20 points (20 × 5 = 100 points). Use the evaluation levels listed below for judging consistency.

Excellent (16–20) Participant demonstrated the performance indicator in a professional manner, exceeds business standards.

Good (10–15) Participant demonstrated the performance indicator in an acceptable manner; meets minimal business standards; there would be no need for additional formalized training at this time.

Fair (4–9) Participant demonstrated the performance indicator with limited effectiveness; performance generally fell below minimal business standards; additional training would be required to improve.

Poor (0–3) Participant demonstrated the performance indicator with little or no effectiveness; a great deal of formal training is needed.

Chapter 1

Chapter 1 Marketing Is All Around Us

Study Skills
Building Vocabulary

Directions Read the tips on building vocabulary. Use them as you review the chapter. Then complete the activity by crossing out the word in each group that does not belong with the others. Write a sentence telling what the remaining terms have in common.

Building Vocabulary
• As you read, circle or jot down unfamiliar or key terms.
• Write the dictionary definition of terms with which you are unfamiliar.
• Describe terms in your own words, and indicate your mental image of each term.
• Use the term in a sentence.

1. selling   financing   pricing   communications skills

_____

2. assemble   inform   persuade   remind

_____

3. lower prices   new products   higher prices   improved products

_____

4. time   possession   sales   information

_____

5. consumer   industrial   segmented   utility

_____

6. product   market   place   price

_____

7. credit cards   promotion   personal checks   layaway plans

_____

8. understanding business   interpersonal skills   economics   research

_____

9. displays   advertising   owner's manuals   charge accounts

_____

10. product   income   ethnic background   age

_____

Chapter 1 Marketing Is All Around Us

Study Skills
Test Preparation

Directions Study the Test-Prep Tips and think about how you can use them to improve your test scores. Write a sentence or two to answer each of the following questions about the main ideas in Chapter 1.

Test-Prep Tips
• Make sure to write an answer for every question on a short-answer or essay test.
• Proofread your answers to eliminate errors.
• Include important details in your answers to short-answer and essay questions.

1. What is the purpose of customer relationship management? _____

_____

2. What is an example of *information utility*? _____

_____

3. How are goods and services alike and different? _____

_____

4. What are the three main types of information companies look for when they conduct marketing research?

_____

5. What are some effects of marketing activity and the competition it generates?

_____

6. Making purchasing easy by accepting credit cards, debit cards, and checks, and offering layaway plans is an example of which type of utility?

_____

7. What characteristics define a market? _____

_____

8. What are the promotional strategies in a marketing campaign designed to do?

_____

Chapter 1 Marketing Is All Around Us

 Test-Taking
Practice Test

Directions Take the practice test. Choose the word or phrase that best completes the sentence or answers the question.

1. Which areas of skill and knowledge are part of the study of marketing?
    a. calculus and statistics
    b. human development and psychology
    c. economics and entrepreneurship
    d. intelligence and mental health

2. What does good marketing planning require?
    a. collecting and analyzing data
    b. understanding business systems
    c. making a profit
    d. informing through advertising

3. What is the main purpose of the selling process?
    a. to consider consumer wants and needs
    b. to create a database about customers
    c. to promote social responsibility
    d. to influence the purchasing decision

4. Which is likely to lower the unit cost of producing a product?
    a. greater variety of product choice
    b. a general softening of the market
    c. decreased demand for a product
    d. increased demand for a product

5. What is most often the main goal of a retail business to which you are selling your product?
    a. satisfying customers
    b. understanding the market
    c. increasing profit
    d. mass merchandising

6. What is a target market?
    a. a group of people most likely to become customers
    b. a group of people most likely to be similar in age
    c. a group of people similar to one already identified
    d. a group of people identified by using market research

Chapter 2 The Marketing Plan

Note Taking
Main Ideas and Supporting Details

Directions As you read, write key words and short phrases in the Cues column. Write notes, facts, and main ideas in the Note Taking column. Then summarize the section in the Summary box.

Cues	Note Taking
• Marketing Planning	• Marketing Planning
• Market Segmentation	• Market Segmentation

Summary

Chapter 2

Chapter 2 The Marketing Plan

 Academic Integration: Social Studies
Analyzing a Database

Needs and Wants In order to be successful, businesses focus on satisfying the needs and wants of their customers. Marketers must clearly define the type of customer they want to reach. Then they need to continuously monitor their customers to determine if they are reaching their target market. Imagine that you own a bakery and have begun to assemble a database of information about your customers, as shown on the printout below.

Customer	Gender	Age	ZIP code	Income Range	Family Size
1	F	B	02138	A	3
2	M	A	02143	A	2
3	F	B	02138	B	4
4	F	B	02138	B	2
5	F	E	02143	B	3

Key: • Age: A=under 21; B=21–35; C=36–45; D=46–55; E=over 55
• Income Range: A=under $35,000; B=$35,000–$65,000; C=over $65,000

Directions Follow these steps to analyze the database and create a profile of your typical customer. Then answer the questions below.
• Turn on your computer and start your database software program.
• Create a database like the one above using database software.
• Sort the data by each of the following categories: gender, age, ZIP code, income range, and family size. After each sort, save your work to a different file.
• Print out a copy of your work if your teacher has instructed you to do so.

1. What is the profile of your core customer based on the data you collected?

_____

_____

2. What can you learn from your customer's ZIP codes? As a marketer, how can you use this information?

_____

_____

3. How does developing a customer profile benefit a marketer?

_____

_____

4. Why is it important for marketers to monitor their customers periodically?

_____

Chapter 2 *(side tab)*

Chapter 2 The Marketing Plan

 Real-World Application
SWOT Analysis

Losing Market Share Futura Fashions, Inc., is a hypothetical 100-store chain that caters to a teenage market. The stores carry male and female clothing and accessories. Sales at Futura Fashions have declined in recent months, and its stock price has dropped 30 percent. An analyst who follows the stock believes that the decline is due to a loss of talent in buying and merchandising. As a result, Futura Fashions has lost market share to its competitors. Competitors, such as American Eagle and Aeropostale, have had increases in sales of 14 percent and 27 percent, respectively. A recent report in *Women's Wear Daily*, a trade publication, indicates that a clothing manufacturer is considering opening its own retail stores that will target teens.

The teenage clothing market is difficult to evaluate. Trends are important. Either you catch them or your business suffers. So, Futura Fashions has recently hired an experienced fashion buyer and merchandise manager. The economy is strong. Consumer confidence is up and so is consumer spending. Recent reports indicate a decrease in jobless claims and an increase in employment. However, inflation is increasing slowly, so the Federal Reserve has increased interest rates a quarter of one percent, which could make consumers less inclined to spend.

Directions Use the information above to prepare a SWOT analysis for Futura Fashions, Inc.

Internal Strengths	Internal Weaknesses
External Opportunities	**External Threats**

Activity

On piece of paper, use the information from the SWOT analysis to develop recommendations for Futura Fashions. What should it do to get back on track?

Chapter 2 The Marketing Plan

 Real-World Application
Market Segmentation

Creating a New Product Line The Research and Development department of a fragrance company has been given the task of developing a new product line for a more price-conscious consumer. Below is a description of its current product line and its target market.

The current product line targets men and women in the baby boom generation with household incomes that exceed $150,000 a year. The men's and women's lines include fragrances, hair and skin care products, soaps, and shower gels. Although packaged differently, the men's and women's price ranges are similar. Prices range from $45 to $100 for individual items and from $90 to $195 for gift sets. Psychographic characteristics of this target market include an active lifestyle and a desire to be considered fashionable and chic. This fragrance is sold in upscale department stores in large U.S. cities and suburbs.

Directions Complete the market segmentation analysis below to create a customer profile for the new target market.

2. Demographics: _____

    Age: _____

    Income: _____

    Gender: _____

    Other: _____

2. Geographics: _____

3. Psychographics: _____

_____

    Activities: _____

    Attitudes: _____

    Personality & Values: _____

4. Behavioral: _____

☑ Activity

On a sheet of paper, list and explain your recommendations for a marketing mix to support the new product line. Describe the four Ps: product features such as design, special capabilities, and product name; place decisions such as type of retail store, Internet, and/or catalog; retail price; and ideas for promotion.

Chapter 2 The Marketing Plan

 ## DECA Connection
Marketing Internship

Role Play You are an intern in the marketing department of a clothing manufacturer. This manufacturer currently makes apparel for infants and toddlers. The demographics are changing, and the teenage market is growing, so the company wants to make clothes for preteens and teens. Since you are the youngest person on staff, the marketing director (judge) has asked for your input.

Directions Role-play a meeting with your marketing director (judge) during which you share your ideas. To prepare for the meeting, use your knowledge of marketing planning to create a written outline of all the information you would include in a formal marketing plan for this new clothing line. Provide examples of your suggestions.

Organize your thoughts around the performance indicators noted below. Use these performance indicators to jot down your ideas during the preparation period. Time your preparation to last 15 minutes and your role-play presentation to last a maximum of ten minutes. After your role play, use the performance indicators to evaluate your efforts.

Assessment You will be evaluated on how well you meet the following performance indicators:

Score:

_____   Explain the role of situational analysis in the marketing planning process.

_____   Identify fashion trends.

_____   Explain the concepts of market and market identification.

_____   Describe current business trends.

_____   Select a target market.

Scoring Each performance indicator equals 20 points (20 × 5 = 100 points).
Excellent (16–20)   **Good** (10–15)   **Fair** (4–9)   **Poor** (0–3)

Chapter 2 The Marketing Plan

Study Skills
Improving Concentration

Directions Use the following tips to help improve your concentration. Then review Chapter 2 using the tips as you answer the questions that follow. If the statement is true, circle **T**. If the statement is false, circle **F** and rewrite the statement so that it is true.

Improving Concentration
• Remove distractions such as telephones and televisions from your study area.   • Keep a clock nearby to time your study sessions. Take a short break every 20 minutes.   • As you are studying, remind yourself about what you are reading.

1. SWOT stands for "strengths, weaknesses, opportunities, and threats."   T   F

   _____

2. Marketers study customers' buying patterns because they provide insights into product offerings and pricing strategies.   T   F

   _____

3. An environmental scan is an analysis of internal company strengths and weaknesses.   T   F

   _____

4. Most companies increase the amount of money spent on research and development in times of recession.   T   F

   _____

5. Understanding key points of difference is important in marketing planning because they point to advantages a company, product, or service has over its competition.   T   F

   _____

6. A sustainable competitive advantage is one that enables a company to survive against its competition over a short period of time.   T   F

   _____

7. The terms Baby Boom, Generation X, and Generation Y segment the population according to income.   T   F

   _____

8. Disposable income is the money a family pays in taxes to the government.   T   F

   _____

Chapter 2 The Marketing Plan

 Study Skills
Test Preparation

Directions Study the Test-Prep Tips and think about how you can use them to improve your test scores. Write a sentence or two to answer each of the following questions about the main ideas in Chapter 2.

Test-Prep Tips
• Prepare for tests over a few days or weeks. Continually review class material.
• When preparing for a test, do not wait until the night before to try to learn everything at once.
• When studying from a textbook, read the chapter summaries. They summarize important points.

1. What aspects of a business should be considered when conducting an analysis of the internal factors that affect business operation?

   _____

2. What questions would you use to analyze a company's internal competitive position?

   _____

   _____

   _____

3. How can a company find opportunities to create a competitive advantage?

   _____

   _____

   _____

   _____

4. What constitutes an effective marketing strategy?

   _____

   _____

   _____

5. By what ways do marketers identify different market segments?

   _____

6. What four factors help marketers describe a target market?

   _____

   _____

Chapter 2

Chapter 2 The Marketing Plan

Test-Taking
Practice Test

Directions Take the practice test. Choose the word or phrase that best completes the sentence or answers the question.

1. When conducting a SWOT analysis, the internal aspect of the analysis is based on
   a. sales, advertising, and promotions.
   b. the company's strengths and weakness.
   c. political, economic, socio-cultural, and technological factors.
   d. market research findings.

2. To direct the marketing activities of a company, communicate its goals, objectives, and strategies, as well as monitor its performance you would
   a. conduct a SWOT analysis.
   b. conduct an environmental analysis.
   c. write a marketing plan.
   d. conduct marketing research.

3. What term is used to describe people born between 1946 and 1964?
   a. the baby boom generation
   b. Generation X
   c. Generation Y
   d. Generation Z

4. What do geographics, demographics, psychographics, and product benefits have in common?
   a. They are methods that can be used to segment a market.
   b. They are examples of mass-marketing approaches.
   c. They are terms used frequently in sales-oriented companies.
   d. They are unrelated to one another and therefore should not be used in combination to market a product.

5. The three phases of the marketing process are
   a. directing, controlling, and evaluating.
   b. planning, implementation, and control.
   c. segmenting a market, targeting a group, and promoting a product.
   d. analyzing, performing, and evaluating.

6. Segmenting the market based on product-related behavior involves looking at
   a. geographics and demographics.
   b. personality and values.
   c. mass marketing opportunities.
   d. benefits desired, shopping patterns, and usage rates.

Chapter 3 Political and Economic Analysis

 Note Taking
Main Ideas and Supporting Details

Directions As you read, write key words and short phrases in the Cues column.
Write notes, facts, and main ideas in the Note Taking column. Then summarize
the section in the Summary box.

Cues	Note Taking
• What Is an Economy?	• What Is an Economy?
• Understanding the Economy	• Understanding the Economy

Summary

Chapter 3

Chapter 3 Political and Economic Analysis

 Academic Integration: Mathematics
Analyzing a Spreadsheet

Productivity Increases in productivity help a company to maintain or increase its profit and keep prices competitive. The Dorris Company has three plants that make plastics used in the manufacturing of other products. Based on the printout below, the company wants to know which plant has the highest productivity.

	A	B	C	D	E	F	G
1	Plant	Workers	Hours	Weeks	Annual Hours	Annual Output	Average Productivity
2					(total worker hours)	(total units produced)	(units produced per worker per hour)
3							
4	A	800	40	52		2,000,000	
5	B	700	40	52		2,600,000	
6	C	900	40	52		1,800,000	

Directions Follow these steps to analyze the spreadsheet. Then answer the questions below.
- Open a spreadsheet software program on your computer.
- Create a spreadsheet like the one above using your spreadsheet application.
- Create a formula for cell E4 to calculate the annual worker hours for each plant by multiplying the number of workers by the hours in each week and the total weeks in a year. Copy the formula to cells E5 and E6. To complete the calculation, create a formula for cell G4 to divide the annual output by the annual hours to find the average productivity. Copy the formula to the remaining rows.
- After completing your calculations, save your work. Print out a copy of your work if your teacher has instructed you to do so. Then answer the questions that follow.

1. Which plant has the highest productivity? The lowest?

   _____

2. Why is worker productivity important to a manufacturing company?

   _____

   _____

3. Plant C uses older technology in its production processes, and the company is considering replacing this plant with a fully automated one in a new location. What are the problems and benefits for the workers and community when a company closes an old plant?

   _____

   _____

   _____

Chapter 3 Political and Economic Analysis

 Real-World Application
Comparing North and South Korea

Directions Read the information taken from the Central Intelligence Agency's *World Factbook* on North Korea and South Korea. Then answer the questions that follow.

North Korea, one of the world's most centrally planned and isolated economies, faces desperate economic conditions. Industrial capital stock is nearly beyond repair as a result of years of underinvestment and shortages of spare parts. Industrial and power outputs have declined in parallel. Due in part to severe summer flooding followed by dry weather conditions in the fall of 2006, the nation has suffered its 12th year of food shortages because of on-going systemic problems, including a lack of arable land, collective farming practices, and chronic shortages of tractors and fuel. In 2004, the regime formalized an arrangement whereby private "farmers' markets" were allowed to begin selling a wider range of goods. In October 2005, the regime reversed some of these policies. External food aid now comes primarily from China and South Korea. Firm political control remains the Communist government's overriding concern, which will likely inhibit the loosening of economic regulations.

Since the 1960s, South Korea has achieved an incredible record of growth and integration into the high-tech modern world economy. Four decades ago, GDP per capita was comparable with levels in the poorer countries of Africa and Asia. In 2004, South Korea joined the trillion dollar club of world economies. Today its GDP per capita is equal to the lesser economies of the EU. Led by consumer spending and exports, growth in 2002 was an impressive 7 percent, despite anemic global growth. Between 2003 and 2006, growth moderated to about 4 to 5 percent. A downturn in consumer spending was offset by rapid export growth. Moderate inflation, low unemployment, an export surplus, and fairly equal distribution of income characterize this solid economy.

1. How do the political systems of North Korea and South Korea differ?

_____

2. How would you categorize North Korea's and South Korea's economic system?

_____

_____

3. Why do you think South Korea's GDP per capita is so much greater?

_____

_____

Chapter 3

Chapter 3 Political and Economic Analysis

Real-World Application
Analyzing the Economy

Directions Read the article below. Then answer the questions that follow.

Despite their jitters, consumers are on track to increase their spending at an annual rate of about 3.5 percent in the third quarter. Second, companies may not be hiring in droves, but they are adding to their payrolls and going ahead with capital-spending projects. Business investment in new equipment accounted for more than a third of the growth in real gross domestic product in the second quarter. Lastly, the Fed sounded a bit more upbeat about the economy after its September 21 meeting than it did in August. As expected, policymakers hiked the federal funds rate by a quarter-point, to 1.75 percent. In its announcement, the Fed said the economy "appears to have regained some traction" and that labor markets have improved modestly, while inflation has eased. Uncertainty has been the hallmark of this recovery. Over the past three years, demand has been buffeted by a host of unknowns, from terrorism to corporate scandals to war. One area where consumers feel no jitters is housing. Americans still see home ownership as one of the best investments around. Low interest rates also suggest that worries about consumer debt levels are overblown. What the economy needs most are the conditions in which businesses and consumers feel more secure about making the investment and spending decisions that will drive this recovery into 2005.

(**Source:** From *BusinessWeek*, October 4, 2004, "What's Everyone So Rattled About?" by James C. Cooper and Kathleen Madigan)

1. Which goals of an economy are addressed in this article? Explain your answer.

_____

_____

_____

2. How are consumer spending and business investments related to growth in the GDP?

_____

_____

3. What factors suggest that the United States was in a period of economic recovery when the article was written?

_____

_____

Chapter 3

Chapter 3 Political and Economic Analysis

 **DECA Connection**
Drugstore Employee

Role Play Imagine you are a drugstore employee. The government recently passed legislation that involves a prescription drug program for Medicare recipients. One of your duties at work is to disseminate information to interested customers. You have been telling potential enrollees that they may be able to save money on brand name drugs as well as generic drugs. However, there is a $30 annual fee for the drug discount card.

Directions Role-play an encounter with an irate customer (judge) who is upset that the government does not provide free prescription drugs to the elderly, as many socialist countries provide.

Organize your thoughts around the performance indicators noted below. Use these performance indicators to jot down your ideas during the preparation period. Time your preparation to last 15 minutes and your role-play presentation to last a maximum of ten minutes. After your role play, use the performance indicators to evaluate your efforts.

Assessment You will be evaluated on how well you meet the following performance indicators:

Score:

_____ Explain the concept of economic resources.

_____ Determine the relationship between government and business.

_____ Describe the nature of current economic problems.

_____ Explain the types of economic systems.

_____ Show empathy for others.

Scoring Each performance indicator equals 20 points (20 × 5 = 100 points).
Excellent (16–20)　　　**Good** (10–15)　　　**Fair** (4–9)　　　**Poor** (0–3)

Chapter 3

Chapter 3 Political and Economic Analysis

 Study Skills
Vocabulary

Directions Match each definition with the correct term.

business cycle	consumer price index	inflation
capital	economy	infrastructure
capitalism	employee productivity	privatization
command economy	gross domestic product	scarcity

1. A measure of the goods and services produced using labor and property in the U.S.

   _____

2. The way a nation makes choices about how to use its resources.

   _____

3. The process of selling government-owned businesses to privat individuals.

   _____

4. Money needed to start and operate a business.

   _____

5. Stages an economy goes through due to recurring slowdown and growth.

   _____

6. Measure of the change in price over a set period of timeof some 400 specific goods and services used by the average urban household.

   _____

7. Measure of output divided by input of worker hours.

   _____

8. Difference between wants and needs on one hand and available resources on the other.

   _____

9. Economic system characterized by private ownership of businesses and marketplace competition.

   _____

10. In this type of economy, the government answers three basic economic questions: what, how, and for whom?

    _____

Chapter 3 Political and Economic Analysis

Study Skills
Test Preparation

Directions Study the Test-Prep Tips and think about how you can use them to improve your test scores. Write a sentence or two to answer each of the following questions about the main ideas in Chapter 3.

Test-Prep Tips
• Stay current on your reading and assignments. It is harder to catch up once you lag behind.
• Review the material on a regular basis.
• Practice taking the test with classmates before test day. Quiz each other on the material that will be on the test.

1. What are the three questions nations ask to define their economic system?

   _____

   _____

2. Who decides what should be produced in a command economy?

   _____

   _____

3. What is the role of the government in socialist countries?

   _____

   _____

   _____

4. What information is used to measure the state of an economy?

   _____

   _____

5. What is the consumer price index and what is it used for?

   _____

   _____

   _____

6. What are the key phases of the business cycle?

   _____

Chapter 3

Chapter 3 Political and Economic Analysis

Test-Taking
Practice Test

Directions Take the practice test. Choose the word or phrase that best completes the sentence or answers the question.

1. Low unemployment, an increase in the output of goods and services, and high consumer spending best illustrates the _____ period of the business cycle.
   a. expansion
   b. recession
   c. trough
   d. peak

2. The government answers all three economic questions in a _____.
   a. mixed economy
   b. market economy
   c. command economy that follows a communist model
   d. command economy that follows a socialist model

3. What can the government do to give a boost to a slowing economy?
   a. raise taxes
   b. lower taxes
   c. increase interest rates
   d. issue more government bonds

4. What is the productivity (output per worker hour) of a bicycle plant with 600 employees who work 40 hours a week for 50 weeks a year and produce 2,400,000 bicycles?
   a. 20
   b. 5
   c. 10
   d. 2

5. Which of the following countries is NOT socialist with a market economy?
   a. Canada
   b. Sweden
   c. Cuba
   d. Germany

6. Which of the following is NOT a factor of production?
   a. growth
   b. labor
   c. land
   d. entrepreneurship

Chapter 4 Global Analysis

 Note Taking
Main Ideas and Supporting Details

Directions As you read, write key words and short phrases in the Cues column.
Write notes, facts, and main ideas in the Note Taking column. Then summarize
the section in the Summary box.

Cues	Note Taking
• International Trade	• International Trade
• The Global Marketplace	• The Global Marketplace

Summary

Chapter 4 Global Analysis

 Academic Integration: Social Studies
Calculating Trade Balances

Trade Balance In today's global marketplace, businesses must be aware of the balance of trade between countries—the difference between what a country exports and imports. A positive balance of trade occurs when a nation exports more than it imports; it has a trade surplus. A negative balance of trade occurs when a nation imports more than it exports; it has a trade deficit. In this computer activity, you will determine whether a trade surplus or a trade deficit exists between the United States and each country listed in the spreadsheet below.

	A	B	C	D
1	Country (Imports from/Exports to)	U.S. Imports in Billions	U.S. Exports in Billions	Trade Surplus or Deficit
2	Austria	8.3	3.0	
3	Belgium	14.4	21.3	
4	Canada	302.4	230.6	
5	France	37.0	24.2	
6	Italy	32.6	12.5	
7	Spain	9.8	7.4	
8	United Kingdom	53.5	45.4	
9	Totals			

Directions Follow these steps to analyze the spreadsheet.
- Turn on your computer and open your spreadsheet software program.
- Create a spreadsheet like the one above using your spreadsheet application.
- Enter a formula to calculate the trade deficit or surplus between the United States and each of the selected countries.
- Enter formulas to calculate the total imports, exports, and balance of trade for the countries listed.
- After completing all your calculations, save your work.
- Answer the questions that follow.

1. Does the United States have a total trade surplus or deficit with the listed countries?

_____

2. List countries with which the United States has a trade surplus and the surplus amount.

_____

3. What are some effects of a negative balance of trade on a nation's economy?

_____

_____

Chapter 4 Global Analysis

Real-World Application
Factors Influencing Global Trade

Global Trade When companies enter the global marketplace they are met with a number of challenges. Among these are cultural, political, and legal factors that influence how and what they can sell.

Directions Read the article below. Then answer the questions that follow.

It is a challenge to persuade a population to adopt novel food tastes, but this PepsiCo subsidiary [Frito-Lay] is making a go of it. Frito-Lay sells chips with such flavoring as "crispy, fragrant French chicken wings" and "fresh, crispy seafood." The goal by 2007: make Lay's the number one snack in the world's most crowded country.

Lay's potato chips didn't show up [in China] until 1997 because China bans potato imports, forcing Frito-Lay to start, quite literally, from the ground up, opening two farms to supply big, round, sturdy potatoes short on sugar (to preserve whiteness). Three years after planting its first spud in China, Lay's launched its first entry—"salty flavored"—and saw an instant hit. But in China Lay's quickly found that dishes popular in one region did not sell as well in others. Shanghai snackers tend to like sweet tastes, southerners prefer salty, westerners go for spicy flavors and northerners prefer meaty ones, forcing Lay's to adjust its marketing.

PepsiCo also had to accommodate yin and yang, the Chinese philosophy that nature and life need to balance opposing elements (like light and dark or sweet and sour). It plays out in the local palate: Chinese consider fried foods to be hot and therefore shun them in the summer because the two hots do not balance; cool would be better.

That discovery last year led to Frito-Lay's most creative effort in China so far: "cool lemon" potato chips. The yellow, strongly lemon-scented chips are dotted with greenish lime specks and mint and are sold in a package featuring images of breezy blue skies and rolling green grass. Lay's launched them with a TV ad featuring Malaysian pop star Angelica Lee, who asks fans in a stadium, "Can you eat just one?" The campaign triggered a spike in sales last summer. (China is a particularly good market for TV ads, given that it has 126 TV sets for every 100 households and still offers relatively few channels, making it harder to zap away from a barrage of commercials.)

1. What political/legal factor affected the launch of Frito Lay potato chips in China?

_____

_____

Chapter 4 Global Analysis

Real-World Application
Factors Influencing Global Trade (continued)

2. What two cultural factors influenced the variety of Chinese Lay's potato chip flavors?

_____

_____

_____

_____

_____

3. How would you classify Frito-Lay's marketing strategy of its Lay's potato chips in China—was it globalization, adaptation, or customization? Explain.

_____

_____

_____

_____

_____

4. Why is China's entry into the WTO important for multinational companies like PepsiCo?

_____

_____

_____

5. Why do you think PepsiCo's direct foreign investment was largely in joint ventures?

_____

_____

_____

_____

6. What factor helped Frito-Lay to decide on TV as a medium for its promotional message?

_____

_____

_____

_____

Chapter 4

Chapter 4 Global Analysis

Real-World Application
Global Competition

Free Trade Agreements Sometimes countries impose trade barriers or restrictions when they want to limit trade. Other times countries will enter into agreements that allow for commercial exchange conducted on free market principles. Trade done without restrictive regulation is referred to as free trade

Directions Read the passage below and answer the questions that follow.

> Long-time trading partners, the United States and Australia entered into a trade agreement that allows both countries to import and export to one another many products duty-free. The United States-Australia Free Trade Agreement took effect on January 1, 2005.
>
> The day the agreement took effect Australia tariffs were eliminated on most American-manufactured goods and agricultural products. The largest U.S. manufacturing segment helped by the agreement is the automotive parts industry. Tariffs on the automobile parts dropped from 15 percent to zero. The agreement also called for the United States to remove a 25 percent tariff on light commercial vehicles and a 50 percent tariff on merchant-ship repairs and maintenance for Australian manufacturers.
>
> The agreement provides for duty-free agricultural products between the two countries. United States food exports to Australia represent about $400 million annually. Australia is able to import to the United States agricultural products, including canned tuna, peanuts, fruit juices, and other food products, all duty free.

1. How does the United States-Australia free trade agreement help manufacturers of automobile parts?

_____

2. How does the agreement help Australian light commercial vehicle manufacturers?

_____

3. How is the U.S. agricultural industry helped by the agreement?

_____

4. How does the agreement affect the price of Australian fruit at your local grocery store?

_____

5. What is a negative effect of free trade agreements?

_____

Chapter 4

Chapter 4 Global Analysis

DECA Connection
International Trade Consultant

International Trade Imagine that you are an international trade consultant in the marketing department of D&J Soft Drink Company. Your company would like to start selling its products in Asian countries. The United States has signed a trade agreement with Vietnam and China, as well as lifted some sanctions against North Korea. As soon as those sanctions were lifted, Coca-Cola began selling its soft drinks in North Korea, one of the few nations in the world where Coca-Cola was not being sold. Your company currently has soft drink products distributed in Europe and South America. One thing your company learned in Europe was that men would not buy diet cola because diet drinks are often perceived as feminine.

Since the three nations (Vietnam, China, and North Korea) have recently opened their doors to U.S. products, your supervisor (judge) wants you to evaluate each country as a potential market for one for your company's products, then recommend a nation to be your company's first Asian market. Any economic, political, or social issues that need to be addressed should be considered along with possible solutions to any obstacles that may be apparent from your research. Cultural sensitivity is a must. Suggest marketing ideas that would help make the product launch successful in your recommended country.

Role Play Based on what you know about Asian cultures and the economies of the three nations under study, make your recommendation of which country's market to penetrate first. Prepare a memo to your supervisor (judge) that details your recommendation, rationale, and ideas for a product name, as well as marketing solutions to the competition you will face in that country, from major soft drink brands such as Coca-Cola. Also address the cultural factors that must be taken into consideration when you are promoting, distributing, and pricing your products.

Directions Organize your thoughts around the performance indicators that follow. Use these performance indicators to write the memo during the preparation period. Time your preparation period to last 20 minutes and your presentation of the memo to last a maximum of 5 minutes, including time for follow-up questions. After your presentation, use the performance indicators to evaluate your efforts.

Chapter 4 Global Analysis

DECA Connection
International Trade Consultant *(continued)*

Assessment You will be evaluated on how well you meet the following performance indicators:
- Explain the nature of international trade.
- Identify the impact of cultural and social environments on world trade.
- Describe the nature of current economic problems.
- Evaluate influences on a nation's ability to trade.

Scoring Each performance indicator equals 20 points (20 × 5 = 100 points).
Excellent (16–20) **Good** (10–15) **Fair** (4–9) **Poor** (0–3)

1. Explain the nature of international trade. **Score** _____

2. Describe the nature of current economic problems. **Score** _____

3. Evaluate influences on a nation's ability to trade. **Score** _____

4. Develop cultural sensitivity. **Score** _____

Chapter 4

Chapter 4 Global Analysis

Study Skills
Time Management for Test Taking

Directions Read the tips to help improve you concentration. Then review the chapter using the tips as you answer the questions that follow. If the statement is true, circle **T**. If the statement is false, circle **F** and rewrite the statement so that it is true

Improving Concentration
• Take a break about every 20 minutes. • Spend a few minutes taking deep and relaxing breaths. As a result more oxygen is carried to the brain, and you are more alert. • Try not to let other thoughts come into your mind.

1. If a U.S. company imports wine from Italy, it can pay the Italian exporter in U.S. dollars.   T   F

   _____

   _____

2. Specialization builds and sustains a market economy.   T   F

   _____

   _____

3. An import quota can limit the monetary value of a product that may be imported.   T   F

   _____

   _____

4. The United States, Canada, and Australia all call their currency *dollars*.   T   F

   _____

5. All countries' currency have the same value.   T   F

   _____

6. When a country imports more that it exports, it has a trade surplus.   T   F

   _____

7. An embargo limits the amount of specific goods that can be imported into a country.   T   F

   _____

   _____

Chapter 4 Global Analysis

 Study Skills
Test Preparation

Directions Study the Test-Prep Tips and think about how you can use them to improve your test scores. Write a sentence or two to answer each of the following questions about the main ideas in Chapter 4.

Test-Prep Tips
• Keep up-to-date on reading the text and reviewing your notes.
• Keep all your notes for each class together so you can find them easily.
• Believe in yourself. Be positive about your memory skills.

1. How does the consumer benefit from international trade?

_____

_____

_____

2. What is a labor-intensive industry and where do such industries do the best?

_____

_____

3. What are the three main types of trade barriers to international trade?

_____

_____

4. What is the difference between a tariff and an embargo?

_____

_____

5. What are the different ways a business could enter the global marketplace?

_____

_____

6. What is the difference between globalization and customization?

_____

_____

_____

Chapter 4

Chapter 4 Global Analysis

Test-Taking
Practice Test

Directions Take the practice test. Choose the word or phrase that best completes the sentence or answers the question.

1. When planning a marketing strategy for the sale of a product in a foreign country, businesses that do not change anything about their product or their promotions are said to be practicing a
   a. globalization strategy.
   b. product adaptation strategy.
   c. customization strategy.
   d. promotion adaptation strategy.

2. What are licensed specialists who know the applicable laws, procedures, and tariffs governing imports called?
   a. maritime brokers
   b. freight forwarders
   c. customs brokers
   d. foreign importing brokers

3. At present the U.S. balance of trade can best be described as a
   a. trade equilibrium.
   b. trade surplus.
   c. positive balance of trade.
   d. negative balance of trade.

4. Because different countries possess unique resources and capabilities, they
   a. practice protectionism.
   b. are independent of one another.
   c. are self-sufficient.
   d. are economically independent.

5. Partnerships made when direct investment in a foreign country occurs with a domestic partner are called
   a. multinationals.
   b. mini-national.
   c. joint ventures.
   d. cooperatives.

6. GATT, NAFTA, and the EU are examples of
   a. trade barriers imposed on nations.
   b. trade agreements and alliances.
   c. agencies that provide financial and advisory support to businesses that want to engage in foreign trade.
   d. free-trade zones.

Chapter 5 The Free Enterprise System

 Note Taking
Main Ideas and Supporting Details

Directions As you read, write key words and short phrases in the Cues column. Write notes, facts, and main ideas in the Note Taking column. Then summarize the section in the summary box.

Cues	Note Taking
• Market Oriented Economic Systems	• Market Oriented Economic Systems
• Business Opportunities	• Business Opportunities

Summary

Chapter 5

Chapter 5 The Free Enterprise System

Academic Integration: Social Studies
Analyzing a Spreadsheet

Supply and Demand In a market economy, it is important for managers to understand the relationship between supply and demand. Demand refers to the amount of goods or services that consumers are willing to buy at certain prices; supply refers to the amount of goods or services that producers are willing to make and sell at certain prices.

You will create a graph to illustrate the supply and demand curves for a product. Look at the printout below, which shows the supply and demand for a product at ten different retail prices. Notice that as the price increases, the quantity supplied increases, but the quantity demanded decreases.

Retail Price	Quantity Supplied	Quantity Demanded
$0.10	10	100
$0.20	20	80
$0.30	30	75
$0.40	40	65
$0.50	50	60
$0.60	60	50
$0.70	70	40
$0.80	80	30
$0.90	90	20
$1.00	100	5

Directions Follow these steps to analyze the spreadsheet. Then answer the questions that follow.
- Create a spreadsheet like that on page 45 using spreadsheet software program.
- Follow the instructions for your software to create a scatter graph of the data. A graph in which two lines cross should be the result.
- After completing your graph, save your work to a new file.

1. On the graph that you have created, what is the equilibrium price for the product?

   _____

2. Explain what the equilibrium price means to a marketer.

   _____

   _____

3. If the supplier used a retail price of 40 cents instead of the equilibrium price, what might happen?

   _____

Chapter 5

Chapter 5 The Free Enterprise System

Real-World Application
Competition the Old Fashioned Way

Directions Read the text below. Then answer the questions that follow.

   An 80-year-old tool company, Snap-On Tools has succeeded because of a unique and extremely effective way of doing business.

   Snap-On Tools makes and sells tools and equipment for the automotive industry. Rather than sell through traditional retail stores, Snap-On's franchisees sell out of big white trucks emblazoned with the red Snap-On logo. Each truck is fully stocked with tools and equipment, a fully mobile retail establishment. Each franchise owner drives to service stations, car dealerships, independent garages, and places where car enthusiasts work. The franchise owner takes the store to them, building a strong relationship with his customers.

   Although Snap-On's tools are generally more expensive than their competitors' tools, Snap-On wins loyal customers by offering high-quality tools and unparalleled customer service. Besides the freedom of being able to shop at work, Snap-On customers can receive interest-free credit on many sales and interest-bearing loans for expensive equipment. In addition, the company, which prides itself on its service and vision, continues to increase its product line to meet the needs of its customers. The company has moved beyond wrenches to products such as computerized diagnostic systems.

1. How would you describe Snap-On Tools' competitive strategy—does it fit a price or non-price model? Explain.

   _____

   _____

2. How are the free enterprise "freedoms" of ownership and profit depicted in this article on Snap-On Tools?

   _____

   _____

   _____

3. Is there any risk for the franchised dealers who purchase the truck, tools, and equipment from Snap-On? Explain your answer.

   _____

   _____

Chapter 5

Chapter 5 The Free Enterprise System

Real-World Application
Supply and Demand

Supply and Demand As prices rise, demand drops. As prices increase, supply increases. The equilibrium point is where supply and demand curves meet.

Price	Number Demanded	Number Supplied	Surplus or Shortage
$20	2,000	500	
$25	1,600	1,200	
$30	1,400	1,400	
$35	1,200	1,600	
$40	1,000	1,800	
$45	750	2,000	

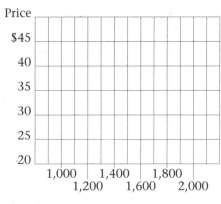

Directions Study the supply-and-demand schedule above. Use it to draw supply-and-demand curves on the grid. Be sure to label both curves, and then answer the questions below.

1. What is the price and number of units at the equilibrium point?

   _____

2. What is the significance of this point for buyers and sellers?

   _____

   _____

3. What happens to demand for backpacks as the price goes down?

   _____

4. What is the significance of this point for buyers and sellers?

   _____

5. Complete the final column of the supply-and-demand schedule provided above. Fill in the difference between the amount supplied and the amount demanded. Indicate whether each entry is a surplus or a shortage by using a plus or minus sign, respectively.

6. Indicate on the graph which area represents surplus and which represents shortage. Code these, using different colors or patterns.

Chapter 5 The Free Enterprise System

DECA Connection
E-Commerce Security Consultant

Role Play Imagine you are an employee of a specialty retail establishment that sells some products online. Your employer has noticed a decline in online sales recently. After spending a lot of money for the design and maintenance of the company's Web site, your employer is concerned. Since you have direct contact with online customers, your employer (judge) wants your input on whether to keep the online business.

Directions Role-play a meeting with your employer (judge) during which you discuss the pros and cons of keeping the online business. To prepare for the meeting, use your knowledge of e-commerce to outline the risks and solutions to the problems.

Organize your thoughts around the performance indicators noted below. Use these performance indicators to jot down your ideas during the preparation period. Time your preparation period to last 15 minutes and your role-play presentation to last a maximum of ten minutes. After your role play, use the performance indicators to evaluate your efforts.

Assessment You will be evaluated on how well you meet the following performance indicators:
- Explain the nature of risk management.
- Identify ways that technology impacts business.
- Explain key factors in building a clientele.
- Demonstrate problem-solving skills.
- Explain routine security precautions.

Scoring Each performance indicator equals 20 points (20 × 5 = 100 points).
Excellent (16–20)   **Good** (10–15)   **Fair** (4–9)   **Poor** (0–3)

Chapter 5

Chapter 5 The Free Enterprise System

 Study Skills
Improving Vocabulary

Directions Use the following tips to help improve your vocabulary. Then complete the following sentences using the correct word from the list below.

Improving Vocabulary
• Most vocabulary words are learned from context. The more words you are exposed to, the better vocabulary you will have.   • Relate new words to words you already know.   • Get in the habit of looking up words you do not know.

business risk	global business	private sector
competition	equilibrium	profit
demand	public sector	domestic business
supply	patent	nonprofit organization

1. A state of _____ exists when the number of products supplied equals the amout of product demanded.

2. It would be a big _____ to spend more money on a new advertising campaign than the campaign would generate.

3. She worries about _____ because a clothing store opened up near hers.

4. When Joe took a job with the local government, it was his first experience working in the _____ .

5. The company was about to become a _____ when it began exporting products to Costa Rica.

6. He made a nice _____ when he sold his car for $1,200 more than what he paid for it.

7. They realized _____ was down for their product when they ran out of room in the warehouse.

8. The board members decided they did not want to sell things to overseas, they were happy being a _____ .

Chapter 5 The Free Enterprise System

 Study Skills
Test Preparation

Directions Study the Test-Prep Tips and think about how you can use them to improve your test scores. Write a sentence or two to answer each of the following questions about the main ideas in Chapter 5.

Test-Prep Tips
• Review tests you have already taken for end-of-chapter or end-of-term tests.
• Read any teacher comments from old tests and homework.
• Correct any questions you missed on previous tests and homework.

1. What are some ways to protect intellectual property?

   _____

2. Explain why competition is an essential part of a free enterprise system.

   _____

   _____

3. What are some of the factors businesses use in non-price competition?

   _____

   _____

4. How are the prices and the quantities of goods produced determined? Explain.

   _____

   _____

   _____

   _____

   _____

5. What is the difference between a domestic and global business?

   _____

   _____

6. What are the five "rights" of merchandising?

   _____

   _____

Chapter 5

Chapter 5 The Free Enterprise System

Test-Taking
Practice Test

Directions Take the practice test. Choose the word or phrase that best completes the sentence or answers the question.

1. Demand for consumer goods and their respective consumer trends
   a. create derived demand in the industrial market.
   b. are not related to demand in the industrial market.
   c. are only useful to businesses in the consumer market.
   d. create problems with suppliers in the industrial markets.

2. Which of the following are economic benefits of profitable businesses?
   a. the value of a company's stock goes down
   b. the demand for a company's product goes down
   c. profitable companies attract competition
   d. profitable businesses can cut back on research and development

3. When evaluating the production function during a SWOT analysis, you would look for
   a. cost.
   b. innovation.
   c. liabilities.
   d. demand of the product.

4. What are four main functions of an organization's operation?
   a. production, marketing, management, and finance
   b. accounting, production, promotion, and sales
   c. management, accounting, finance, and advertising
   d. marketing, management, accounting, and finance

5. Intellectual property rights for inventions are known as
   a. trademarks.
   b. copyrights.
   c. design plans.
   d. patents.

6. A business that uses the money it makes to fund a cause is called a
   a. global business.
   b. domestic business.
   c. nonprofit business.
   d. for profit business.

Chapter 6 Legal and Ethical Issues

Note Taking
Main Ideas and Supporting Details

Directions As you read, write key words and short phrases in the Cues column.
Write notes, facts, and main ideas in the Note Taking column. Then summarize
the section in the Summary box.

Cues	Note Taking
• Government and Laws	• Government and Laws
• Social Responsibility and Ethics	• Social Responsibility and Ethics

Summary

Chapter 6 Legal and Ethical Issues

 ## Academic Integration: English Language Arts
Word Processing

Code of Ethics In most companies a code of ethics is provided to managers to guide them in responding to different business situations.

Imagine you are a sales manager at Beta Corporation, which produces and markets office furniture. You manage 45 salespeople and are responsible for developing a code of ethics that addresses three specific topics listed in the box below. Creating a handout that address these topics. You will be giving the handout to all the sales managers at the next sales meeting. You may revise the wording of the heading or add to the handout.

Code of Ethics Topics
1. Salespeople's use of gift or payments to obtain business
2. Obtaining and using information about competitors
3. Honest and accurate completion of expense reports

Directions Follow these steps to create your handout. Then answer the questions that follow.
- Turn on your computer and open your word processing software.
- Develop and write a code of ethics for the three areas listed. Proofread and edit your work to make sure that it is correct and concise.
- Save your work. Print out a copy of your completed code of ethics if your teacher has instructed you to do so.

1. What would you include in an ethical code regarding payments of money or gifts by salespeople to obtain business?

_____

_____

_____

2. What would you include in an ethical code concerning the acquisition and use of information about competitors?

_____

_____

_____

3. Why might offering money or gifts to potential customers be considered unethical?

_____

_____

Chapter 6 Legal and Ethical Issues

Real-World Application
Legal and Ethical Issues

Directions Read the text below. Then answer the questions that follow.

Washington, DC—(June 17, 2004)—The Better Business Bureau system, Visa USA, Call For Action, and the Federal Trade Commission (FTC) today announced a joint education campaign to help consumers "cut the line on phishing scams."

During the campaign, the BBB and its partners will educate consumers on how to identify phishing scams; how to avoid becoming a victim; and how to report a suspicious e-mail. Comprehensive phishing resources will be available on the Internet for consumers by all parties involved in this campaign.

Phishing is an e-mail scam in which fraudsters attempt to convince consumers to reveal personal information—such as their credit or debit account numbers, checking account information, Social Security numbers, and banking account passwords—though official-looking fake Web sites or in a reply e-mail. According to the Anti-Phishing Working Group, phishing scams grew 178 percent from March to April of 2004.

1. Which of the groups involved in this national campaign is

   A. a government agency? _____

   B. an organization involved in business self-regulation? _____

   C. an example of consumerism? _____

2. Why would the four organizations noted in this article want to fight against phishing?

   _____

   _____

   _____

3. If you were suspicious of an e-mail and thought it might be phishing, what would you do?

   _____

   _____

4. What else could the organizations do to educate consumers about phishing scams?

   _____

   _____

   _____

Chapter 6 Legal and Ethical Issues

Real-World Application
Social Responsibility

Social Responsibility Ethics and social responsibility have become important business topics as trust in corporations has deteriorated due to scandals. It is important for businesses and their employees to act in an ethical manner in order to regain consumers' trust.

Directions Use the situations described below to clarify your views on the social responsibility of businesses. Study each situation and answer the questions that follow.

1. You own and operate a small fast-food restaurant located on the main street of town. Both businesspeople and shoppers stop in to eat. The junior high school is also just a half-block away, so many students eat there.

   Garrick Hughes, an old friend of yours, stops in for lunch. Garrick works for a vending machine company. He wants to install a cigarette machine in your restaurant. It would give your customers a choice of 20 brands of cigarettes.

   You know that cigarette companies need about 1,000 new smokers every day to replace those who die from smoking-related illnesses. Garrick knows this too, so he offers you a special inducement—a sales promotion that will net you more than $500 every month. All you have to do is let him put in the vending machine. What will you tell Garrick? Why?

   _____

   _____

   _____

   _____

2. You are a middle-level manager of a large chemical products company. You have just learned that one of your plants is disposing of chemical waste by draining it underground into a nearby river.

   You are not sure whether top management knows about the situation. The people who live in the community do not. There has been a modest die-off of fish in the river, but no one has made the connection to your company.

   The local plant manager asks you to keep what you have discovered a secret. What will you do?

   _____

   _____

   _____

Chapter 6 Legal and Ethical Issues

Real-World Application
Social Responsibility *(continued)*

3. You are the owner of a music store. You are having trouble competing with the large discount stores that offer CDs at lower prices than the suppliers charge for them. One day someone offers you 1,000 CDs for a fraction of the usual cost. You are tempted to buy them, even though you think they might be stolen. The low price would enable you to make some money and pay the store's bills. What will you do?

_____

_____

_____

_____

4. You work for a large auto parts chain. The company that owns the chain is about to merge with a larger, more profitable company. If the companies do merge, it would mean that the price of the company's stock would increase in value.

   You learn from someone higher up in the company that the merger is definitely going to happen. The person is a close friend, and she asks you to keep the news to yourself. Another close friend later asks you about the merger, wondering if he should purchase some stock, hoping to make some money when the price goes up. What do you tell him?

_____

_____

_____

_____

_____

_____

_____

_____

Chapter 6 Legal and Ethical Issues

 **DECA Connection**
Volunteer Coordinator

Role Play Imagine you are an employee of a locally owned small business. The business owner (judge) feels strongly that his/her employees should be involved in volunteer work within the community. Your employer is uncertain, however, about the best way to implement such an activity.

Directions Role-play a meeting with the members of your team. You are the team leader, and you are trying to develop a proposal for employee participation in community volunteer work.

Organize your thoughts around the performance indicators noted below. Use these performance indicators to jot down your ideas during the preparation period. Time your preparation period to last 15 minutes and your role-play presentation to last a maximum of ten minutes. After your role play, use the performance indicators to evaluate your efforts.

Assessment You will be evaluated on how well you meet the following performance indicators:
- Develop a project plan.
- Develop criteria for deciding which activities will qualify for the incentive.
- Explain the role of business in society.
- Participate as a team member.
- Demonstrate appropriate creativity.

Scoring Each performance indicator equals 20 points (20 3 5 5 100 points).
Excellent (16–20)   **Good** (10–15)   **Fair** (4–9)   **Poor** (0–3)

Develop a project plan.   **Score** _____

_____

_____

Chapter 6 Legal and Ethical Issues

 DECA Connection
Volunteer Coordinator (continued)

Develop criteria for deciding which activities will qualify for the incentive. **Score** _____

_____

_____

Explain the role of business in society. **Score** _____

_____

_____

Participate as a team member. **Score** _____

_____

_____

Demonstrate appropriate creativity. **Score** _____

_____

_____

Chapter 6 *(sidebar)*

Chapter 6 Legal and Ethical Issues

Study Skills
The Role of Ethics

Directions Read the tips for studying ethical situations. Then read the scenario and answer the questions.

Studying Ethical Situations
• Read the scenario the first time for general ideas, the second time for specific points, and, if possible, a third time for ideas.
• Note the different alternatives regarding the situation.
• Reason out what is the right thing to do.

During the summer you have a part time job with a painting company. The company has had a busy summer and has dozens of paint cans with small amounts of paint in them. It needs to dispose of the paint cans. Local ordinances require that the cans of paint can only be disposed of in certain places to prevent the paint from getting into the local water supply. Most of your coworkers follow the company's policy of hauling the paint cans to the proper disposal site. However, one of the employees is known to have dumped the paint cans in a wooded area near a stream.

1. Is this action against the law?

_____

_____

2. Based on your reading, why do you think a government would enact a law regarding the proper treatment of old paint?

_____

_____

3. Do you think the action taken by the one employee is contrary to company values? How do you know?

_____

_____

4. How would you respond to the employee if he suggested you put the old paint cans in the woods too?

_____

_____

Chapter 6 Legal and Ethical Issues

 **Study Skills**
Test Preparation

Directions Study the Test-Prep Tips and think about how you can use them to improve your test scores. Write a sentence or two to answer each of the following questions about the main ideas in Chapter 6.

Test-Prep Tips
• Gather all the materials you will need, including your textbook and old tests.
• Identify all the text material that you will need to know for the test.
• Study all your notes from the text.

1. What are the three branches of the U.S. government and what does each include?

_____

_____

_____

_____

2. Explain what the Consumer Product Safety Commission (CPSC) does?

_____

_____

3. What are the responsibilities of the Environmental Protection Agency (EPA)?

_____

_____

4. What are some benefits socially responsible companies might give employees? Why?

_____

_____

5. Explain two things socially responsible companies are doing to protect the environment?

_____

_____

6. What is the Sarbanes-Oxley Act?

_____

_____

Chapter 6 Legal and Ethical Issues

 Study Skills
Practice Test

Directions Take the practice test. Choose the word or phrase that best completes the sentence or answers the question.

1. The Sarbanes-Oxley Act of 2002 has provisions for all of the following except
    a. protection for whistle-blowers.
    b. holding executives and their consulting firms accountable.
    c. proper reporting of a corporation's financial situation.
    d. workplace safety.

2. This workplace benefit helps to reduce employee absenteeism and employee turnover.
    a. Health care benefits
    b. Extended family leave
    c. On-site child care
    d. Time off with pay when sick

3. Voluntary product recalls are examples of good
    a. marketing.
    b. business ethics.
    c. resource management.
    d. environmental safety.

4. The bureau under the direction of the Federal Trade Commission that has the responsibility for enforcing laws related to clothing labels, scams related to marketing practices, and truth in advertising is the Bureau of
    a. Consumer Protection.
    b. Competition.
    c. Economics.
    d. Finance.

5. When selling goods and services to the government for use in government agencies, vendors often must do all of the following except
    a. follow guidelines for price bidding.
    b. show proof that they use minority suppliers.
    c. show proof that they are an equal opportunity employer.
    d. offer their products at cost.

6. The branch of government responsible for interpreting, applying, and administering the laws of the United States is the
    a. executive branch.
    b. legislative branch.
    c. judicial branch.
    d. state government.

Chapter 7 Basic Math Skills

Note Taking
Main Ideas and Supporting Details

Directions As you read, write key words and short phrases in the Cues column. Write notes, facts, and main ideas in the Note Taking column. Then summarize the section in the Summary box.

Cues	Note Taking
• Math Fundamentals	• Math Fundamentals
• Interpreting Numbers	• Interpreting Numbers

Summary

Chapter 7 Basic Math Skills

 Academic Integration: Mathematics
Spreadsheet

Activity

As the owner of the Holiday Gift Shop, you have monitored the sales output of each of your employees. The printout below shows sales information for several employees. For each employee, it shows the number of hours worked, the number of sales transactions, and the dollar sales that resulted from those transactions. Because each employee has worked a different number of hours, averages must be calculated before any comparisons can be made. Use your spreadsheet program to calculate the average number of transactions that each employee had per hour. Then calculate the average hourly sales that each employee generated.

	A	B	C	D	E	F
1		Hours	Number of	Dollar	Mean	Mean
2	Employee	Worked	Transactions	Sales	Transactions	Sales
3	Name	Per week	Per week	Per week	Per hour	Per hour
4	Jenny B.	35	378	$11,368.98		
5	Kyle A.	43	420	$13,440.33		
6	Maia R.	37	356	$10,324.50		
7	All Employees					

Directions Follow these steps to create a spreadsheet. Then answer the questions below.

- Turn on your computer and open your spreadsheet software program.
- Create a spreadsheet like the one above using your spreadsheet application.
- Enter a formula to calculate the mean number of transactions per hour for Jenny B. Copy the formula to appropriate cells in all remaining rows.

- Enter a formula to calculate the mean hourly sales for Jenny B. Copy the formula to appropriate cells in all remaining rows.
- Calculate the mean number of transactions per hour and the mean hourly sales for all employees.

1. What were the mean transactions per hour figures for each and all employees?

   Jenny B. _____   Maia R._____   Kyle A. _____   All Employees _____

2. What were the mean hourly sales figures for each and all employees?

   Jenny B. _____   Maia R. _____   Kyle A. _____   All Employees _____

3. How can you use this data to help your salespeople and improve business?

   _____

   _____

Chapter 7 Basic Math Skills

 Real-World Application
Writing Checks

Directions Complete the checks below using the following information.

Check No. 321 To Mr. Arnold Gilbert for $324.57 (cleaning services)
Check No. 352 To Windsor Grocery for $80.29 (weekly groceries)
Check No. 353 To Realty Associates for $17,500 (deposit on house)

Laura Michaels	_____, 2 _____ 321
4793 Aldon Drive	18-24/979
Midland, TX 77002	1202 (7)

PAY TO THE ORDER OF _____ $ _____

_____ DOLLARS

First State Bank
1800 Plains Avenue
Midland, TX 77002

Memo_____   _____

Laura Michaels	_____, 2 _____ 325
4793 Aldon Drive	18-24/979
Midland, TX 77002	1202 (7)

PAY TO THE ORDER OF _____ $ _____

_____ DOLLARS

First State Bank
1800 Plains Avenue
Midland, TX 77002

Memo_____   _____

Laura Michaels	_____, 2 _____ 353
4793 Aldon Drive	18-24/979
Midland, TX 77002	1202 (7)

PAY TO THE ORDER OF _____ $ _____

_____ DOLLARS

First State Bank
1800 Plains Avenue
Midland, TX 77002

Memo_____   _____

Chapter 7

Chapter 7 Basic Math Skills

Real-World Application
Estimates, Rounding Off, and Decimals

Directions A   Estimate the answer to each of the following problems. Then use a calculator to solve the problems. Write and compare both of your answers.

1. $385 + 694 + 918 + 42$ Estimate _____   Answer _____

2. $\$18,918.47 - \$3,298.95$ Estimate _____   Answer _____

3. $36,916 \times 2.74$ Estimate _____   Answer _____

4. $696/12$ Estimate _____   Answer _____

Directions B   Round each of the following decimals to the nearest tenth. Write your answers.

5. 22.762   Nearest Tenth _____

6. 77.097   Nearest Tenth _____

7. 8.541   Nearest Tenth _____

Directions C   Convert the following fractions to decimals. Round to the nearest hundredth. Write your answers.

8. $1/4 =$ _____

9. $2/3 =$ _____

10. $1/3 =$ _____

Chapter 7 Basic Math Skills

DECA Connection
Assistant Manager

Role Play You are to assume the role of assistant manager of an interior design shop. You must often provide customers with estimates for time and materials necessary to complete a job. You have noticed that some of your fellow employees have difficulty with the concept of estimating. Their mistakes cause problems for the shop owner and the customers.

Directions The shop owner (judge) has asked you to plan a practice session to improve the skills of the employees. You must demonstrate to the shop owner that you can teach the employees how to improve their estimating skills.

Organize your thoughts around the performance indicators noted below. Use these performance indicators to jot down your ideas during the preparation period. Time your preparation period to last 15 minutes and your role-play presentation to last a maximum of ten minutes.

Assessment You will be evaluated on how well you meet the following performance indicators:

Score:

_____ Explain the role of situational analysis in the marketing planning process.

_____ Identify fashion trends.

_____ Develop a marketing plan.

_____ Explain the concepts of market and market identification.

_____ Select a target market.

Scoring Each performance indicator equals 20 points (20 × 5 = 100 points).
Excellent (16–20)   **Good** (10–15)   **Fair** (4–9)   **Poor** (0–3)

Chapter 7

Chapter 7 Basic Math Skills

Study Skills
Understanding Numbers

Directions Use the following tips to help you master new material. Then review your understanding of the important concepts in this chapter by answering the questions that follow.

Mastering New Material
• Study a little each day instead of trying to learn large amounts of material at once.   • Choose a study area that is free from distractions such as television and radio.   • Use flashcards when studying math facts such as fraction and decimal equivalents.

1. Write the digits used in our numbering system.

_____

2. Write the number 234,056,008 in words.

_____

3. Which digit in 234,056,008 represents

millions?   _____

tens?   _____

thousands?   _____

4. What is a fraction?

_____

5. Write a fraction with a numerator of 96 and a denominator of 30.

_____

6. Write the above fraction as a mixed number.

_____

7. Write the above fraction as a decimal number.

_____

8. Write the above decimal number in words.

_____

9. What does percentage mean?

_____

10. When a percentage is written as a fraction, what number is the denominator?

_____

11. What are graphs?

_____

Chapter 7 Basic Math Skills

 Study Skills
Test Preparation

Directions Study the Test-Prep Tips and think about how you can use them to improve your test scores. Write a sentence or two to answer each of the following questions about the main ideas in Chapter 7.

Test-Prep Tips
• Relate the information you are learning to what you already know and you will be better able to understand and retain it.
• Budget your time, make sure you have sufficient time to study so that you are well prepared for the test.

1. What is the two-step process for multiplying decimal numbers?

_____

_____

_____

2. What are some helpful techniques for learning to use a 10-key keypad?

_____

_____

3. In a fraction, what does the numerator represent?

_____

4. What are statistics used for?

_____

_____

5. What is a line graph? What is it useful for?

_____

_____

_____

6. What are the five steps for solving percentage problems?

_____

_____

Chapter 7 Basic Math Skills

Study Skills
Practice Test

Directions Take the practice test. Choose the word or phrase that best completes the sentence or answers the question.

1. To write a fraction or mixed number as a percentage, first
   a. move the decimal point two places to the left.
   b. convert the fraction to decimal form.
   c. switch the numerator and dominator.
   d. multiply the decimal equivalent of the percentage by the number.

2. The two basic types of calculators are the
   a. the algebraic entry system and the geometric entry system.
   b. reverse-entry system and the forward-reverse entry system.
   c. algebraic entry system and the reverse-entry system.
   d. the estimate-entry system and the algebraic entry system.

3. What are the three steps in rounding decimal amounts?
   a. **1.** Find the decimal place you are rounding to. **2.** Look at the digit to the right of that place. **3.** If the digit to the right is less than 5, leave the first digit as it is. If the digit is 5 or greater, round up.
   b. **1.** Find the decimal place you are rounding to. **2.** Shift the decimal point one place to the left. **3.** Round the digit to the left of the decimal up one number.
   c. **1.** Find the decimal place you are rounding to. **2.** Look at the digit to the left of that place. **3.** If the digit to the left is less than 5, leave the first digit as it is. If the digit is 5 or greater, round up.
   d. **1.** Find the decimal place you are rounding to. **2.** Shift the decimal point one place to the right. **3.** Round the digit to the right of the decimal up one number.

4. What information is presented in a frequency table?
   a. geometric representations of parts of a whole
   b. numbers, fractions, or percentages observed for different intervals
   c. drawings of parallel bars with lengths proportional to the qualities measured
   d. a numerator and a denominator

5. The home row of keys on a 10-key keypad are
   a. 1, 2, and 3.
   b. 4, 5, and 6.
   c. 7, 8, and 9.
   d. 0, 1, and 2.

6. Which is the most common way of describing central tendency in statistics?
   a. the average
   b. the median
   c. the mode
   d. the mean

Chapter 8 Communication Skills

Note Taking
Main Ideas and Supporting Details

Directions As you read, write key words and short phrases in the Cues column.
Write notes, facts, and main ideas in the Note Taking column. Then summarize
the section in the Summary box.

Cues	Note Taking
• Defining Communication	• Defining Communication
• Elements of Speech and Writing	• Elements of Speech and Writing

Summary

Chapter 8 Communication Skills

Academic Integration: English Language Arts
Oral and Visual Presentation

Persuasive Oral Communications Most jobs in business, especially in marketing, require good communication skills. Successful marketers constantly use verbal communication to sell their ideas and products or services. Sometimes this is done in a formal setting, such as a meeting, but most of the time, verbal communication is informal. In this computer activity, you will make an oral presentation to persuade your classmates to support your viewpoint on an issue. It should be supported by a computer-aided presentation that you create using presentation software.

The topic of your presentation should be approved by your instructor and be of interest to you and your classmates. Topics such as "All business should be conducted in a socially responsible manner," or "Ethics should be the number one consideration when doing business," are possibilities.

Prepare an outline of your presentation, listing the key points. Be sure to include examples that can be used to illustrate the important points. Think about what counterpoints might be raised by your classmates, and plan responses to opposing positions. Use your key points, examples, and planned counterpoint rebuttals to develop oral and slide presentations. Develop a title screen and at least three other screens to support your viewpoint.

Directions Follow these steps to create a presentation. Then answer the questions that follow.
- Turn on your computer and open your presentation software program.
- Follow the instructions for your software to create a title screen for your presentation. Save the file as CH8PROB.
- Based on your ideas, develop at least three more screens to support your argument.
- Save your work and print out a copy of your screens for your instructor.

1. In what situations might verbal communications be used on the job?

_____

_____

_____

_____

_____

_____

_____

Chapter 8 Communication Skills

 Academic Integration: English Language Arts
Oral and Visual Presentation *(continued)*

2. Why should you consider who your audience is before planning an oral presentation?

_____

_____

_____

_____

_____

_____

_____

3. In what situations might verbal communications be used on the job?

_____

_____

_____

_____

_____

_____

_____

4. In what situations might verbal communications be used on the job?

_____

_____

_____

_____

_____

_____

_____

_____

Chapter 8 Communication Skills

Real-World Application
Communication Channels

Directions Consider the situations described below and answer the questions that follow.

1. Tell which channel you think would be most effective in each of the situations. Explain your answers.

   a. An invitation to an informal gathering after work

   _____

   _____

   _____

   _____

   _____

   _____

   b. A new idea you would like your supervisor to consider

   _____

   _____

   _____

   _____

   _____

   _____

   c. A progress report on an important project

   _____

   _____

   _____

   _____

   _____

   _____

Chapter 8 Communication Skills

Real-World Application
Communication Channels *(continued)*

2. Describe with detail the appropriate setting for each of the following.

   a. A team meeting to celebrate reaching an important goal

   _____

   _____

   _____

   b. A training session to explain new office procedures

   _____

   _____

   _____

   _____

3. Describe a situation in which each of the following barriers to listening is present

   a. Distractions

   _____

   _____

   _____

   b. Emotional Barriers

   _____

   _____

   _____

   c. Planning a Response

   _____

   _____

   _____

Chapter 8

Chapter 8 Communication Skills

 Real-World Application
Appropriate Business E-Mail

E-mail Just as a business person is more careful with spoken language at work than at home, the business person needs to follow certain rules when e-mailing as well. E-mails should use the standard business e-mail format (informative subject line, traditional greeting, clear body, formal closing, and signature, including contact information).

Directions Consider the situations described below. Then write a business e-mail appropriate to each.

1. You are a buyer for the Fun-4-U toy stores. You have just received a shipment of defective rocking horses from Schlock Rockers, Inc. It is the third time you have received defective merchandise from the company.

   Write a business e-mail advising the firm that you are returning its latest shipment and wish to cancel any pending orders. Be sure to explain why you are taking this action.

   _____

   _____

   _____

   _____

   _____

   _____

2. You are a sales representative for American Classics, a furniture company. You have decided to try marketing your company's products to a hotel chain in another part of the country.

   Your first step is to write a business e-mail introducing your company and its product lines. Address your e-mail to the purchasing agent of the hotel chain. Describe the company and its merchandise in a way that will make the agent want to buy. Also write that you will be sending some catalogs of your furniture, and finish by asking for an appointment to meet with the agent in person.

   _____

   _____

   _____

   _____

   _____

Chapter 8 Communication Skills

 DECA Connection
Volunteer Coordinator

Role Play Imagine that you are a member of a large clerical staff for a catalog company. Management has announced a very strict policy stating that employees may not use the company computers for personal business of any sort. You and your fellow employees feel that this policy is too strict. You would like to have the privilege of using the company computers during your break times and during lunch hours or after work. You have been selected as the representative to convey these feelings to the office manager (judge).

Directions Role-play a meeting with your office manager to make your case on behalf of you and your fellow employees.

Organize your thoughts around the performance indicators noted below. Use these performance indicators to jot down your ideas during the preparation period. Time your preparation period to last 15 minutes and your role-play presentation to last a maximum of 10 minutes. After your role play, use the performance indicators to evaluate your efforts.

Assessment You will be evaluated on how well you meet the following performance indicators:

Score:

_____   Persuade others.

_____   Demonstrate ethical work habits.

_____   Describe the nature of organizational conflict.

_____   Demonstrate responsible behavior.

_____   Foster positive working relationships.

Scoring Each performance indicator equals 20 points (20 × 5 = 100 points).
Excellent (16–20)   **Good** (10–15)   **Fair** (4–9)   **Poor** (0–3)

Chapter 8 Communication Skills

Study Skills
Learning New Vocabulary

Directions Use the following tips to help improve your vocabulary. Then study the lists below and the Magic Square. To solve the puzzle, select a definition for each term from the numbered list. Then write each definition's number in the appropriately labeled puzzle cell. If you have correctly matched all the terms and definitions, the total of the numbers will be the same across each row and down each column.

Learning New Vocabulary
• Choose a vocabulary word you need to learn, write it on a sticky-note, and then write its definition in your own words. Post it where you will see it throughout your day.
• Have a friend or family member quiz you on key vocabulary words.
• Create a mental picture or "word picture" to go along with the meaning of the word. For example, feedback might look like an audience using a giant fork for feeding words back to a original speaker on a stage.

A. jargon

B. barriers

C. feedback

D. communication

E. distractions

F. messages

G. channels/media

H. emotional barriers

I. setting

1 Circumstances under which communication takes place

2. The process of exchanging ideas, information, and feelings

3. Obstacles that interfere with the understanding of a message

4. Things that compete with the message for the listener's attention

5. The receiver's response to the message

6. The avenues through which messages are delivered

7. Specialized vocabulary, used by members of a particular group

8. Biases against the opinion expressed that prevent a listener from understanding

9. The information, ideas, or feelings that the sender wants to communicate

A	B	C
D	E	F
G	H	I

Chapter 8 Communication Skills

 Study Skills
Test Preparation

Directions Study the Test-Prep Tips and think about how you can use them to improve your test scores. Write a sentence or two to answer each of the following questions about the main ideas in Chapter 8.

Test-Prep Tips
• When taking a test, always read the directions before you work on a section. Circle key words such as *not, contrast, similar,* and *different.* Failing to read directions can cause you to completely misjudge what the test is asking.
• Use the *Focus on Key Points, Review Vocabulary,* and *Review Facts and Ideas* at the end of each chapter to study for your test.

1 What are the three basic considerations when writing in business?

_____

_____

_____

2. What is the first step in persuasion for a marketer?

_____

_____

_____

3. What is the relationship between parliamentary procedure and a quorum?

_____

_____

_____

4. Why is it important for businesspeople to be aware of cultural differences?

_____

_____

_____

Chapter 8

Chapter 8 Communication Skills

Study Skills
Practice Test

Directions Circle the letter of the choice that best completes each of the following sentences.

1. Things that get in the way of effective listening are called
   a. annoyances.
   b. barriers.
   c. enumerations.
   d. feedback.

2. Skills that help you read with more understanding include focusing your mind, improving your vocabulary, and
   a. comparing and contrasting.
   b forming pictures.
   c. knowing the purpose of your reading.
   d. planning a response.

3. People usually speak in order to inform, to entertain, and to
   a. draw a conclusion.
   b. enumerate.
   c. generalize.
   d. persuade.

4. It is important when writing that you know your purpose, your subject, and your
   a. interest.
   b. jargon.
   c. audience.
   d. setting.

5. When speaking on the telephone, enunciate clearly, use your most pleasant tone, and
   a. draw on your extensive vocabulary.
   b. interrupt as necessary.
   c. shout.
   d. speak loudly enough to be heard.

6. The trend in business writing is toward
   a. a direct, conversational style.
   b. frequent generalization.
   c. heavy reliance on jargon.
   d. overuse of abbreviations.

Chapter 8

Chapter 9 Technology Applications for Marketing

 Note Taking
Main Ideas and Supporting Details

Directions As you read, write key words and short phrases in the Cues column. Write notes, facts, and main ideas in the Note Taking column. Then summarize the section in the Summary box.

Cues	Note Taking
• Computer Applications	• Computer Applications
• Computer Technology and Marketing	• Computer Technology and Marketing

Summary

Chapter 9 Technology Applications for Marketing

Academic Integration: Mathematics
Using and Analyzing a Regional Sales/Expense Spreadsheet

Hi-Tech Information Gathering The Exerfit Corporation manufactures exercise equipment that it sells to retail stores around the country. The company has seven sales regions, as shown in the computer printout below. The managers of these regions all report to the national sales manager. You are assisting the sales manager in evaluating the cost of salaries, sales, and marketing for each region. Total annual sales for each region are shown on the printout, along with salary, sales, and marketing expenses.

Region	Sales	Salaries & Benefits	Salaries as Percentage of Sales	Sales Expenses	Sales Expenses as Percentage of Sales	Marketing Expenses	Marketing Expenses as Percentage of Sales
North-east	$2,458,000	$148,900	6.1%	$225,000	9.2%	$250,000	10.2%
South-east	$3,242,000	$132,700		$218,000		$267,400	[8.2%]
South	$2,898,000	$124,400		$197,500		$245,000	[8.5%]
Midwest	$4,012,111	$169,600		$242,400		$291,200	[7.3%]
Central	$1,950,000	$108,000		$131,600		$162,700	[8.3%]
North-west	$3,982,000	$151,300		$232,500		$485,000	[12.2%]
South-west	$2,624,000	$118,000		$167,000		$251,700	[9.6%]

Chapter 9 Technology Applications for Marketing

 ## Academic Integration: Mathematics
Using and Analyzing a Regional Sales/Expense Spreadsheet (continued)

Directions Follow these steps to complete the spreadsheet and analyze the profitability of each region. Then answer the questions below about the completed spreadsheet.

- Open your spreadsheet software program on your computer.
- Create a spreadsheet like the one on Page 72 using your spreadsheet application.
- Write a formula to calculate salaries as a percentage of sales, rounding to the tenths place. Do the same for sales and marketing expenses. Copy these formulas to the remaining rows. [Salaries as a percentage of sales = (salaries $\times$ 100) $\div$ sales.]
- Save your work. Print out a copy of your work if you have been instructed to do so.

1. Which region has the highest salary cost as a percentage of sales? The lowest?

_____

_____

2. Which region has the highest marketing expenses in dollar amounts? As a percentage of sales?

_____

_____

3. Assume the Exerfit Corporation has a budget goal of keeping sales expenses below 6.5 percent of sales and marketing expenses below 8 percent of sales. Which regions are below budget in each category?

_____

_____

4. Looking at the spreadsheet results, you can see that marketing costs in the Northwest region are quite a bit higher than in other regions, while salary costs are lower. Suppose the Northwest regional manager has been using part-time or freelance marketing help, which explains the higher marketing costs and lower salary costs. What are some reasons why the manager might not use full-time employees?

_____

_____

_____

_____

Chapter 9

Chapter 9 Technology Applications for Marketing

 Real-World Application
Software Recommendations

Directions Read the situations described below. Assume you are a salesperson for a computer software dealer. What software would you recommend to the customer in each of the situations? Explain your answers.

1. Jake is a cartographer. He needs to scan aerial photographs and use the scans as templates over which he draws a map of the area photographed. He uses a large number of maps to produce an atlas (a book of maps). What software does he need?

   _____

   _____

   _____

   _____

2. Emily is the manager of sales and distribution for a small publisher. She deals with about 400 clients and needs to collect, organize, and continually update information about her clients, mostly small retail stores. She needs to know the following about each store: contact name, telephone number, fax number, e-mail address, address, resale number, store hours, and credit limit. She often corresponds with clients via both form letters and individualized letters. What software must she have?

   _____

   _____

3. George designs sundials as a hobby. To design a sundial he needs to know the latitude and longitude of the sundial's location. With that information and a set of equations, he can calculate the angle of the sun's shadow on the sundial face given the time of day. His sundials are marked every 15 minutes. George wants to quickly calculate the angles from 6 a.m. to 6 p.m. for any location. What software does he need?

   _____

   _____

4. George, Jake, and Emily decide to form a small company that markets Jake's maps and George's sundials. Naturally they want to set up a Web site, but they also want to go on the road giving presentations, and do old-fashioned things like mass-mailing brochures. What software will they need over and above what they already have?

   _____

   _____

Chapter 9 Technology Applications for Marketing

Real-World Application
Mock Online Seller

Directions Online shopping services are an important new venue for marketing. Use the following exercise to explore this market. Select a product that you would like to sell using an online marketing approach. Answer the questions to help you think about a marketing plan.

1. What is the name of the product?

   _____

2. Why did you select this product?

   _____

   _____

   _____

3. How is this product currently marketed?

   _____

   _____

4. What value does online marketing add to this product?

   _____

   _____

   _____

5. What disadvantages might a consumer experience in shopping for this product through an online service as compared to the way it is primarily marketed?

   _____

   _____

   _____

6. Do you believe that online services will become a significant part of the market in the future? Explain your answer.

   _____

   _____

   _____

Chapter 9

Chapter 9 Technology Applications for Marketing

DECA | **DECA Connection**
| **E-Commerce Consultant**

Role Play Imagine you are an e-commerce consultant working for a map publishing business. The owner of the business has asked you to investigate ways in which the company's products could be marketed online. Your research indicates that the cost of hiring a company to design and implement a Web site can cost up to $200,000, depending on the complexity of the Web site. The company you contacted has Web designers who get paid $170 to $340 per hour, and the job may take six months to a year to complete. If the business wants the ability to take orders, send confirmations, track customer preferences, and provide the necessary security for the business and its customers, the total cost could be as high as $400,000.

This firm will review your client's requirements and help you decide on a strategy, as well as design, implement, test, and roll out the Web site. A simpler version of a Web site, one that is used for advertising the product and then providing a toll-free number to place orders, may only take a few months and cost a lot less money.

You have been asked to make a recommendation regarding the design and implementation of a Web site for the company. After reviewing the costs and benefits of online marketing of the company's maps with the business owner (judge), suggest what you think would be the best method(s) to use.

Directions Role-play a meeting with the business owner (judge) in which you suggest what you think would be the best method(s) to use. To prepare for the meeting, be ready to summarize the costs and benefits of each method for the owner (judge).

Organize your thoughts around the performance indicators noted below. Use these indicators to jot down your ideas during the preparation period. Time your preparation period to last 15 minutes and your role-play presentation to last a maximum of 10 minutes. After your role play, use the performance indicators to evaluate your efforts.

Chapter 9 Technology Applications for Marketing

DECA Connection
E-Commerce Consultant *(continued)*

Assessment You will be evaluated on how well you meet the following performance indicators:

Score:

_____   Analyze technology for use in the sales function.

_____   Identify ways that technology impacts business.

_____   Use communication technologies.

_____   Determine services to provide to customers.

_____   Present report findings and recommendations.

Scoring Each performance indicator equals 20 points ($20 \times 5 = 100$ points).
Excellent (16–20)   **Good** (10–15)   **Fair** (4–9)   **Poor** (0–3)

Chapter 9

Chapter 9 Technology Applications for Marketing

Study Skills
Learning New Vocabulary

Directions Use the following tips to help improve your vocabulary. Then fill in the blanks by key terms. Finally, read the circled letters to discover the Mystery Phrase.

Learning New Vocabulary
• For many of these new words, you may already be familiar with their abbreviations, which are often used. This may help you remember meanings and spellings better.
• Create your own vocabulary flashcards. On one side write the word and its abbreviation, on the other, write its definition. Have a classmate quiz you, and then switch roles.

1   This links together documents on the Internet.
2. The entry point for a Web site
3. Electronic mail
4. Programs used to create text documents
5. Software that lets users edit text and graphics in one document
6. A network of computer networks, allowing the free flow of information
7. This outlines what can be found on each page within a Web site.
8. Software for producing slide shows or multimedia presentations
9. Programs that let computer users electronically communicate
10. A collection of interlinked electronic documents that is a subset of the Internet
11. This establishes a wireless Internet connection using radio frequencies.
12. Software used to organize, calculate, and analyze numerical data
13. Checkpoint that protects information on networked computers
14. Software that stores and organizes information
15. Also known as the Web address, this protocol identifies and locates Web pages.
16. Software that integrates all parts of a company's business management

1. _ _ _ _ _ _ _ _ _ _ _ _ _ _ _ _ _ _ _ _ _ _ _ _○_ _
2. _○_ _ _ _ _ _ _.
3. _ -○_ _ _
4. _ _ _ _ _○_ _ _ _ _ _ _ _ _
5. _ _ _ _ _ _ _ _○_ _ _ _ _ _ _ _ _
6. _ _○_ _ _ _ _ _
7. _ _○_ _ _ _ _
8. _○_ _ _ _ _ _ _ _ _ _ _
9. _○_ _ _ _ _ _ _ _ _ _ _ _○
10. _○_ _ _ _ _ _ _ _ _
11. _ _ -○_ _
12. _ _ _ _ _ _ _ _ _ _○_
13. _ _ _ _○_ _ _
14. _○_ _ _ _ _○
15. _ _ _ _ _○_ _ _ _ _ _ _ _ _ _ _ _ _
16.○_ _ _ _ _ _ _ _ _ _ _ _ _ _ _ _ _ _ _ _ _ _ _ _ _ _ _ _

Mystery Phrase: _____

Chapter 9 Technology Applications for Marketing

 Study Skills
Test Preparation

Directions Study the Test-Prep Tips and think about how you can use them to improve your test scores. Write a sentence or two to answer each of the following questions about the main ideas in Chapter 9.

Test-Prep Tips
• At home, find a regular place to study. Try to study at the same time every day. Train others to leave you alone during your study time.
• When answering an essay question on a test, focus on one main idea. Do not write long introductions and conclusions; spend most of your time answering the question asked.
• Do not spend too much time on questions that are confusing. If you do not know the answer to a question, circle the question number and move on. Come back to it later after you have answered the questions of which you are more sure.

1. Where can you find a site map and why would one be useful?

_____

2. What is interactive TV and who uses it?

_____

_____

3. How is a database program different from a spreadsheet program?

_____

_____

4. How is broadband different from Wi-Fi? How are they the same?

_____

_____

_____

5. How can businesses use graphics programs to market their products?

_____

_____

6. What are some specialized software that marketers use?

_____

_____

Chapter 9

Chapter 9 Technology Applications for Marketing

Test-Taking
Practice Test

Directions Take the practice test. In each series of terms, circle the one that does not belong. Explain your choice on the line below.

1.
Hypertext transfer protocol (HTTP)   Uniform resource locator (URL)
Firewall   Browser
Search engine

_____

2.
Word processing   Video game
Database   Presentation
Desktop publishing

_____

3.
Site map   Dial-up
Wi-Fi   Power grid
Digital subscriber line (DSL)

_____

4.
Videoconferencing   Instant messaging
E-mail   Telephone
Enterprise resource planning (ERP)

_____

5.
Touch-screen computers   E-mail
Interactive TV   Database
Internet

_____

6.
Touch-screen computers   Interactive TV
Web sites   Search engines
Enterprise resource planning software

_____

Chapter 10 Interpersonal Skills

Note Taking
Main Ideas and Supporting Details

Directions As you read, write key words and short phrases in the Cues column. Write notes, facts, and main ideas in the Note Taking column. Then summarize the section in the Summary box.

Cues	Note Taking
• Personal Strengths and Interpersonal Skills	• Personal Strengths and Interpersonal Skills
• Working Together: Leadership and Teamwork	• Working Together: Leadership and Teamwork

Summary

Chapter 10

Chapter 10 Interpersonal Skills

 ## Academic Integration: English Language Arts
Customer Service

Word Processing Skills You work in the customer service department for a mail-order company that sells gardening equipment and supplies. Ms. Jamie Winter has written a letter explaining that the workbench she ordered is missing the hardware that is needed for assembly. Write a letter apologizing for the missing hardware. Tell Ms. Winter that you are enclosing the hardware in the package with your letter. The address for the letter is shown below. Remember to leave one blank line after the salutation. Also leave one blank line between paragraphs of your letter and between the last line of the last paragraph and the closing. Include an enclosure notation after the closing to indicate that the hardware is being sent with this letter. Add an appropriate closing at the end of your letter and sign your name.

Ms. Jamie Winter
2403 Bremerton Avenue
Westerville, OH 43081

Directions Follow these steps to write a letter to Ms. Winter, then answer the questions that follow.
- Turn on your computer and open your word processing software program.
- Write a letter to Ms. Winter in response to her complaint.
- Save your work. Print out a copy of your work if you have been instructed to do so.

1. What is the purpose of your letter?

_____

_____

_____

_____

_____

_____

_____

_____

Chapter 10 Interpersonal Skills

Academic Integration: English Language Arts
Customer Service *(continued)*

2. Reread your letter and imagine that you are the person receiving the letter. Does it make you feel that your problem has been handled efficiently? Does it leave you with a positive impression of the company?

_____

_____

_____

_____

_____

_____

_____

_____

_____

3. What are some general guidelines that you think should be followed in writing letters responding to a customer's complaint?

_____

_____

_____

_____

_____

_____

_____

_____

_____

Chapter 10

Chapter 10 Interpersonal Skills

Real-World Application
Using Interpersonal Skills on the Job: Case 1

Directions Use the situations described below to explore your grasp of interpersonal skills. Study each situation and then answer the questions that follow.

1. Meg is a sales representative for an engineering services company. She has called on her customer, Tom, just a couple of times. Each time he has purchased services, but he has been very cold and abrupt with Meg. Meg is determined to break the ice with him. The next time she calls on Tom, she comments on some photos in his office of him skiing. Soon they are talking about favorite skiing locations and sharing stories. That day, Tom purchased more engineering services than usual from Meg and treated her in a much friendlier manner.

   a. What caused Tom to change his attitude?

   _____

   _____

   _____

   b. What other things could Meg have done to improve her relationship with Tom?

   _____

   _____

   _____

2. Bill performed so well in his entry-level position at a marketing firm that he was quickly promoted to a managerial position. In his new job, Bill seemed to undergo a personality change. He was no longer friendly with his coworkers; instead, he became very formal and bossy. He was very critical of the people he supervised and rarely gave praise. The members of his team soon began to complain about him.

   a. Why do you think Bill behaved the way he did?

   _____

   _____

   _____

   b. If you were his supervisor, what would you do?

   _____

   _____

   _____

Chapter 10

Chapter 10 Interpersonal Skills

 Real-World Application
Using Interpersonal Skills on the Job: Case 2

Directions Use the situations described below to explore your grasp of inter-personal skills. Study each situation and then answer the questions that follow.

1. Dan is a member of a four-person sales team in a gourmet kitchen shop. All of the sales team members have been cross-trained in the daily assignments that must be completed. Their first task each day is to restock shelves, clean, and prepare the store for opening. Dan is often late to work, arriving just a few minutes before opening time. He is an excellent salesperson and loves to work with customers on the floor. He will often trade his cashiering shift with another team member so that he can work with customers. His excellent sales record helps to ensure that his team always meets their sales goal. However, some of the team members are complaining that he is not a good team player.

   a. How would you feel about working with Dan?

   _____

   _____

   b. What would you do if you were the store manager?

   _____

   _____

2. Sara's team at the pizza parlor was working toward a bonus that their manager had offered to whichever team received the fewest customer complaints. Sara noticed that one of her team members, Julie, often made mistakes when writing up customer orders. Sara tried to encourage her to be more careful, but Julie seemed to resent her suggestions.

   a. What would you do if you were in Sara's situation?

   _____

   _____

   _____

   b. What would you do if you were the manager?

   _____

   _____

   _____

Chapter 10

Chapter 10 Interpersonal Skills

DECA Connection
E-Commerce Consultant

Role Play Imagine you are the supervisor of a group of customer service representatives at a franchised auto dealership. The dealership's mission for handling customer complaints is: "Do what needs to be done in order to ensure customer satisfaction." This policy is part of the franchise agreement with the auto manufacturer. A recent report from the auto manufacturer indicated that your customer service representatives are not handling customer complaints uniformly, nor are they receiving good grades in follow-up customer satisfaction surveys. This poor evaluation has led to problems among your employees, who are trying to put the blame elsewhere.

The general manager of the auto dealership (judge) wants to know how you plan to resolve this problem with your employees. He has asked you to prepare a plan for an upcoming staff meeting, where you address this issue. He wants to see an outline of your plan and hear exactly how you will conduct that staff meeting.

Directions Role-play a meeting with the business owner (judge) where you suggest what you think would be the best method(s) to use. To prepare for the meeting, be ready to summarize the costs and benefits of each method for the owner (judge).

Organize your thoughts around the performance indicators noted below. Use these indicators to jot down your ideas during the preparation period. Time your preparation period to last 15 minutes and your role-play presentation to last a maximum of ten minutes. After your role play, use the performance indicators to evaluate your efforts.

Assessment You will be evaluated on how well you meet the following performance indicators:
- Explain the nature of positive customer/client relations.
- Foster positive working relationships.
- Give directions for completing job tasks.
- Conduct staff meetings.
- Establish standards for job performance.

Chapter 10

Chapter 10 Interpersonal Skills

DECA Connection
E-Commerce Consultant *(continued)*

Explain the nature of positive customer/client relations.   **Score** _____

_____

_____

Foster positive working relationships.   **Score** _____

_____

_____

Give directions for completing job tasks.   **Score** _____

_____

_____

Conduct staff meetings.   **Score** _____

_____

_____

Establish standards for job performance.   **Score** _____

_____

_____

Scoring Each performance indicator equals 20 points (20 × 5 = 100 points).
Excellent (16–20)   **Good** (10–15)   **Fair** (4–9)   **Poor** (0–3)

Chapter 10

Chapter 10 Interpersonal Skills

 Study Skills
Learning New Vocabulary

Directions Use the following tips to help improve your vocabulary. Read each sentence below and circle the word or phrase that comes closest in meaning to the underlined word or phrase. Then write a sentence using the word or phrase.

Learning New Vocabulary
• Play word games and do crossword puzzles. Many are available for free on the Internet and you do not even need a partner to play them.
• When learning a new word, make as many connections and associations as you can. For example, the word *empathetic* is similar in meaning and form to the word *sympathetic*.

1. Maria was <u>assertive</u> when asking her supervisor to assign her more responsibility.
   angry   firm   honest   understanding

   _____

2. George <u>empathized</u> with Kelly's dilemma.
   criticized   tried to resolve   understood   was interested in

   _____

3. Carmen had <u>an agreement</u> with her supervisor to complete four computer classes.
   instructions from   a suggestion from   an arrangement   a written contract

   _____

4. Amy's <u>ethics</u> helped her gain the trust of her coworkers.
   self-esteem   negotiation skills   basic values   good looks

   _____

5. Robert was skilled at getting his team to reach a <u>consensus.</u>
   an agreement   an understanding   its goals   varied opinions

   _____

6. As a supervisor, Ramon values Dan's <u>initiative</u>.
   honesty   responsibility   creativity   drive to get things done

   _____

7. Before hiring any employees, the owners of B's Books decided to treat all with <u>equity.</u>
   basic values   honesty   equality   understanding

   _____

8. The actor was in <u>negotiations</u> for awhile, trying to get time off to see his children.
   an agreement   process of bargaining   drive to get things done   goals

   _____

   _____

Name _____ Date _____ Class _____

Chapter 10 Interpersonal Skills

 Study Skills
Test Preparation

Directions Study the Test-Prep Tips and think about how you can use them to improve your test scores. Then complete each sentence using a term from the Word Bank. Use all of the words in completing this exercise. (Some sentences will require more than one answer.)

Test-Prep Tips
• When studying in small groups, make sure your study group includes only students who are serious about studying. Some should be at your level of ability or better.
• Study old homework problems, unassigned problems in the textbook, and problems on old exams. Do not leave a problem until you are sure you can do it by yourself.

Word Bank			
listening	initiative	shared leadership	creativity
integrity	shared responsibility	enthusiasm	interest
establishing a plan	self-awareness	roles	team goals
self-esteem	equity	honesty	

1 Two procedures that will help you in dealing with customer complaints are
_____

2. Ethical behavior includes the personal traits of
_____

3. The first step to making personal changes is
_____

4. Personal traits that foster a positive attitude are
_____

5. Confidence is enhanced by good
_____

6. Two important elements of teamwork are
_____

7. Consensus is an important element in setting
_____

8. Using your imagination and acting on your ideas demonstrate the personal traits of
_____

9. Establishing standards so all employees have equal rights and opportunities creates
_____

10. Cross-training makes it possible for team members to be assigned many
_____

Chapter 10

Chapter 10 Interpersonal Skills

Test-Taking
Practice Test

Directions Take the practice test. For each item, circle the letter of the option that best answers the question.

1. Which is not a personality trait that would help someone be a better team player?
   a. empathy
   b. ethics
   c. initiative
   d. conflict

2. What is another word for equity?
   a. negotiation
   b. fairness
   c. management
   d. self-esteem

3. What is cross-training in the business world?
   a. playing on the company team
   b. being flexible
   c. being able to do different tasks on a business team
   d. training different people in a company

4. How does a good team leader get a consensus?
   a. by being aggressive
   b. by convincing everyone to agree
   c. by being a good listener
   d. by having team goals

5. What is the most important part of good customer service?
   a. keeping happy customers
   b. taking the customer aside
   c. not losing money
   d. improving the product or service

6. Which is part of good teamwork?
   a. planning
   b. delegation
   c. time management
   d. all of the above

Chapter 10

Chapter 11 Management Skills

Note Taking
Main Ideas and Supporting Details

Directions As you read, write key words and short phrases in the Cues column. Write notes, facts, and main ideas in the Note Taking column. Then summarize the section in the Summary box.

Cues	Note Taking
• Management Structures	• Management Structures
• Management Functions	• Management Functions

Summary

Chapter 11 Management Skills

Chapter 11

 Academic Integration: English Language Arts
Memo to the Delegate

Delegation You are the general manager for Somer's Plumbing Supplies, Inc. You have observed that none of the six departmental managers you supervise use delegation to get their work done quickly and effectively. Use your word processing software to create a memo to your departmental managers. In the memo, stress the benefits of delegating tasks and responsibilities to others. The heading for the memo is shown below.

To: Department Managers, Somer's Plumbing Supplies, Inc.

From: Your Name

Re: Using Delegation More Effectively

Date: Today's Date

Directions Follow these steps to create the memo. Then answer the questions below.
- Open your word processing software program on your computer.
- Write the memo. Proofread and edit your work to make sure that it is correct and concise.
- Save your work. Print out your memo if your teacher has instructed you to do so.

1. What primary benefits of delegating responsibility should be included in the memo?

_____

_____

_____

_____

_____

2. What tips on how to delegate effectively should be included in the memo?

_____

_____

_____

_____

_____

Chapter 11 Management Skills

Real-World Application
Organization

Directions Read the situation described below. Then write a description telling how you would organize the group to reach the goal. Tell whether your plan illustrates vertical or horizontal organization. Explain why you chose this organizational structure.

Fund Raising You are the leader of an 18-member jazz band at Belmont High School. The group recently took top honors in a national competition and as a result has been invited to perform at the White House. Unfortunately, the band's travel budget for the year was used up attending the nationals. In order to accept this invitation, you and the band will have to raise $12,600 in the next two months.

_____

_____

_____

_____

_____

_____

_____

_____

_____

_____

_____

_____

_____

_____

_____

_____

_____

_____

_____

_____

_____

Chapter 11

Chapter 11 Management Skills

 Real-World Application
Evaluating Work Performance

Directions Use the situation described below to practice your management decision-making skills. Study the situation carefully, and then answer the questions that follow.

Different Work Styles Jason works in the editorial department at Resorts Unlimited. A two-year veteran, he has edited three major directories. He always works more hours than anyone in the office. By working nights for several weeks, Jason was able to complete the editing on two of the three directories on schedule. The last directory, however, was late getting into production because some of Jason's calls to resorts were not returned.

The delay cost the company several thousand dollars. Now, Jason is editing a directory of tennis resorts. Since he started this project, he has been arriving at the office an hour early and always stays at least an hour after everyone else leaves. However, he mentioned that he may be delayed again because he is having difficulty contacting a few resort managers.

Derrick, who had no previous editing experience, was also hired by Resorts Unlimited two years ago. He comes to the office at 8 a.m. and goes home at 5 p.m. He worked late only one evening when he was finishing his last project, a directory of ski resorts. Twice, when he felt he could not get all the information he needed on the telephone, he visited resorts in Colorado and New Mexico. Each time, he left the office on Thursday evening, flew to the resort, spent the weekend skiing, and returned by noon Monday. On his first three projects, Derrick finished editing a few days ahead of schedule, and he appears to be on schedule for his current one.

1. How would you evaluate the performance of each man? If an opening were to occur for editorial director, which would you promote? Why?

   _____

   _____

2. Within three months of the publication of Derrick's ski directory, complaints start coming in with regularity from users and listed resorts. It seems that large blocks of information are either inaccurate or out-of-date. The result is an early reprint with heavy alteration costs and a disturbing loss of goodwill. Would these facts alter your earlier evaluations of Jason and Derrick? Explain why or why not.

   _____

   _____

Chapter 11 Management Skills

 DECA Connection
Marketing Internship

Role Play You are to assume the role of an assistant manager of a catalog company that specializes in high quality casual clothing for men and women. The vice president of sales (judge) has set new goals that she wants the company to achieve in the next 12 months, including increasing sales by 20 percent and generating a minimum of 15 new customers per month. She thinks the best way to achieve those objectives is through an employee incentive program that focuses on your staff of 10 full-time and 20 part-time telephone order takers. You have been given a budget of $2,500 to implement an incentive program. You think a more realistic budget would be $5,000.

Directions Role-play a meeting with your vice president of sales (judge) during which you share your ideas. To prepare for the meeting, use your knowledge of management skills to create a written outline of all the information you would include a new incentive program. Provide examples of your suggestions.

Organize your thoughts around the performance indicators noted below. Use these performance indicators to jot down your ideas during the preparation period. Time your preparation to last 15 minutes and your role-play presentation to last a maximum of ten minutes. After your role play, use the performance indicators to evaluate your efforts.

Assessment You will be evaluated on how well you meet the following performance indicators:

Score:

_____ Develop strategies to achieve company goals/objectives.

_____ Explain the concept of staff motivation.

_____ Explain the nature of staff communication.

_____ Demonstrate appropriate creativity.

_____ Persuade others.

Scoring Each performance indicator equals 20 points (20 × 5 = 100 points).
Excellent (16–20)   **Good** (10–15)   **Fair** (4–9)   **Poor** (0–3)

Chapter 11 Management Skills

Study Skills
Memorization

Directions Use the following tips to help improve your ability to memorize information. Then, review Chapter 11 using the tips as you answer the questions that follow. If the statement is true, circle **T**. If the statement is false, circle **F** and rewrite the statement so that it is true.

Memorization Skills
• Three focused, 15-minute study sessions per day are better than one 1-hour session.
• Do not try to memorize fifty words in one sitting; try six or eight words.
• Go back and repeat things often to reinforce what you have already learned.

1. Horizontal organization is a management structure characterized by   T   F
   self-managing teams.

   _____

2. Top management is the link between the top and supervisory levels.   T   F

   _____

   _____

3. Empowerment involves setting goals and determining how to reach them.   T   F

   _____

   _____

4. In supervisory-level management, managers supervise the activities of   T   F
   employees who carry out tasks determined by plans of middle and top management.

   _____

5. Controlling includes establishing a time frame in which to achieve the goal, T   F
   assigning employees to the project, and determining a method for approaching the work.

   _____

6. Remedial action focuses on managing employees in a way that prevents   T   F
   behavior that might require disciplining an employee.

   _____

   _____

7. Management is defined as getting work done through the effort of others.   T   F

   _____

8. When an employee leaves the company, the human resources department   T   F
   will typically arrange a mission statement.

   _____

Chapter 11 Management Skills

Study Skills
Test Preparation

Directions Study the Test-Prep Tips and think about how you can use them to improve your test scores. Write a sentence or two to answer each of the following questions about the main ideas in Chapter 11.

Test-Prep Tips
• Understand how the test content is organized. Ask your teacher if the test will include multiple choice, true or false, and/or essay-style questions. Just knowing how the questions are organized will help you prepare for a test.

1. What are the three basic levels of management in the traditional, vertically organized company?

_____

_____

2. What is the difference between a vertical and a horizontal company?

_____

_____

_____

3. What are three characteristics of a horizontal company?

_____

_____

_____

_____

4. What are the basic functions of management?

_____

5. What does it mean to delegate responsibility?

_____

_____

_____

6. What is the purpose of assessing employee performance?

_____

Chapter 11 Management Skills

 Test-Taking
Practice Test

Directions In each series of terms, circle the one that does not belong. Then explain your choice on the line below.

1. CEO   Executive   Supervisor
   Top management   Vice president

   _____

2. Customer orientation   Empowerment   Functional divisions
   Organization by process   Self-managing teams

   _____

3. Evaluating performance   Setting standards   Solving problems
   Assigning duties   Suggesting changes

   _____

4. Be consistent.   Be firm.   Define the problem.
   Give clear directions.   Set a good example.

   _____

Directions Complete the following statements by filling in the blanks.

5. The process of reaching goals through the use of human resources, technology, and

   material resources is called _____.

6. Flattening the organization is an expression describing _____.

7. The practice of encouraging employees to contribute and take responsibility for the

   management process is called _____.

8. Providing frequent feedback, rewarding smart work, and encouraging creativity are

   important in _____ employees.

9. Recruiting, hiring, and providing in-service training programs are responsibilities of the

   _____ department.

Chapter 12 Preparing for the Sale

 Note Taking
Main Ideas and Supporting Details

Directions As you read, write key words and short phrases in the Cues column.
Write notes, facts, and main ideas in the Note Taking column. Then summarize
the section in the Summary box.

Cues	Note Taking
• What Is Selling?	• What Is Selling?
• Getting Ready To Sell	• Getting Ready to Sell

Summary

Chapter 12

Chapter 12 Preparing for the Sale

 Academic Integration: Social Studies
Using and Analyzing a Spreadsheet

Evaluating Customer Preferences on Buying Decisions A local car dealer has collected information about the preferences of new car buyers. The spreadsheet below lists car features and customer ratings for each feature. The list shows how many male and female customers ranked each feature as a key factor in a buying decision. The dealer will use this information to plan future advertising campaigns and sales personnel will use the information in discussing the various car models with potential customers.

Features	Men who want the feature (total men polled: 260)	Percentage of total men who want the feature	Women who want the feature (total women polled: 248)	Percentage of total women who want the feature
Airbags	220		230	
Air conditioning	208		180	
Antilock brakes	240		215	
Automatic transmission	180		196	
CD player	170		150	
High performance tires	190		130	
Maintenance costs	198		200	
Power seat adjustments	150		170	
Repair record	210		180	
Standard transmission	85		68	
Satellite radio	88		80	
Variety of colors	100		90	

Chapter 12 Preparing for the Sale

Academic Integration: Mathematics
Using and Analyzing a Spreadsheet (continued)

Directions Follow these steps to complete the spreadsheet and analyze the profitability of each region. Then answer the questions below.

- Open your spreadsheet software program on your computer.
- Create a spreadsheet like the one on the previous page using your spreadsheet application.
- Write formulas to calculate the percentages of men and women who ranked each feature as a major reason for buying a car. Then copy the formulas to the remaining rows. (Percentage of men = (Number of men × 100) ÷ Total number of men polled.
- Save your work. Print out a copy of your work if you have been instructed to do so.

1. Which feature is rated as most important by men? By women? What is the percentage for each?

   _____

   _____

   _____

   _____

2. Which feature is the least important for men? For women? What is the percentage for each?

   _____

   _____

   _____

3. If you were the sales manager for this car dealer, how would you use this information in planning special sales promotions or in sales situations?

   _____

   _____

   _____

   _____

   _____

   _____

   _____

Chapter 12

Chapter 12 Preparing for the Sale

 ## Real-World Application
Features and Benefits

Directions Prepare a detailed feature-benefit chart for the Sony CFD-970
Sports Series MP3 Player/Satellite Radio Player. Remember, to develop customer benefits, you need to answer these two questions:

1) How does the feature help the product's performance?

2) How does performance information give customers a personal reason to buy?

Feature-Benefit Chart
Sony CFD-970 Sports Series MP3 Player/Satellite Radio Player

Product Feature: High-impact plastic case with waterproof seals

Customer Benefits: Rugged and splash-resistant to help keep out water, moisture, and dirt,
which allows you to take the recorder anywhere you go

Product Feature: Built-in MP3 and satellite radio (with a 1-year subscription to the satellite
radio service of your choice)

Customer Benefits: _____

_____

Product Feature: Sony Mega Bass® sound system.

Customer Benefits: _____

Product Feature: Satellite radio tuner

Customer Benefits: _____

Product Feature: Two-way power supply (two AAA batteries or household current)

Customer Benefits: _____

Product Feature: Two four-inch speakers

Customer Benefits: _____

Product Feature: Weight: 4 oz., 5 oz. with batteries

Customer Benefits: _____

What additional features would you add to the feature-benefit chart?

_____

Chapter 12 Preparing for the Sale

 Real-World Application
Preparing for a Sale

Directions Read the scenario below, and then answer the questions about preparing for making a sale.

Marketing Scenario Imagine you were just hired as a sales representative for a new start-up company that sells men's and women's fashion accessories. The deal is that you will be paid on straight commission at a rate of 8 percent. You only get paid if you sell these products. So, you must begin by studying the products and industry trends, and by prospecting. You need to develop your own leads. How do you prepare for the sale?

1. **Developing Product Information**—What will you do to develop the product information you need to be knowledgeable about the product line?

   _____

   _____

   _____

   _____

2. **Industry Trends**—How will you learn about industry trends?

   _____

   _____

   _____

3. **Prospecting**—What will you do to locate potential leads?

   _____

   _____

4. **Qualifying Leads**—What will you do to qualify potential customers (leads)?

   _____

   _____

5. **Last Step in the Pre-approach**—After finding a qualified prospect, what will you do?

   _____

6. **Commission Sales**—If one of your leads buys $2,000 worth of products, how much will you get paid? (Show your work.)

   _____

Chapter 12 Preparing for the Sale

 **DECA Connection**
Marketing Consultant

Role Play Imagine you are a volunteer in the children's ward at a local hospital. The hospital's new public relations/marketing director (judge) wants to raise money for the children's ward in order to renovate it and buy much-needed equipment. A celebrity fashion show is being planned as the fundraiser.

With your sales background and knowledge of the community, the public relations director (judge) has asked you to help. He would like you to compile a list of prospects for the sale of fashion show fundraiser tickets. The list should include individuals who would be willing to pay $75 for a ticket, as well as companies and organizations that might buy blocks of tickets (10 tickets = $750). Organizations and businesses should also be asked to provide door prizes and raffle prizes that will be given away during the fashion show. Additionally, you have been asked to write a sales letter and a telemarketing script that can be used to qualify the prospects (and identify the hopeless prospects so future sales efforts can be directed to the most promising leads).

Directions Role-play a meeting with the new PAGER director (judge) where you outline your plan and take suggestions from the new director. To prepare for the meeting, have your letters and script ready or outlines of each and an idea of prospects or where to find them and how to identify serious prospects to pursue.

Organize your thoughts around the performance indicators noted below. Use these indicators to jot down your ideas during the preparation period. Time your preparation period to last 15 minutes and your role play presentation to last a maximum of ten minutes. After your role-play, use the performance indicators to evaluate your efforts.

Assessment You will be evaluated on how well you meet the following performance indicators:
- Differentiate between consumer and organization buying behavior.
- Prospect for customers.
- Persuade others.
- Write sales letters.
- Use proper grammar and vocabulary.

Chapter 12 Preparing for the Sale

 **DECA Connection**
Marketing Consultant (continued)

Differentiate between consumer and organization buying behavior.   **Score** _____

_____

_____

Prospect for customers.   **Score** _____

_____

_____

Persuade others.   **Score** _____

_____

_____

Write sales letters.   **Score** _____

_____

_____

Use proper grammar and vocabulary.   **Score** _____

_____

_____

Scoring Each performance indicator equals 20 points (20 × 5 = 100 points).
Excellent (16–20)   **Good** (10–15)   **Fair** (4–9)   **Poor** (0–3)

Chapter 12 Preparing for the Sale

 Study Skills
Learning New Vocabulary

Directions Use the following tips to help improve your vocabulary. Then match each definition with the correct term from the Word Bank. (Not all terms will be used.)

Learning New Vocabulary
• When learning new words, concentrate on only a few terms at a time instead of trying to learn many words at once. When you are truly comfortable with the new words, only then should you move on to learn the next set.
• Look for words in bold or italicized print as you read. These are often key terms. Make sure you know what these words mean before you read the next section.

Word Bank		
cold canvassing	extensive decision making	product features
feature-benefit selling	prospect or lead	customer benefits
limited decision making	rational motive	emotional motive
personal selling	routine decision making	pre-approach
telemarketing		

_____ 1. Matching product characteristics to a customer's needs and wants.

_____ 2. Advantages or personal satisfaction a customer will get from a good or service

_____ 3. Used when a person buys goods and services that he or she has purchased before, but not on a regular basis

_____ 4. Direct contact between a salesperson and a customer

_____ 5. A potential customer

_____ 6. Basic, physical, or extended attributes of a product or purchase

_____ 7. Conscious, factual reason for a purchase

_____ 8. Used when there has been little or no previous experience with an infrequently purchased item

_____ 9. Getting ready for the face-to-face selling encounter

_____ 10. Technique used when a salesperson tries to locate potential customers with little or no direct help

Chapter 12 Preparing for the Sale

 Study Skills
Test Preparation

Directions Study the Test-Prep Tips and think about how you can use them to improve your test scores. Write a sentence or two to answer each of the following questions about the main ideas in Chapter 12.

Test-Prep Tips
• When studying for a test, write key ideas, definitions, and formulas on flash cards. Record your notes. Use these tools to review and prepare for test day.
• When working on a test, keep things moving along. Work on a problem until you get stuck. Think about it for a minute or two, and if nothing comes to mind then circle it and go on to another problem. Go back to it at the end if you have time.
• Eat well before taking a test. Have a good breakfast or lunch and avoid junk food. Studies show that you need good nutrition to concentrate and perform your best.

1. When does a customer do routine decision making? What kinds of product might a customer buy that requires this type of decision making?

   _____

   _____

2. Why do companies offer employee discounts?

   _____

   _____

3. When a drug representative visits a doctor's office to inform them about a new painkiller, what type of marketing would this be?

   _____

4. What types of motives do customers have when making decisions to make a purchase?

   _____

   _____

5. Under which selling category would telemarketing fall?

   _____

6. How do salespeople prepare for the sale?

   _____

   _____

   _____

Chapter 12 Preparing for the Sale

Test-Taking
Practice Test

Directions Take the practice test. Circle the letters of ALL choices that accurately complete each of the following sentences.

1. Salespeople can get product information they need through
   a. direct experience with the product.
   b. formal training.
   c. friends, relatives, coworkers, and customers.
   d. printed resources (such as packaging, labels, user's manuals, and publications like *Consumer Reports*).

2. Extended product features for a Reebok running shoe might include the
   a. Duratech rubber sole.
   b. Reebok brand name.
   c. removable molded sock liner.
   d. limited warranty.

3. When buying an automobile, a customer may have
   a. rational reasons for making the purchase, such as monetary savings gained through gas economy.
   b. emotional motives for making the purchase, such as social approval and prestige generated by the image associated with a high-priced car.
   c. both rational and emotional reasons for the purchase based on features such as air bags and a 24-hour emergency roadside service.
   d. reasons different from those of other customers who purchased the same vehicle.

4. The two goals of selling are
   a. to persuade customers to buy something regardless of their need for the item.
   b. to help customers make satisfying buying decisions.
   c. to create an ongoing, profitable relationship with a customer.
   d. to make management's sales quotas any way you can.

5. When a salesperson researches a prospect to determine if he or she needs the product the salesperson is selling, has the financial resources to pay, and is the person who has the authority to buy, we say the salesperson is
   a. prospecting.
   b. using the endless chain method.
   c. cold canvassing.
   d. qualifying the lead.

6. Two pressures on sales staff that can lead to illegal or unethical selling practices if not handled properly by sales personnel are
   a. commission sales.
   b. sales quotas.
   c. sales training requirements.
   d. company policies that address team work.

Chapter 13 Initiating the Sale

Note Taking
Main Ideas and Supporting Details

Directions As you read, write key words and short phases in the Cues column. Write notes, facts, and main ideas in the Note Taking column. Then summarize the section in the Summary box.

Cues	Note Taking
• The Sales Process	• The Sales Process
• Determining Needs in Sales	• Determining Needs in Sales

Summary

Chapter 13

Chapter 13 Initiating the Sale

Academic Integration: Mathematics
Spreadsheet Application

Demographics The Home Supply Store is planning to build a new retail store in one of five areas of a large city. The population, total income, and number of people over age 30 in each area are listed in the spreadsheet below. Home Supply has found that its stores do better in areas with a population of at least 55,000 over age 30 and average income of $28,000. About 70 percent of the store's regular customers are over 30.

	A	B	C	D	E	F
1		Population	Total	Average	Population	Percentage
2		Chapter 13 Initiating the Sale				
3		CD player	Income	Income	Over 30	Over 30
4	North	84,600	$2,453,400,000		57,700	
5	South	78,400	$2,138,600,000		55,890	
6	East	67,600	$1,876,000,000		48,690	
7	West	82,700	$2,670,000,000		68,600	
8	Central	76,800	$1,958,000,000		49,500	

Directions Follow these steps to create a spreadsheet. Then answer the questions below.

Spreadsheet Directions
- Open your spreadsheet software program on your computer.
- Create a spreadsheet like the one above using your spreadsheet application.
- Create a formula to calculate average income in each area, then copy it to the remaining rows. Create a formula to calculate the percentage of the population over age 30 in each area, and then copy the formula to the remaining rows.

- Save your work. Print out a copy of your work if your teacher has instructed you to do so.

1. Which of the areas meets Home Supply's guidelines for establishing a new store?

   _____

   _____

2. Which area offers the highest percentage of residents over 30?

   _____

3. Which area has the highest average income?

   _____

Chapter 13 Initiating the Sale

 Real-World Application
Approaching the Customer

Directions Read the following scenarios and write an appropriate approach for the initial face-to-face meeting with the customer. After writing the approach, practice saying it to a classmate to check that what you wrote is how you would actually speak.

Situation 1: You work in the sales department of The Delta Hotel, a large hotel with a conference center that includes several meeting rooms, a business center where guests can send and receive faxes, and nicely furnished guest rooms. The hotel also has two restaurants and offers catering services for special events in its ballroom. Ms. Rodriguez, a representative from a local business, is in the out-side office waiting to meet with you. Since she made her appointment through your assistant, you have yet to speak with her directly. She did tell your assistant that her company was considering holding a three-day business conference in your hotel.

_____

_____

Situation 2: You work as a sales associate in a camera store. You observe a woman looking at a digital camera.

_____

_____

Situation 3: You work as an in-house sales representative in the New York showroom of a men's apparel manufacturer. John Armstrong, an out-of-town buyer whom you have known for the past five years, has an appointment with you to see the new fall line. You see him walking into the showroom 30 minutes early and you are still working with a buyer who had the first appointment of the day.

_____

_____

_____

Situation 4: As a sales clerk in a self-service stationery store, you are often asked to work at the service desk where customers come for assistance. One such customer is now approaching the service desk.

_____

Chapter 13 Initiating the Sale

 Real-World Application
Features and Benefits

Directions Imagine that you work in a retail store that specializes in outdoor
apparel and sporting goods. After you approach a customer who is looking at
the Canyon Meadow jacket, made by Colombia Sportswear Company, you begin
to determine her needs.

1. Write one question that you could use to determine why the customer is looking at the
   jacket.

   _____

   _____

2. Write two questions to determine the customer's previous experience with the Columbia
   Sportswear Company (manufacturer of the Canyon Meadow jacket) and its products.

   a. _____

   _____

   b. _____

   _____

3. Write four questions related to specific features of the jacket that will help you decide if
   it is the one that will satisfy your customer's needs and wants.

   a. _____

   _____

   b. _____

   _____

   c. _____

   _____

   d. _____

   _____

Chapter 13 Initiating the Sale

 DECA Connection
Sales Representative

Role Play You are to assume the role of sales representative for a manufacturer of insulated clothing and accessories for use in business-to-business situations that involve cold environments. Your primary customers are wholesalers that have large warehouses of refrigerated and frozen foods they sell to retail stores and restaurants. Your company manufactures insulated clothing with varying levels of insulation for the different temperatures. The clothing includes jackets, pants, footwear, headwear, and gloves.

Directions Your sales manager (judge) wants to put together a training manual for new sales employees. She has asked you to write and present the section on approaching new customers and determining their needs at the next sales meeting. Generate at least ten questions that can be used to determine the customer's needs. Tell why and when these questions should be asked. Prepare three introductions you might use when approaching a purchasing agent face-to-face for the first time.

Time your preparation to last 15 minutes and your role-play presentation to last a maximum of ten minutes. After your role play, use the performance indicators to evaluate your efforts.

Assessment You will be evaluated on how well you meet the following performance indicators:

Score:

_____ Establish a relationship with the client/customer.

_____ Address the needs of individuals.

_____ Determine customer/client needs.

_____ Prepare for the sales presentation.

_____ Address people properly.

Scoring Each performance indicator equals 20 points (20 × 5 = 100 points).
Excellent (16–20)   **Good** (10–15)   **Fair** (4–9)   **Poor** (0–3)

Chapter 13 Initiating the Sale

📄 Study Skills
Improving Writing Skills

Directions Use the following tips to help improve your writing skills. Then, in the space below, write a brief scenario (story) of a selling situation that illustrates at least three terms from the Word Bank. Select the product of your choice. Underline the words from the Word Bank when they appear in the story. Products you might want to consider using are a computer, a copier, running shoes, a camera, luggage, or a CD player.

Writing
• Before answering a question that asks you to write a paragraph, consider how you will organize your paragraph. For example, you might present a statement and then follow it with supporting details. You might tell how two things are alike and different, describe a sequence of events, or list possible solutions to a problem. Good organization is important and will help you get a better grade.

Word Bank	
greeting approach method	merchandise approach method
nonverbal communication	open-ended questions
service approach method	

_____

_____

_____

_____

_____

_____

_____

_____

_____

_____

_____

Chapter 13 Initiating the Sale

Study Skills
Test Preparation

Directions Study the Test-Prep Tips and think about how you can use them to improve your test scores. Write a sentence or two to answer each of the following questions about the main ideas in Chapter 13.

Test-Prep Tips
• During study time, reward yourself with short breaks to stretch your body and your mind.
• When studying for a test, take a ten-minute break every hour and reward yourself with a call to a friend, a walk, a bike ride, or a healthy food or drink treat.
• Set an alarm or keep an eye on your watch. Breaks should only last about ten minutes.

1. What role does the salesperson play in the selling process?

_____

_____

2. What are the seven steps to the selling process?

_____

_____

_____

3. Which type of approach is most effective in retail sales? Why?

_____

_____

_____

4. When determining needs, why is it important for you to discover your customer's motivation for buying?

_____

_____

5. What should you look for when observing a customer? How can this help your sale?

_____

_____

_____

Chapter 13

Chapter 13 Initiating the Sale

Test-Taking
Practice Test

Directions Circle the letter of the word or phrase that completes each of the following questions.

1. The three purposes of the approach include all of the following except
   a. to begin conversation.
   b. to establish rapport with the customer.
   c. to focus on the merchandise.
   d. to handle customer objections.

2. "Good morning, Mr. Escalona. How's your golf game?" This is an example of
   a. an unacceptable retail approach.
   b. the greeting approach method.
   c. the merchandise approach method.
   d. the service approach method.

3. "You are looking at the newest tennis racket in the Prince line. It has a bigger sweet spot than any of the previous models." This is an example of
   a. the greeting approach method.
   b. the merchandise approach method.
   c. the research approach method.
   d. the service approach method.

4. General concepts that industrial salespeople would use in their opening statements to prospective customers during the initial approach include all of the following except
   a. having the financial resources to pay.
   b. being a better competitor.
   c. increasing productivity.
   d. reducing costs and expenses.

5. Determining needs is an important step in the sales process because
   a. it helps you focus everything you say and do on your customer's needs and wants.
   b. it gives you an opportunity to show and tell the customer everything you know about the product.
   c. you cannot handle customers' objections without having first determined their needs.
   d. it is the first contact that you have with the customer and therefore can make or break the sale.

6. A salesperson should begin determining a customer's needs
   a. after the product presentation begins.
   b. as soon as possible in the sales process.
   c. before closing the sale.
   d. when the customer introduces an objection.

7. Determining needs can best be achieved by
   a. observing, asking questions, and listening to your customers.
   b. presenting product features.
   c. asking easy, yes/no questions.
   d. asking many questions in a row to gather all the facts you need before showing a customer any products.

Chapter 14 Presenting the Product

Note Taking
Main Ideas and Supporting Details

Directions As you read, write key words and short phrases in the Cues column. Write notes, facts, and main ideas in the Note Taking column. Then summarize the section in the Summary box.

Cues	Note Taking
• Produce Presentation	• Produce Presentation
• Objections	• Objections

Summary

Chapter 14

Chapter 14 Presenting the Product

Academic Integration: Mathematics
Spreadsheet Application

Analyzing Sales You are the sales rep with a company that manufactures doors and windows for use in residential and commercial buildings. Much of your time is spent traveling from site to site presenting the company's product lines to building contractors. Your manager has asked you to analyze the amount of time you spend making sales calls and how many of those calls actually result is sales. You have collected the information shown in the spreadsheet below. This information includes the number of sales calls you have made during each of the last eight months. Also included are average times per sales call, number of sales made, and the total dollar volume in sales each month.

	A	B	C	D	E	F	G
1		Sales Calls Made	Average Time per Call	Number of Sales Made	Percentage of Calls Resulting	Dollar Amount	Average Sale per
2	Chapter 14 Presenting the Product						
3	January	80	43	40		$408,000	
4	February	76	48	32		$350,000	
5	March	82	40	38		$378,000	
6	April	78	50	41		$280,000	
7	May	74	62	42		$397,800	
8	June	74	58	36		$358,600	
9	July	70	60	38		$419,400	
10	August	72	64	40		$465,000	

Directions Follow these steps to analyze the spreadsheet. Then answer the questions that follow.
- Turn on your computer and open your spreadsheet software program.
- Create a spreadsheet like the one above.
- Create a formula to calculate the percentage of sales calls that resulted in sales. Then copy the formula to the remaining rows.
-
-
- Create a formula to calculate the average sales dollar per sales call made during the month. Copt the formula to the remaining rows.
-
- Save your work. Print out a copy of your work if your teacher has instructed you to do so.

Chapter 14 Presenting the Product

 Academic Integration: Mathematics
Spreadsheet Application *(continued)*

1. What relationship do you see between the number of minutes spent on sales calls and the percentage of calls that result in sales?

_____

_____

_____

_____

2. What is the highest percentage of sales calls resulting in sale? the lowest?

_____

_____

_____

_____

3. Using the information in the spreadsheet, develop a plan to increase your sales for the next several months. Explain the data on which you have based your conclusions for how to increase sales.

_____

_____

_____

_____

_____

_____

_____

_____

_____

Chapter 14

Chapter 14 Presenting the Product

Real-World Application
Presentation Preparation

Directions Plan a product presentation for a Sharp Digital Viewcam. Write exactly what you would say and do to present the product features listed below.

1. Dimensions, (W × H × D inches) 16.2 × 3.8 × 2.9, and approximate weight, 1.2 pounds, without tape or battery.

   a. _____

   _____

   _____

   _____

   b. _____

   _____

   _____

   c. _____

   _____

   _____

   _____

2. Write two questions to determine the customer's previous experience with the Sharp Digital Viewcam.

   a. _____

   _____

   _____

   _____

   _____

   b. _____

   _____

   c. _____

   _____

   _____

Chapter 14 Presenting the Product

 Real-World Application
Dealing with Customer Objections

Directions For each customer objection below, write a salesperson's response using the indicated method. For ideas, refer to the feature-benefits chart for the Canyon Meadows jacket found in Chapter 12 of Marketing Essentials.

1. **Objection:** "This jacket is so thin. It can't possibly keep out the rain."

   Response: (Use the boomerang method.)

   _____

   _____

   _____

   _____

2. **Objection:** "I like this jacket, but I'm not sure my daughter really needs all of its features. She just needs a jacket to wear to school."

   Response: (Use the third party method.)

   _____

   _____

   _____

   _____

3. **Nonverbal Objection:** The customer has a skeptical look in his face when you tell him how easy is it to pack up the jacket into a pouch.

   Response: (Use the demonstration method.)

   _____

   _____

   _____

   _____

Chapter 14

Chapter 14 Presenting the Product

DECA Connection
Sales Associate

Role Play Imagine that you are a sales associate at Luggage & Bags Unlimited. You are responsible for selling a variety of luggage, attaché cases, backpacks, and related products. You know that it is important to use layman's terms, show how product features translate into consumer benefits, involve the customer in the sale, demonstrate the product features, and use sales aids. You also realize that during a product presentation it is common to handle objections that may occur. Another sales associate has started helping a customer who is entering high school next month, but the customer (judge) is the teen's mother, who will be paying for the purchase.

Directions You are responsible for presenting the features and benefits of a backpack and handling any objections the consumer and customer (judge) may have. Some of those objections may involve the price, durability, capacity, and ergonomic issues. Use your own backpack or bag to make your product presentation to the customer.

Organize your thoughts around the performance indicators noted below. Use these performance indicators to jot down your own ideas during the preparation period. Time your preparation period to last 15 minutes and your role-play presentation to last a maximum of ten minutes. After your role play, use the performance indicators to evaluate your efforts.

Assessment You will be evaluated on how well you meet the following performance indicators.
- Analyze product information to identify product features and benefits.
- Prescribe a solution to customer needs.
- Demonstrate the product.
- Convert customer/client objections into selling points.
- Recommend a specific product.

_____

_____

_____

_____

_____

_____

_____

Chapter 14

Chapter 14 Presenting the Product

 DECA Connection
Sales Associate *(continued)*

Assessment Assume each performance indicator is worth 20 points (20 × 5 = 100 points). Use the evaluation levels listed below for judging consistency.

Analyze product information to identify product features and benefits   **Score** _____

_____

_____

Prescribe a solution to customer needs.   **Score** _____

_____

_____

Demonstrate the product.   **Score** _____

_____

_____

Convert customer/client objections into selling points.   **Score** _____

_____

_____

Recommend a specific product.   **Score** _____

_____

_____

Scoring Each performance indicator equals 20 points (20 × 5 = 100 points).
Excellent (16–20)   **Good** (10–15)   **Fair** (4–9)   **Poor** (0–3)

Chapter 14

Chapter 14 Presenting the Product

 Study Skills
Improving Vocabulary

Directions Use the following tips about improving your vocabulary. Then review the vocabulary in Chapter 14 and answer the questions that follow. If the statement is true, circle **T**. If the statement is false, circle **F** and rewrite the statement so that is it true.

Improving Vocabulary
• Using specialized vocabulary in your profession will help you express your thoughts. • Using the specialized vocabulary of your profession with ease will help you create a good impression with your peers and bosses.

1. Jargon is technical or specialized vocabulary used by members of a particular profession or industry.   T   F

   _____

2. To paraphrase is to restate the meaning of the customer's concern in different words.   T   F

   _____

3. The superior point method is used to handle an objection by recommending a different product that would still satisfy a customer's needs.   T   F

   _____
   _____

4. The third party method uses a pervious customer or another neutral person who can give a testimonial about the product.   T   F

   _____

5. An excuse is a concern, a hesitation, a doubt, or another honest reason a customer has for not making a purchase.   T   F

   _____

6. Layman's terms are words the average customer can understand.   T   F

   _____

7. The substitution method is a technique that permits a sales person to acknowledge objections as valid, yet still offset them with other product features.   T   F

   _____
   _____

8. An objection analysis sheet enumerates common customer objections and possible responses to those objections.   T   F

   _____

Chapter 14 Presenting the Product

 Study Skills
Test Preparation

Directions Study the Test-Prep Tips and think about how you can use them to improve your test scores. Write a sentence or two to answer each of the following questions about the main ideas in Chapter 24.

Test-Prep Tips
• Think productively while you are studying. Look at problems in several ways and try to find new ways of thinking about what you are studying.   • Think about relationships and connections between subjects that seem to be dissimilar.

1. What items might be found on a receiving record?

_____

_____

_____

2. Explain the blind-check method. Is this the most accurate checking method?

_____

_____

_____

3. What is inventory and what does it include?

_____

_____

_____

4. How are retail businesses expected to maintain their inventory?

_____

_____

_____

5. What are the steps in the stock handling process?

_____

_____

_____

Chapter 14

Chapter 14 Presenting the Product

 **Study Skills**
Practice Test

Directions Take the practice test. Circle the letters of the choice that accurately complete each of the following sentences.

1. The goal of the product presentation is to
   a. answer all of the customer's questions.
   b. match the customer's needs with appropriate product features and benefits.
   c. persuade a customer to buy the most expensive model in the product line.
   d. show the customer as many products as time permits.

2. During the product presentation in the sale of running shoes, a salesperson should not
   a. show a video tape of Olympic runners wearing specific running shoes.
   b. use a model of a running shoe cut in half to show its construction and hidden features.
   c. have the customer try on a running shoe and walk around in it.
   d. present the customer with five or six models of running shoes to consider at one time.

3. When you do not know the customer's price range and your knowledge of the intended use is insufficient to determine a price range
   a. begin by showing the medium-priced product in the line.
   b. begin by showing the highest-priced product line.
   c. begin by showing the lowest-priced product line.
   d. ask the customer how much he or she wants to spend.

4. You are a sales representative for a manufacturer of strep throat testing equipment and supplies. When you call on a physician who is too busy to see you, you should
   a. tell the receptionist that you will not be in the area again for a very long time.
   b. leave your business card and literature about your product.
   c. sit in the office until all the patients have been seen and the doctor has time to see you.
   d. simply leave the office and make a note to return another day.

5. You are a retail sales associate in a clothing store. After speaking with you for a few minutes, a customer explains that she is just browsing and did not plan on buying anything today. At this point, you should
   a. tell the customer how annoyed you are that she wasted your time.
   b. simply leave her alone.
   c. encourage the customer to look around and ask you any questions she may have.
   d. follow the customer around the store just in case she is a shoplifter. .

6. If a customer said, "That's more than I wanted to spend on a bicycle built for tow. I had no idea they were so expensive," you would use the
   a. superior point method.   c. demonstration method.
   b. direct denial method.   d. third party method.

Chapter 15 Closing the Sale

Note Taking
Main Ideas and Supporting Details

Directions As you read, write key words and short phases in the Cues column.
Write notes, facts, and main ideas in the Note Taking column. Then summarize
the section in the Summary box.

Cues	Note Taking
• How To Close a Sale	• How To Close a Sale
• Customer Satisfaction and Retention	• Customer Satisfaction and Retention

Summary

Chapter 15

Chapter 15 Closing the Sale

Academic Integration: Mathematics
Analyzing a Database

Calculating Room Rates The manager of the Pine Mountain Ski Resort is making a budget for the upcoming season. One of the first things the manager does is forecast revenue from room rentals for each of the five months of the season. Those months are December through April. The manager uses past experience to estimate the number of rooms that will be filled during each month. This is the occupancy rate. The spreadsheet below shows the price of the rooms per night and the occupancy rate for each month.

	A	B	C	D	E
1		Number of Rooms	Average Room Rate	Occupancy Rate	Revenue
2	Chapter 15 Closing the Sale				
3	December	100	$128	95%	
4	January	100	$128	92%	
5	February	100	$128	89%	
6	March	100	$128	74%	
7	April	100	$128	48%	
8					
9	Total Revenue				

Directions Follow these steps to analyze the database. Then answer the questions that follow.

- Turn on your computer and open your spreadsheet software program.
- Create a spreadsheet like the one above using your spreadsheet application.
- Input a formula to determine the estimated revenue for the month of December. Copy the formula to the remaining cells.

- Calculate the total revenue by entering the appropriate formula to add the revenue column.
- Save your work to a new file. Print out a copy of your work if your teacher has instructed you to do so.

1. What is the total revenue based on the projections of occupancy for the months of December through April?

   _____

   _____

2. Which month has the highest revenue from the rooms? The lowest?

   _____

Chapter 15

Chapter 15 Closing the Sale

🌐 Real-World Application
Closing the Sale

Directions Write what you would say to close the sale in each situation.

1. **Situation 1:** You work as a sales associate for Carol's electronics.

   a. Your store is having a one-day sale to celebrate your town's bicentennial. All merchandise in the store is marked down 10 percent for one day. Your customer says, "I like the Sharp Digital Viewcam, but I didn't expect to buy anything today. I'd like my wife to see it before I make a final decision." (Use the standing-room-only close in combination with an appropriate service close).

   _____

   _____

   _____

   _____

   _____

   b. Your customer says, "I can't wait to start videotaping using the power zoom." (Use a direct close).

   _____

   _____

2. **Situation 2:** You work as a sales representative for the Sharp Sales Company.

   a. You just finished showing the buyer for JTS Electronics, a retailer, all the features and benefits of the Sharp Digital Viewcam, and you think it is time to try a close. (Use a non-threatening question as a trial close).

   _____

   _____

   b. A buyer for PNC Electronic Wholesalers asks, "If I order six dozen Sharp Digital Viewcams to start and they sell well, how quickly can I get a reorder?" (Use a direct close).

   _____

   _____

Chapter 15

Chapter 15 Closing the Sale

Real-World Application
Selling and Customers

Directions Study the sales situations below. Then, in each case, tell what additional merchandise or service you would suggest and what you would say to recommend it.

1. You work in a bicycle store and have just sold a bicycle to a couple for their young daughter.

   Suggested item: _____

   What would you say? _____

   _____

2. You are a sales representative for the Sharp Manufacturing Company. The company is offering free shipping on all orders that exceed $5,000, if the order is placed within the next week. You just closed a sale with a retail store buyer who wants to place a $4,500 order.

   Suggested item: _____

   _____

   What would you say? _____

   _____

Directions Study the sales situations below. Then, in each case, tell what you would do establish a relationship with the customer.

3. You are a sales representative for the Sharp Manufacturing Company. A retail store buyer has just placed an order with you for $100,000 with specifications regarding delivery.

   _____

   _____

   _____

4. You are a sales associate for an upscale clothing store.

   _____

   _____

   _____

   _____

Chapter 15 Closing the Sale

 DECA Connection
Computer Salesperson

Role Play You are to assume the role of sales associate for Computers Etc. Within 20 minutes you have determined a customer's (judge) needs, and presented the features and benefits of a computer and monitor that meets those needs. You now feel it is time to close the sale and suggest additional items that will compliment the computer. The customer (judge) is interested in a 15" monitor and a computer with a high-speed modem, a CD writeable drive, and a DVD drive, at a retail price of $1,299. In addition to printers and computer software, your company offers several services that the customer (judge) may be interested in, such as leasing, extended warranty (at a cost of $49.99 for three years). You are expected to see if customers are having any problems or have any questions. To ensure customer satisfaction, an independent market research company conducts a customer follow-up survey. It might be a good idea to tell your customer (judge) about the survey so he will respond to it.

Directions Close the sale with the customer (judge) and suggest appropriate goods and services to enhance the original purchase.

Organize your thoughts around the performance indicators noted below. Use these performance indicators to jot down your ideas during the preparation period. Time your preparation period to last 15 minutes and your role-play presentation to last a maximum of ten minutes. After your role play, use the performance indicators to evaluate your efforts.

Assessment You will be evaluated on how well you meet the following performance indicators:

Score:

_____ Facilitate customer-buying decisions

_____ Close the sale.

_____ Demonstrate suggestion selling.

_____ Explain the role of customer service as a component of selling relationships.

_____ Plan follow-up strategies for use in selling.

Scoring Each performance indicator equals 20 points (20 × 5 = 100 points).
Excellent (16–20)   **Good** (10–15)   **Fair** (4–9)   **Poor** (0–3)

Chapter 15

Chapter 15 Closing the Sale

Study Skills
Time Management

Directions Use the following tips to help improve how you manage your time.
Then, review Chapter 15 using the tips as you answer the questions that follow.
If the statement is true, circle **T**. If the statement is false, circle **F** and rewrite
the statement so that it is true.

Time Management
• Prepare a hard copy or electronic calendar at the beginning of each semester. Use it to record assignments and due dates and to keep track of testing schedules. Review and update your schedule weekly as the semester progresses.

1. Suggestive selling means selling additional goods or services to the customer.　　T　F

　_____

2. An initial effort to close a sale is called a direct close.　　T　F

　_____

3. A closing method in which you ask for the sale is called a which close.　　T　F

　_____

4. Customer relationship management involves finding customers and keeping them satisfied.　　T　F

　_____

5. A standing-room-only close is a closing method used when a product is in short supply or when the price will be going up in the near future.　　T　F

　_____

6. A closing method that explains services that overcome obstacles or problems is called a direct close.　　T　F

　_____

　_____

7. Obtaining positive agreement from the customer to buy is known as a buying signal.　　T　F

　_____

8. Buying signals are things that a customer does or says to indicate a readiness to buy.　　T　F

　_____

Chapter 15

Chapter 15 Closing the Sale

 Study Skills
Test Preparation

Directions Study the Test-Prep Tips and think about how you can use them to improve your test scores. Write a sentence or two to answer each of the following questions about the main ideas in Chapter 15.

Test-Prep Tips
• Anxiety about tests can contribute to poor performance. Maintain a positive attitude. Think of a test as an opportunity to show what you have learned.
• If you feel anxious during a test, take several slow deep breaths to help you relax.

1. Why is it important for salespeople to remain flexible with potential buyers?

_____

2. What types of words can be used to create an ownership mentality in the customer?

_____

3. What are some things salespeople can do to keep customers?

_____

4. How do salespeople, customers, and firms benefit from suggestive selling?

_____

_____

_____

5. What are five basic rules for using suggestive selling?

_____

_____

_____

_____

6. What are four follow-up ideas salespeople should use?

_____

_____

_____

_____

Chapter 15

Chapter 15 Closing the Sale

 Study Skills
Practice Test

Directions Take the practice test. Choose the word or phrase that best completes the sentence or answers the question.

1. You should close the sale
   a. at the same point in each sales presentation.
   b. after a customer says, "I'll take it."
   c. only after you have finished presenting all of your product's selling points.
   d. when your customer is ready to buy.

2. When a customer is having difficulty making a buying decision,
   a. leave the customer alone.
   b. help by summarizing the major features and benefits of the product.
   c. rush the customer.
   d. show the customer additional merchandise.

3. Continuing to tell a customer about the features and benefits of a product that he or she is ready to buy
   a. is an effective sales practice.
   b. helps reduce a customer's doubts about a product.
   c. is especially important in the sale of expensive merchandise.
   d. may cause the salesperson to lose the sale.

4. A specialized closing technique that should be used only when the situation warrants is the
   a. direct close.
   b. service close.
   c. standing-room-only close.
   d. which close.

5. Suggestion selling
   a. can make the original purchase more enjoyable.
   b. hurts a firm because of increased sales-related expenses.
   c. means loading customers down with unwanted goods or services.
   d. should only be attempted when salespeople have time.

6. Customer Relationship Management suggests that
   a. the sale is the first step in developing a relationship with your customer, not the final one.
   b. taking payment or taking the order is the last step in the sales process.
   c. if you did not close the sale today, the sale is lost forever.
   d. after-sale activities are just that and, as such, not part of the formal sales process.

Chapter 16 Using Math in Sales

Note Taking
Main Ideas and Supporting Details

Directions As you read, write key words and short phrases in the Cues column.
Write notes, facts, and main ideas in the Note Taking column. Then summarize
the section in the Summary box.

Cues	Note Taking
• Sales Transactions	• Sales Transactions
• Cash Registers	• Cash Registers
• Purchase Orders, Invoices, and Shipping	• Purchase Orders, Invoices, and Shipping

Summary

Chapter 16 Using Math in Sales

Academic Integration: Mathematics
Spreadsheet Application

Calculating Growth You want to invest in a high-growth business. You have studied market and economic factors and you have narrowed your choices to the business sectors listed below. You want to choose the sector that has the highest growth rate.

The printout below shows data that you have collected about current sales, as well as anticipated sales in five years. To calculate the growth rate for each business sector, first subtract the current sales from the anticipated sales in five years. Then divide the result by current sales totals.

	A	B	C	D
1	**Business Category**	**Current Sales**	**Anticipated Sales in Five Years**	**Growth Rate**
2	Chapter 16 Using Match in Sales			
3	Restaurants	$48,926	$86,109	
4	Retailing (non-food)	$18,790	$33,530	
5	Hotels/Motels	$14,631	$22,511	
6	Convenience Store	$12,309	$19,377	
7	Business Services	$12,076	$21,282	
8	Automotive Products and Services	$10,604	$15,944	
9	Food Retailing	$10,370	$14,544	
10	Rental Service	$5,282	$8,900	
11	Construction and Home Services	$3,720	$9,255	
12	Recreational/Entertainment/ Travel	$1,840	$6,573	

Directions Follow these steps to calculate the growth rates for each business sector. Then answer the questions on the next page.
- Open your spreadsheet software program on your computer.
- Create a spreadsheet like the one above.
- Enter a formula to calculate growth rate for each of the business sectors listed.
- After completing your calculations, save your work.
- Print out a copy of your work if your teacher has instructed you to do so.

Chapter 16 Using Math in Sales

 Academic Integration: Mathematics
Spreadsheet Application *(continued)*

Directions Write what you would say to close the sale in each situation.

1. Which business sector shows the largest growth rate?

_____

_____

_____

2. Which business sector shows the smallest growth rate?

_____

_____

_____

3. Based on your calculations, which business sector would be the best investment choice? Why?

_____

_____

_____

_____

_____

_____

4. Based on your calculations about growth rate, which of these business sectors would be the least desirable investment opportunity? Explain.

_____

_____

_____

_____

_____

_____

_____

Chapter 16 Using Math in Sales

 Real-World Application
Register Training

Directions Study the illustration of a cash drawer below. Then on the appropriate line write the name of the currency or coin that is customarily placed in each compartment.

1	2	3	4	5
6	7	8	9	10

1. _____

2. _____

3. _____

4. _____

5. _____

6. _____

7. _____

8. _____

9. _____

10. _____

Directions Imagine yourself in the following sales situation: Your friend Howie comes into Stepworth Audio, where you work. He buys two used CDs for a total cost of $18.37 and gives you $20.

1. Name the coins and bills you will give Howie. (Be sure to sue the proper order for making change).

_____

_____

_____

2. How would you verbally count the change back to Howie?

_____

_____

3. How would you count the change if you had a POS system?

_____

_____

Name _____ Date _____ Class _____

Chapter 16 Using Math in Sales

 Real-World Application
Preparing Sales Slips

Directions You are a salesclerk (ID No. 38760, Dept 6) at Old West Togs 'n Tack. Prepare sales slips for your first two customers of the day. Their purchases are described below. Use the current date, and assume the state sales tax is six percent.

Customer 1
3 shirts @ $29.95
2 belts @ $36.95
2 pairs of boots @ $125.00
3 halters @ $37.95

Customer 2
2 pairs of jeans @ $ 34.95
3 shirts @ $32.95
2 saddle racks @ $28.50

OLD WEST TOGS 'N TACK			
400 Mesquite Hwy., Mina, NV 89824			
Sold To:			
Address:			
Date		Dept.	Clerk #
Qty	Description	Price	Amount
		Subtotal	
		Sales Tax	
		Total	

OLD WEST TOGS 'N TACK			
400 Mesquite Hwy., Mina, NV 89824			
Sold To:			
Address:			
Date		Dept.	Clerk #
Qty	Description	Price	Amount
		Subtotal	
		Sales Tax	
		Total	

Chapter 16 Using Math in Sales

 **DECA Connection**
Sales Team Member

Role Play Imagine that you are a member of a sales team for a stationary store. Most of the store's business comes from custom invitation orders. When taking custom orders, many special charges must be calculated for custom inks, special printing, quality of paper, shipping and handling, etc.

Directions Your boss (judge) has asked you to design a generic sales check that can be used to record charges for these orders. Your boss also wants you to train new employees on how to use the sales checks to record sales.

Organize your thoughts around the performance indicators noted below. Use these performance indicators to jot down your ideas during the preparation period. Time your preparation period to last 15 minutes and your role-play presentation to last a maximum of ten minutes. After your role play, use the performance indicators to evaluate your efforts.

Assessment You will be evaluated on how well you meet the following performance indicators:
- Describe the nature of business records.
- Sell a good/service/idea to groups.
- Conduct training class/program.
- Prepare simple written reports.
- Demonstrate appropriate creativity.

_____

_____

_____

_____

_____

_____

_____

_____

_____

_____

_____

_____

Chapter 16 Using Math in Sales

 DECA Connection
Sales Team Member *(continued)*

Scoring Each performance indicator equals 20 points (20 × 5 = 100 points).
Excellent (16–20)   **Good** (10–15)   **Fair** (4–9)   **Poor** (0–3)

Describe the nature of business records.   **Score** _____

_____

_____

Sell a good/service/idea to a group.   **Score** _____

_____

_____

Conduct training class/program.   **Score** _____

_____

_____

Prepare simple written reports.   **Score** _____

_____

_____

Demonstrate appropriate creativity.   **Score** _____

_____

_____

Chapter 16 Using Math in Sales

 Study Skills
Improving Vocabulary

Directions Use the following tips to help improve your vocabulary. Then review the vocabulary in Chapter 16 using the tips as you answer the questions that follow. If the statement is true, circle **T**. If the statement is false, circle **F** and rewrite the statement so that is it true.

Improving Vocabulary
• To improve your vocabulary, play word games that incorporate new words and terms you are learning.

1. On approval is a type of sale that permits a customer to take an item home for further consideration.   T F

   _____

   _____

2. An exchange is a trade of one item for another.   T F

   _____

   _____

3. A partial refund (usually because of a flaw in the merchandise) is called an allowance.   T F

   _____

4. UPC is a type of sale involving payment by check or currency.   T F

   _____

5. A COD is a sale, a return, or an exchange.   T F

   _____

6. A return is when you get money or credit back.   T F

   _____

7. A till is a money drawer in a cash register.   T F

   _____

8. An invoice is also known as a will-call.   T F

   _____

   _____

Chapter 16 Using Math in Sales

Study Skills
Test Preparation

Directions Study the Test-Prep Tips and think about how you can use them to improve your test scores. Write a sentence or two to answer each of the following questions about the main ideas in Chapter 16.

Test-Prep Tips
• Develop self-discipline about studying by scheduling a specific study task for a particular time of day. For example, you might plan to study math for 15 minutes at 4:15 p.m. each day.
• Set an alarm or keep an eye on your watch. Wait for the scheduled time to start the task.
• Stick to this schedule for a semester. Track your progress on math homework and tests.

1. What items might be found on a receiving record?

_____

_____

_____

2. Explain the blind-check method. Is this the most accurate checking method?

_____

_____

_____

3. What is inventory and what does it include?

_____

_____

_____

4. How are retail businesses expected to maintain their inventory?

_____

_____

_____

5. What are the steps in the stock handling process?

_____

_____

_____

Chapter 16 Using Math in Sales

 Study Skills
Practice Test

Directions Take the practice test. Circle the letters of ALL the choices that accurately complete each of the following sentences.

1. Cash registers serve the function of
   a. providing receipts.
   b. recording sales.
   c. issuing vendor marketing codes.
   d. storing cash and sales documents.

2. Money placed in the cash register at the beginning of each day is
   a. used for making change.
   b. called an opening cash fund.
   c. part of the day's sales.
   d. deposited in the bank.

3. Optical scanners make it easier to record sales by relieving salesclerks of the responsibility for
   a. authorizing credit card purchases.
   b. manually entering prices.
   c. calling out prices.
   d. figuring discounts.

4. Adding up all the recorded sales and counting the cash at the end of a business day is called
   a. balancing the cash.
   b. computing a percentage.
   c. balancing the till.
   d. putting an item on layaway.

5. Advantages of using debit cards for both customers and businesses include
   a. immediate payment.
   b. convenience.
   c. theft protection.
   d. protection against bad checks.

6. In a business-to-business transaction, a buyer who wants to take advantage of the discount offered on a January 21 invoice that has dating terms of 20/10 net 45, could do so if he or she made payment on
   a. January 31.
   b. February 12.
   c. March 15.
   d. March 31.

Chapter 17 Promotional Concepts and Strategies

Note Taking
Main Ideas and Supporting Details

Directions As you read, write key words and short phrases in the Cues column.
Write notes, facts, and main ideas in the Note Taking column. Then summarize
the section in the Summary box.

Cues	Note Taking
• Promotion and Promotional Mix	• Promotion and Promotional Mix
• Types of Promotion	• Types of Promotion

Summary

Chapter 17 Promotional Concepts and Strategies

Academic Integration: Mathematics
Analyzing a Database

Calculating Growth You want to invest in a high-growth business. You have studied market and economic factors and you have narrowed your choices to the business sectors listed below. You want to choose the sector that has the highest growth rate.

The printout below shows data that you have collected about current sales, as well as anticipated sales in five years. To calculate the growth rate for each business sector, first subtract the current sales from the anticipated sales in five years. Then divide the result by current sales totals.

	A	B	C	D	E
1	Model	Price	Estimated Units	Discount	Discount Cost
2	Chapter 17 Promotional Concepts and Strategies				
3	640A CD	$124	18,420	12.0%	
4	750A CD	$160	24,640	12.0%	
5	Stereo 2244	$178	32,380	8.0%	
6	Stereo 2264	$158	28,960	8.0%	
7	TOTAL COST				

Directions Follow these steps to analyze the database. Answer the questions that follow.
- Open your spreadsheet software program on your computer.
- Create a spreadsheet like the one above using your spreadsheet application.
- Create a formula to calculate the discount cost for each product. Then create a formula to calculate the total of all discount costs.
- Perform the calculations, and then save your work.
- Print out a copy of your work if your teacher has instructed you to do so.

1. What is the total cost of offering the discounts for this new product line?

   _____

2. If the company has budgeted a total of $2,000,000 for promotional discounts, how much money is available? If the response from dealers results in a total promotional cost that is 10 percent higher than the current figure, will the cost be under or over budget?

   _____

   _____

   _____

   _____

Chapter 17 Promotional Concepts and Strategies

Real-World Application
Public Relations

Directions Classify each of the following public relations activities as primarily targeted to employees (E), customers (C), or the general community (GC).

_____ 1. Perkins Restaurants provides complimentary meals for the Give Kids The World Foundation.

_____ 2. A medical center sponsors a free health and wellness seminar for its staff members.

_____ 3. The U.S. Department of Transportation and the Council run a print advertisement with a logo that reads, "You Could Learn a Lot From A Dummy. Buckle Your Safety Belt."

_____ 4. The Eaton Corporation offers 100 percent tuition reimbursement for marketing support specialists.

_____ 5. A local marketing education program sponsors an end-of-the-year student recognition dinner for students and parents.

_____ 6. A new office building sponsors a free breakfast for area businesspeople followed by a tour of the complex.

_____ 7. A department store offers a free gift wrapping service for the holiday season.

_____ 8. A company recognizes an employee for her work with the Little League in a company newsletter.

_____ 9. A regional sales manager of the AT&T Phone Center allows his store managers to act as judges at a state DECA Career Development Conference.

_____ 10. A local radio station allows its manager to serve as a business advisor to a Junior Achievement program at the high school.

_____ 11. Company associates at the Outback Restaurant get a discount on a dinner for two people.

_____ 12. Stacey and Theo's restaurant provides a free meal to the homeless for Thanksgiving.

_____ 13. The Ford Motor Company provides an employee suggestion awards program.

_____ 14. A local community college plans an open house to celebrate the opening of a new downtown campus location.

_____ 15. A furniture store provides free delivery to customers in a 15-mile radius of the store.

_____ 16. A personal care consultant is available to advise customers on cosmetics selection.

_____ 17. Harding's supermarkets offer to bag your groceries and take them to your car for free.

_____ 18. Pharmacia becomes a civic theater patron and has its name printed in the program.

_____ 19. The Steelcase Company promotes people from within the company.

_____ 20. Northwest Airlines supports the Make a Wish Foundation by giving 500 bonus miles to frequent fliers who donate $50 or more.

Chapter 17 Promotional Concepts and Strategies

 Real-World Application
Promotions

Directions Read the case study below. Then answer the questions that follow.

Fantastic Prizes and Free Gifts Offered through Sweepstakes

Sweepstakes have been popular ways to attract customers for years, but until recently were advertised primarily through print and broadcast media, particularly through targeted mailings. Now, companies are turning to the Internet with their sweepstakes and are finding big audiences. A recent survey ranked several Internet sweepstakes sites among the top 50 sites in numbers of unique visitors.

On iwon.com, Web surfers earn sweepstakes entries for every click. Other sites, such as alladvantage.com and freeride.com, award points redeemable for prizes when users leave an advertising banner visible at the top of the page as they surf. Other companies offer contests as opposed to sweepstakes. In contests, users must demonstrate some skill. Webmillion.com gives points redeemable for sweepstakes entries for correct trivia answers. Web-based giveaways are often cash, but can also be prepaid phone cards, gift certificates for stores and restaurants, and free CDs and books.

The strategy of most Web-based sweepstakes companies is to attract repeat users and then sell the users' demographic information to advertisers. Some simply use the sweepstakes to attract people, and then try to sell them magazines, household products, time-share vacations, cruises, books, and flowers. Although purchases are not required to enter most sweepstakes, companies are clearly trying to lure buyers with the chance at winning free cash. Companies strongly suggest that purchases should be made, and even provide different instructions for entering without a purchase. Two established sweepstakes companies, Publishers Clearing House and American Family Publishers, earn commissions on the products they sell through the sweepstakes.

1. What is the difference between a contest and a sweepstakes?

_____

_____

2. Sweepstakes are an example of a consumer incentive. Why might businesses use sweepstakes as a sales promotional device?

_____

3. Most sweepstakes do not require a participant to purchase anything to enter, but many companies highly suggest that you do. Think of techniques to encourage participants.

_____

_____

Chapter 17 Promotional Concepts and Strategies

 DECA Connection
Sales Promotion Planner

Role Play You are to assume the role of assistant manager for a small independent retailer. The store has a very good community reputation for offering
quality merchandise at fair prices. Your store is not large enough to qualify for
quantity discounts on its orders, nor does it buy sufficient quantities to acquire
its own private label. Because of this, your store needs creative non-price sales
promotions to compete with larger retail chains at full margin prices. Your larger
competitors, on the other hand, can and do offer constant sale prices, off-price
promotions, and markdowns. You have been asked by the store owner (judge)
to come up with a list of several non-price sales promotions based upon three
overall store objectives:

* Increase customer traffic into store
* Design creative and fun non-price sales promotions
* Increase sales revenues by using effective sales promotions

Directions Explain your sales promotion ideas to the owner (judge). Detail the
suggested strategies to meet each of these three objectives. Be sure to include
ideas that will increase customer traffic through sales promotions that do not
emphasize sale prices, off-price reductions, or markdowns, since to compete
you must sell at near or full margins.

Organize your thoughts around the performance indicators noted below. Use
these performance indicators to jot down your ideas during the preparation
period. Time your preparation period to last 15 minutes and your role-play presentation to last a maximum of 10 minutes. After your role play, use the performance indicators to evaluate your efforts.

Assessment You will be evaluated on how well you meet the following performance indicators:

Score:

_____   Analyze use of specialty promotions.

_____   Develop a sales promotion plan.

_____   Explain the types of promotion.

_____   Explain the nature of effective communications.

_____   Persuade others.

Scoring Each performance indicator equals 20 points (20 × 5 = 100 points).
Excellent (16–20)   **Good** (10–15)   **Fair** (4–9)   **Poor** (0–3)

Chapter 17 (side tab)

Chapter 17 Promotional Concepts and Strategies

Study Skills
Time Efficiency

Directions Use the following tips to help improve how you use your time. Then, review Chapter 17 using the tips as you answer the questions that follow. If the statement is true, circle **T**. If the statement is false, circle **F** and rewrite the statement so that it is true.

Procrastination
• People procrastinate for many reasons. They may lack confidence in their ability, be unsure about how to start, find a task unpleasant, or have set an impossibly high a standard for themselves.
• To avoid procrastination, motivate yourself by giving yourself a reward upon completing a task. Break complicated tasks into small more manageable parts. Work on the unpleasant parts of a task first, so you get them out of the way.

1. A promotion is any form of communication used by a business to inform, persuade, or remind people about its products and improve its public image.   T   F

   _____

2. A news release refers to any activity designed to create goodwill toward a business.   T   F

   _____

   _____

3. A promotional mix is used by a business to convince potential customers to buy products from it instead of a competitor.   T   F

   _____

   _____

4. Advertising is a paid form of non-personal presentation and promotion of ideas, goods, or services by an identified sponsor.   T   F

   _____

5. Incentives are low-cost items given to customers at a discount or for free.   T   F

   _____

6. A combination of strategies and a cost-effective allocation of resources is is called a "product promotion."   T   F

   _____

Chapter 17 Promotional Concepts and Strategies

 Study Skills
Test Preparation

Directions Study the Test-Prep Tips and think about how you can use them to improve your test scores. Write a sentence or two to answer each of the following questions about the main ideas in Chapter 17.

Test-Prep Tips
• Eat well before taking a test. Have a good breakfast or lunch and avoid junk food. Studies show that you need good nutrition to concentrate and perform your best.
• If you are allowed to use a calculator at a testing site, make sure it is one that is authorized. Also check to see that other electronic devices such as phones, pagers, and alarms are turned off.

1. What are the five basic categories in the promotional mix?

   _____

   _____

2. What are the goals of direct marketing?

   _____

3. What are the roles of advertising, direct marketing, and public relations when a company engages in a promotional mix?

   _____

   _____

4. What are some types of major trade promotions?

   _____

   _____

5. What are some types of major consumer promotions devices?

   _____

   _____

   _____

6. What is the fundamental concept behind premium marketing?

   _____

   _____

Chapter 17 Promotional Concepts and Strategies

Study Skills
Practice Test

Directions Take the practice test. Choose the word or phrase that best completes the sentence or answers the question

1. Companies rely on promotion to
   a. release newsworthy developments about their products.
   b. engage in a one-way communication to the customer.
   c. distinguish between public relations and publicity.
   d. inform people about their products and services.

2. The main function of publicity is to
   a. enable an organization to influence a target audience.
   b. develop a positive perception or awareness of the organization in the marketplace.
   c. stimulate sales, reinforce advertising, and support selling efforts.
   d. increase sales, inform potential customers about new products, and create a positive image.

3. Direct marketing is a type of advertising directed to
   a. the general public in an attempt to increase store traffic.
   b. large retailers in order to convince the retailer to stock the product.
   c. a mass audience rather than a targeted group of prospects an customers.
   d. a targeted group of prospects and customers rather than to a mass audience.

4. Sales promotion activities designed to get support for a product from manufacturers, wholesalers, and retailers are called
   a. coupons.
   b. sales force promotions.
   c. trade promotions.
   d. consumer promotions.

5. Premiums are
   a. low cost items given to consumers at a discount or for free.
   b. certificates that entitle customers to cash discounts on goods or services.
   c. higher priced products earned and given away through contests, sweepstakes, and rebates.
   d. a payment fee for the right to promote products or services at or on a set location.

6. Point-of-purchase displays are
   a. designed by public relations departments to increase revenue.
   b. designed by wholesalers to attract the general public's interest.
   c. designed primarily by manufacturers to hold and display their products.
   d. designed primarily by retailers to hold and display their products.

Chapter 17

Chapter 18 Visual Merchandising and Display

Note Taking
Main Ideas and Supporting Details

Directions As you read, write key words and short phrases in the Cues column. Write notes, facts, and main ideas in the Note Taking column. Then summarize the section in the Summary box.

Cues	Note Taking
• Display Features	• Display Features
• Artistic Design	• Artistic Design

Summary

Chapter 18

Chapter 18 Visual Merchandising and Display

Academic Integration: Mathematics
Spreadsheet Application

Analyzing Test Results Lantana, a maker of cosmetics and beauty supplies, provides visual displays to the retailers that sell its products. The company has created two new display models and has tested those models in several stores. Total customers passing the display, the number of customers who stopped to look, and the number of customers who bought an item from the product line were all counted. Both display models gained more attention than the display model currently used. Model A will cost $189,800 to place in all stores, while Model B will cost $154,500. Based on the test results, the marketing manager estimates the percent if the Model B display is used. The results of the test are shown in the spreadsheet below.

	A	B	C	D	E
1	Chapter 18 Visual Merchandising Display				
2		**Model A**	**Model B**		
3	Total number of customers passing display	2,890	3,120		
4	Number who stopped at display	980	1,044		
5	Number who bought item	540	520		
6	Of total customers, percentage that bought item	18.7%	16.7%		
7	TOTAL COST				
8		**Estimated Percentage Increase**	**Total Current Sales**	**Sales Increase**	**Total Projected Sales**
9	Model A	5.0%	$1,200,000		
10	Model B	3.0%	$1,200,000		

Chapter 18 Visual Merchandising and Display

 Academic Integration: Mathematics
Spreadsheet Application *(continued)*

Directions Follow these steps to analyze the spreadsheet. Then answer the questions below.

- Turn on your computer and open your spreadsheet software program.
- Create a spreadsheet like the one on the previous page.
- For model A and Model B create a formula to calculate the percentages of total customers who bought an item.

- Create formulas to calculate the estimated increase in sales for each display model and total projected sales.

- Perform all calculations then save your work.
- Print out a copy of your work if your teacher has instructed you to do so.

1. What is the percentage of total customers who bought an item?

   _____

   _____

   _____

2. What is the amount of projected increase in sales for each display model?

   _____

   _____

   _____

3. Make a recommendation to the marketing manager for the display model to be placed in all retail stores. Explain your reasons.

   _____

   _____

   _____

   _____

   _____

   _____

Chapter 18

Chapter 18 Visual Merchandising and Display

Real-World Application
Promotional Display

Directions Form teams of two and prepare a promotional display using the various artistic considerations involved with display preparation. Depending on the space available and the directions of your instructor, your display can be an interior display or window display for your school store or classroom.

Activity

Use another piece of paper to design your display before you create it. Your instructor will rate you on your team's completed display by using the following rating scale.

Rating Scale:	1-4 Poor	5-6 Fair	7-8 Good	9-10 Excellent

Categories   **Your Score**

1. **Selling power**
   Does the display give a strong sales message?   _____

2. **Attention-grabbing effect**
   Does the display make striking use of all materials?   _____

3. **Contribution to product image**
   Does the display emphasize and enhance product image?   _____

4. **Timeliness**
   Is the product seasonally appropriate?   _____

5. **Theme usage**
   Does the display use a creative theme appropriate for the product?   _____

6. **Use of color**
   Does the display use color effectively?   _____

7. **Use of artistic elements**
   Were the artistic elements of balance, line, shape, direction,   _____
   texture, proportion, motion, and lighting used creatively?

8. **Arrangement of materials and props**
   Are display materials and props aesthetically pleasing?   _____

9. **Display cards and signs**
   Are display cards and signs easy to read? Do they coordinate and   _____
   match the display?

10. **Overall appearance**
    Was the display clean, neat, and orderly?   _____

Comments: _____

_____

Chapter 18

Chapter 18 Visual Merchandising and Display

Real-World Application
Case Study

Taking a Different Approach In a major departure from its established merchandising approach, the Walgreen Company has made a shift from strip mall to stand-alone stores. Although Walgreens had historically steered clear of competition with major grocery and discount stores, the company's new strategy puts it in direct competition with discounting behemoths and is so far producing profitable results. Research shows the typical Walgreens customer spends only about $10 per visit and stays in the store only 14 minutes.

By leasing strip-mall space, the company avoided huge cash outlays when opening stores, and could count on each store being profitable very quickly. A freestanding store can cost $3 million to build and usually takes two to three years to show a profit. Even so, the Walgreen Company has been aggressive in its move to freestanding stores. In 1992, only 230 Walgreens stores were stand-alones; today, half of the 3.051 Walgreens stores in 43 states are freestanding.

The new Walgreen stores, at approximately 15,000 square feet, are miniscule compared to the typical Wal-Mart, which can top 150,000 square feet. However, the Walgreen Company is banking that they can attract customers with conveniences, such as 24-hour drive-through, and by ensuring customers have a quick, hassle-free visit.

One new store in Buffalo Grove, Illinois, is close to both a Jewel/Osco supermarket and a Wal-Mart. This prototype store showcases the company's new store design strategy. The new store has wide aisles and a center aisle for prominent display of seasonal items. The store carries a larger assortment of high-margin food items like snacks, cereals, and frozen foods than the Walgreens strip-mall stores. The company's core business remains prescription drugs, and the company has an e-commerce pharmacy to increase customer convenience and prescription drug sales.

Research by the store design firm Retail Design Associates showed that improved theme, colors, lighting, and signage can improve a store's sales from 10 to 300 percent. Effective store design can entice shoppers into a store; the right mix of merchandise and competitive prices can keep them as customers. The Walgreen Company has seen the concrete proof of this theory. Customer traffic in strip-mall stores that were converted to stand-alones increased 10 percent. More importantly, store revenue in those same stores increased 30 percent.

Chapter 18

Chapter 18 Visual Merchandising and Display

Real-World Application
Case Study (continued)

Directions Answer these questions about the case study.

1. Explain why the Walgreen Company is changing its store location to compete more directly with large supermarkets and discount stores?

_____

_____

_____

_____

_____

2. The look of every store should conform to customer expectations. What would you suggest to a retailer considering a store design change?

_____

_____

_____

_____

3. Speculate on why the Walgreen Company is willing to take the risk of moving its stores away from strip-malls.

_____

_____

_____

_____

4. In tough economic times, retailers often decide to cut back on staff or inventory, but are reluctant to skimp on store design. Explain this decision and some possible problems it may create.

_____

_____

_____

_____

_____

Chapter 18 Visual Merchandising and Display

DECA Connection
Sales Associate

Role Play You are to assume the role of a sales associate in the women's apparel department of a large department store. Your department has a reputation for its appealing interior displays. A weeklong storewide sales promotion for a new line of clothing has been so successfully received that the store has sold out of the advertised clothing in five days. The department manager is not on duty and the store display manager is also unavailable.

A customer (judge) who has driven several miles to buy the advertised clothing approaches you. You inform her that the clothing line is currently out of stock. The customer is very upset. However, she notices that the mannequin in the interior display is wearing the outfit she wants and insists that you sell it to her. You must make a decision on whether to sell the outfit or not.

Directions Organize your thoughts around the performance indicators noted below. Use these performance indicators to jot down your ideas during the preparation period. Time your preparation period to last 15 minutes and your role-play presentation to last a maximum of ten minutes. After your role play, use the performance indicators to evaluate your efforts

Assessment You will be evaluated on how well you meet the following performance indicators:

Score:

_____ Explain company selling policies.

_____ Make decisions.

_____ Demonstrate problem-solving skills.

_____ Demonstrate a customer service mindset.

_____ Demonstrate appropriate creativity.

Scoring Each performance indicator equals 20 points (20 × 5 = 100 points).
Excellent (16–20) **Good** (10–15) **Fair** (4–9) **Poor** (0–3)

Chapter 18 Visual Merchandising and Display

 Study Skills
Improving Vocabulary

Directions Read the tips on improving vocabulary. Then read each sentence, noting the underlined word or phrase. Then, from the four choices that follow, select the term that could best replace the underlined text. Circle your choice.

Improving Vocabulary
• Be alert for new or specialized vocabulary words and terms as you read your textbook. Keep track of them in your notebook and review them until they become part of your language.

1. The <u>total exterior</u> of a business includes the entranceways, display windows, marquee, and the design and setting of the building itself.
   display   entrance   layout   storefront

2. The <u>exhibit</u> of spring clothing was visually appealing to customers.
   display   formal balance   marquee   store layout

3. Placing large items on each side creates <u>a regular arrangement</u> in a display.
   direction   formal balance   informal balance   proportion

4. A <u>canopy</u> extends out over a store's entrance.
   banner   marquee   storefront   signs

5. The <u>floor space allocation</u> is used to facilitate sales and serve the customer.
   display   storefront   store layout   personnel space

6. Red and green are <u>opposite colors</u> and create great contrasts.
   adjacent colors   complementary colors   analogous colors   transparent colors

7. The <u>coordination of all the physical elements</u> projected the right image to the customers.
   direction   display   shape   visual merchandising

8. Props and signs should always be <u>in the correct relationship</u> to the merchandise.
   aisles   direction   line   proportion

9. Blue and green are <u>located next to each other</u> on the color wheel and blend well.
   adjacent colors   matching colors   complementary colors   transparent colors

10. The <u>object used to display a store's name</u> should be original and easily recognizable.
    billboard   exterior   sign   spectacular

11. The <u>interactive point-of-purchase display</u> is playing an increasingly important role in sales merchandising.
    fixture   interior display   kiosk   window display

12. The <u>strongest visual element of a display</u> attracts the viewer's attention first, above all else.
    direction   focal point   informal balance   line

Chapter 18 Visual Merchandising and Display

Study Skills
Improving Vocabulary

Directions Study the Test-Prep Tips and think about how you can use them to improve your test scores. For each series of items, circle the one that does not belong. Then write a sentence or two explaining your choice.

Test-Prep Tips
• Read all of the choices before choosing your answer.
• Think about how the answer choices are related. Look for the connections among them.

1. advertising   interior displays   storefront   store layout   store interior

   _____

   _____

2. entrances   marquee   store layout   window displays

   _____

   _____

3. dressing rooms   personnel space   restaurant space   recreational areas for children

   _____

   _____

4. fixtures   floors   interior displays   store layout   walls

   _____

   _____

5. abstract setting   color   direction   line   proportion

   _____

   _____

6. adjacent   complementary   color   lighting

   _____

   _____

7. balance   formal   informal   proportion

   _____

   _____

Chapter 18 Visual Merchandising and Display

Study Skills
Practice Test

Directions Take the practice test. Circle the letters of all the choices that accurately complete each of the following sentences.

1. Which is the most important goal of visual merchandising?
   a. to use bright colors and bold designs effectively
   b. to create a positive shopping environment
   c. to enhance customer convenience
   d. to create an attractive storefront

2. Which list includes the four aspects of store layout?
   a. selling space, storage space, personnel space, and customer space
   b. landscaping, ambience, convenient location, and bold graphics
   c. entrances, exits, window displays, and signage
   d. color, graphics, lighting, and paint

3. Well-designed interior displays are most important because they
   a. can be used to display advertising.
   b. encourage passersby to come into the store.
   c. are used to promote a particular product or brand.
   d. enable customers to make a selection without the assistance of a sales clerk.

4. Which is an example of a POP (point-of-purchase display)?
   a. an interior display
   b. an architectural display
   c. a functional prop
   d. a vending machine

5. Which term refers to a merchandising display that features garden rakes and hoes, plants, potting soil, garden gloves, and a wheelbarrow?
   a. cross-mix of items
   b. similar products
   c. related products
   d. equipment items

6. Adjacent colors are also called
   a. vivid colors.
   b. complementary colors.
   c. triadic colors.
   d. analogous colors.

Chapter 18

Chapter 19 Advertising

Note Taking
Main Ideas and Supporting Details

Directions As you read, write key words and short phases in the Cues column. Write notes, facts, and main ideas in the Note Taking column. Then summarize the section in the Summary box.

Cues	Note Taking
• Advertising Media	• Advertising Media
• Media Measurement and Rates	• Media Measurement and Rates

Summary

Chapter 19

Chapter 19 Advertising

Academic Integration: Mathematics
Analyzing a Database

Advertising Media The Apollo Company recently completed a survey of customers who had purchased a bottle of its Spring Joy perfume. The company wanted to know the number of customers who learned about the product from its magazine, newspaper, billboard, or television ads, or from its in-store promotions. The survey results are shown below. The number beside each type of ad is the number of customers who bought the product after seeing it advertised.

	A	B	C
1	**Source of Customer Product Knowledge**	**Number of Buyers**	**Percentage of total**
2	Chapter 19 Advertising		
3	Magazines	180	
4	Newspapers	94	
5	Television	108	
6	Billboards	14	
7	In-store promotions	41	
8	Other	34	
9	TOTAL BUYERS		

Directions Follow these steps to analyze the database. Then answer the questions that follow.

- Open your spreadsheet software program on your computer.
- Create a spreadsheet like the one above using your spreadsheet application.
- Enter a formula to calculate the total number of buyers responding to the survey.
- Enter a formula to calculate the percentage of the total for each type of ad.

- Save your work. Print out a copy of your work if your teacher has instructed you to do so.

1. Of the advertising media given, which had the ads that were seen by the largest percentage of buyers? The smallest?

   _____

   _____

2. If you had 1,200,000 customers, how many of them might you expect to see your ad if it were placed on a billboard?

   _____

   _____

   _____

Chapter 19 Advertising

Real-World Application
Public Relations

Directions Read the case study below. Then answer the questions that follow.

Changing an Advertising Approach After years of relying on television to advertise its products, Procter & Gamble (P&G) changed its strategy to focus more on direct mail, the Internet, and staged events. In 1999, P&G reduced its advertising costs, which included decreasing the total amount spent on television advertising to $1.18 billion, a 7 percent drop. The company pulled back significantly from local TV, decreasing expenses by 30 percent, but increased magazine advertising expenditures by 17 percent and tripled its newspaper advertising. The company hopes to more accurately reach its target market this way.

P&G also changed the way it handles its advertising agencies and campaigns. Company personnel are involved in advertising campaigns from the beginning. P&G now consults with its advertising, public relations, Internet, and direct marketing staff before launching any campaign. In addition, P&G no longer reimburses advertising agencies based on a straight 15 percent of advertising dollars spent. Under the new policy, agencies will be rewarded based on the success of their assigned products in the marketplace. Sales growth, rather than advertising expenditures, will be an incentive to spend more wisely.

The changed policies have already resulted in different advertising campaigns. The launch of Physique, a hair-care line, depended heavily on direct mail rather than television. P&G spent 60 to 80 percent on direct mail teasers, product samples, and specialty advertising. Only then did television and print advertising begin. Finally, the company sent a mass distribution of Physique to more than 60,000 grocery, drug, and warehouse discount stores. The type of launch may not be successful with products such as laundry detergent, but P & G felt it was successful for Physique.

1. Speculate on why P&G has reduced TV spending in favor of increased spending for magazine and local newspapers.

   _____

   _____

2. Why did P&G change the way it reimburses advertising agencies? Will this newer approach lower its operating costs? Why or why not?

   _____

Chapter 19 Advertising

 Real-World Application
Making Choices about Advertising

Directions Read each of the following scenarios. Determine which type of advertising method would be best in each case.

1. A women's clothing designer is seeking a cost effective way to market their newest line of dress shoes to women who dress professionally, yet seek comfort.

   _____

   _____

2. A new car dealership wishes to inform current customers about a sale on luxury sedans. They hope to retain as many customers as possible when the new stock arrives.

   _____

   _____

   _____

3. A coffee and tea company has opened a café in a new city. With their advertising campaign they wish to reach business professionals, blue collar workers, and students in an urban setting, who they feel would be most likely to patronize their café on the morning commute to work or school.

   _____

   _____

   _____

4. A popular music venue in a large city is trying to attract a large audience to attend their five year anniversary party. They have organized a full day of live music with prizes and contests. Their target audience consists of individuals over 12 years old who enjoy reggae and hip-hop music.

   _____

   _____

5. A soft drink company has changed the ingredients in their diet soda. They feel that the new taste is a sure thing. They wish to inform a wide audience on their new ingredients and fantastic new taste. Also, they are hoping that the increased exposure to their diet soda will boost sales for all of their drinks.

   _____

   _____

Chapter 19 Advertising

DECA Connection
Retail Marketing

Role Play You are to assume the role of marketing specialist for the advertising department of a large retail store chain that seeks to promote its new e-commerce Web site. You must promote the Web site based upon three overall company objectives:

- Increase store revenues through gaining new customers
- Increase store revenues through increasing sales to existing customers
- Reduce operating costs involved with servicing existing customers

Directions Provide ideas to promote the store's new Web site to your promotional manager (judge). Be sure to include existing advertising methods to promote the site and other plans to increase sales to new and existing customers. Also address how the new site could be used to reduce costs.

Organize your thoughts around the performance indicators noted below. Use these performance indicators to jot down your ideas during the preparation period. Time your preparation period to last 15 minutes and your role-play presentation to last a maximum of ten minutes. After your role play, use the performance indicators to evaluate your efforts

Assessment You will be evaluated on how well you meet the following performance indicators:

Score:

_____ Develop Web site design/components.

_____ Explain the nature of overhead/operating costs.

_____ Identify ways that technology impacts business.

_____ Explain the types of advertising media.

_____ Demonstrate appropriate creativity.

Scoring Each performance indicator equals 20 points (20 × 5 = 100 points).
Excellent (16–20)　　　**Good** (10–15)　　　**Fair** (4–9)　　　**Poor** (0–3)

Chapter 19 Advertising

 Study Skills
Reading for Different Purposes

Directions Use the following tips to help improve your reading skills. Then review Chapter 19 using the tips as you complete the statements that follow. Write the correct term from Chapter 19 to complete each statement.

Varying Your Reading Strategy
Good readers know how to select and use different reading strategies for different purposes.

- **Study reading** is used when first encountering difficult material. You read slowly with focus to insure high comprehension.
- **Skimming** is used to preview new material and other times when you want to get a general idea about an article. When you skim, you look for main ideas and key terms.
- **Scanning** is helpful when you are looking for the answer to a specific question you have. You move your eyes quickly over the text to spot key words or phrases and locate what you are looking for.

1. _____ is advertising that is designed to increase sales.

2. _____ tries to create a favorable image for a company and foster goodwill in the marketplace.

3. Newspapers, magazines, direct mail, and billboards are examples of _____.

4. Radio and television are both examples of _____.

5. _____ uses public transportation facilities to advertise.

6. Items with an advertiser's name printed on them are called _____.

7. The _____ is the cost of exposing 1,000 readers to an ad.

8. A banner ad or pop-up ad is a common form of _____.

9. _____ is the number of times an audience sees or hears an advertisement.

10. _____ are the agencies, means, or instruments used to convey messages.

11. A single exposure to an advertising message is called an _____.

12. The number of homes or people exposed to an ad is called the _____.

Chapter 19 Advertising

Study Skills
Test Preparation

Directions Study the Test-Prep Tips and think about how you can use them to improve your test scores. Write a sentence or two to answer each of the following questions about the main ideas in Chapter 19.

Test-Prep Tips
• When taking a multiple choice test, read the question before you look at the answer choices. If you come up with the answer in your head before looking at the possible answers, the choices given on the test will not throw you off or trick you.   • Eliminate answers you know are not right. Read all the choices before choosing your answer. If there is no guessing penalty, always take an educated guess and select an answer.

1. Business-to-business magazines are also known as
   a weeklies.
   b. monthlies.
   c. newspapers.
   d. trade publications.

2. The two types of direct marketing are
   a. television and radio advertisements that focus on a specific customer.
   b. direct mail sent to a home and electronic mail sent to an e-mail address.
   c. newspapers and magazines available in a retail store.
   d. telephone directories and direct mail sent to a home.

3. Most television advertisements are
   a. 5- or 10-minute spots.
   b. 1- or 2-second spots.
   c. 30- or-60-minute spots.
   d. 30- or 60-second spots.

4. Magazine rates are based on circulation, the type of readership, and
   a. contracts.
   b. popularity.
   c. production techniques.
   d. location.

5. To reach customers, advertising uses a set format that is defined in terms of
   a. time or space.
   b. quality or quantity.
   c. radio or television.
   d. newspaper or magazine.

6. The three types of radio advertising are
   a. mass radio advertising, network radio advertising, and national radio advertising.
   b. spot radio advertising, transit radio advertising, and national radio advertising.
   c. network radio advertising, national spot radio advertising, and local radio advertising.
   d. national radio advertising, direct radio advertising, and spot radio advertising.

Chapter 19

Chapter 19 Advertising

Study Skills
Practice Test

Directions Take the practice test. For each of the following statements determine whether the information provided reflects an advantage or disadvantage for the type of advertising media identified.

_____ 1. Newspapers have a high readership and a high level of reader involvement.

_____ 2. Magazines are often read more slowly and thoroughly than newspapers.

_____ 3. Many people think of direct-mail advertising as junk mail.

_____ 4. Outdoor advertising is usually viewed very quickly.

_____ 5. Telephone directories are in 98 percent of U.S. households.

_____ 6. Transit advertising is restricted to certain travel routes.

_____ 7. Radio advertising is a mobile medium.

_____ 8. Television can use all of the necessary elements to produce a creative advertising message.

_____ 9. Online advertising response rates are often as low as one percent.

_____ 10. Radio advertising has a short life span.

_____ 11. Transit advertising has a defined market.

_____ 12. Yellow Pages directories are usually printed yearly.

_____ 13. Outdoor advertising permits easy repetition of a message.

_____ 14. Direct marketing can be flexible and keep competitors from seeing the advertisements.

_____ 15. Magazines have less mass appeal when compared to newspapers within a geographical area.

_____ 16. The life of an advertisement in a newspaper is limited.

_____ 17. Online advertisements can be interactive and reach a global audience.

_____ 18. Magazine advertisers can target regular readers because the characteristics of the readers are known.

Chapter 20 Print Advertisements

Note Taking
Main Ideas and Supporting Details

Directions As you read, write key words and short phrases in the Cues column.
Write notes, facts, and main ideas in the Note Taking column. Then summarize
the section in the Summary box.

Cues	Note Taking
• Essential Elements of Advertising	• Essential Elements of Advertising
• Advertising Layout	• Advertising Layout

Summary

Chapter 20

Chapter 20 Print Advertisements

 Academic Integration: English Language Arts
Oral and Visual Presentations

Creating Ad Copy You have been asked to write a print ad to promote a new line of umbrellas. Use the following information to write a headline (15 words or fewer) and copy for the ad.
- Giant size
- All nylon
- Crayon-box solid colors; Rainbow plaids
- Bamboo handle
- Price: $14

Directions Follow these steps to create copy for the ad. Then answer the questions below.
- Open your word processing program on your computer.
- Write copy for the ad.
- Edit and proofread your work to make sure it is correct.
- Save your work. Print out a copy of your work if your teacher has instructed you to do so.

1. How does the copy give reasons why the umbrella is a good buy?

_____

_____

_____

_____

_____

_____

_____

_____

_____

_____

Chapter 20 Print Advertisements

Academic Integration: English Language Arts
Oral and Visual Presentations *(continued)*

2. What kind of writing techniques did you use in your ad in order to make it more effective?

_____

_____

_____

_____

3. Would your headline and ad copy work in all media?

_____

_____

_____

_____

4. What images would you add to make your ad ready for publication in a magazine, and why?

_____

_____

_____

_____

5. What is the target audience for your ad, and how does your ad speak to that audience?

_____

_____

_____

_____

_____

_____

_____

_____

Chapter 20

Chapter 20 Print Advertisements

 ## Real-World Application
Case Study

Directions Read the case study below. Then answer the questions that follow.

Yellow Pages Remain Popular with Advertisers The Internet may be the fastest way to find some information, but when someone needs to find a restaurant, doctor, mechanic, or a pizza, they are still more likely to reach for the good, old-fashioned phone book. That is one of the reasons why print Yellow Pages are still profitable.

Internet Yellow Pages are growing dramatically, but spending on print Yellow Pages ads continues to rise because businesses know that they will get a very high return on their advertising dollars. Yellow Pages ads average $29 of return for every $1 spent, according to research by CRM Associates. Not surprisingly, one-third of all American businesses advertise in at least one Yellow Pages directory.

Even so, print Yellow Pages usage has declined over the past ten years. In 1989, people referred to the Yellow Pages 17.7 billion times, according to the Yellow Pages Publishers Association. By 1999, the Yellow Pages was receiving only 15.6 billion annual references. Despite that drop, advertising expenditures in print Yellow Pages for both local and national businesses continue to grow, rising 5.5 percent in 1999—from $11.99 billion to $12.65 billion—according to a report from New York's McCann-Erickson.

Several Yellow Pages publishers around the world have created their own Internet directories: AT&T produces YellowPages.com in the United States. They are even bundling print and online advertising options for their customers. Online directory assistance has become increasingly popular. The Kelsey Group estimates that online directory advertising lookups in the United States reached 2.4 billion in 2002.

1. Why are Yellow Pages publishers not afraid of online versions of this type of print media?

   _____

   _____

2. Why do print versions of the Yellow Pages still dominate the online versions of the Yellow Pages?

   _____

   _____

   _____

Chapter 20 Print Advertisements

Real-World Application
Create an Ad

Directions Create a one-item newspaper advertising layout for a real or invented store of your choice using a piece of paper or a posterboard. Your advertising layout must contain five elements: a headline, an illustration, copy, the price, and a signature. Use one of the standard layouts illustrated below. Your layout can use illustrations or artwork produced by yourself or obtained from newspapers or magazines.

Your completed advertising layout will be judged using the following rating scale and the performance areas noted below:

Rating Scale:

1–2   Needs significant improvement
3–4   Needs minor improvement
5–7   Good
8–9   Excellent
10   Exceptional

Standard Layouts:

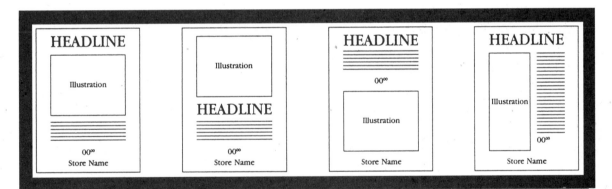

Performance areas: **Your score**

General format

  1. Ad is well organized and easy to follow.   _____

  2. Ad is clean and uncluttered.   _____

  3. White space is appropriate.   _____

Headline

  4. Headline attracts attention.   _____

  5. Aimed at a target audience.   _____

Chapter 20

Chapter 20 Print Advertisements

🌐 Real-World Application
Create an Ad (continued)

Headline   **Your score**

6. Illustration demonstrates a benefit or shows product in use.   _____

7. Illustration is large enough.   _____

Copy

8. Text is written in terms of benefits.   _____

9. Copy is complete and specific.   _____

10. Grammar and spelling are appropriate.   _____

Price

11. The price is clear and visible.   _____

Signature   _____

12. The signature is complete (name, address, telephone, hours,   _____
and slogan).

Chapter 20 Print Advertisements

 **DECA Connection**
Advertising Proofreader

Role Play Imagine that you are an intern at a local newspaper. The manager (judge) of the advertising department has asked you to proofread and edit advertising copy written for a firm of CPAs (certified public accountants). The firm hopes to attract new clients, either businesses or individuals. They have requested that the newspaper advertising department design the rest of the ad. They would like to see a sketch of the proposed ad layout that makes use of the copy they provided. Your job is to proofread the ad copy and make corrections necessary for spelling, grammar, punctuation, and accuracy. Run-on sentences should be corrected and missing information should be added.

Directions Rewrite the ad copy and sketch an ad layout for the firm. Include all parts of a print ad in your sketch. Present the rewritten ad copy and your proposed ad layout on two separate sheets of paper to your manager (judge).

Organize your thoughts around the performance indicators noted below. Use these performance indicators to jot down your ideas during the preparation period. Time your preparation period to last 15 minutes and your role-play presentation to last a maximum of ten minutes. After your role play, use the performance indicators to evaluate your efforts.

Ad Copy

GROAN! It's that time of year again! No, it's not time to set your clocks ahead, but it is time too get a head start on your tax return. Roderick & Stacey, CPAs, is a full-service accounting firm that provides financial services to businesses and to individuals and we can make your life a lot easier by relieving you of the burden of keeping up with the latest changes in tax laws. Call us today for free a estimate.

Assessment You will be evaluated on how well you meet the following performance indicators:
- Explain parts of a print advertisement.
- Write promotional messages that appeal to targeted markets.
- Use proper grammar and vocabulary.
- Evaluate effectiveness of advertising.
- Make oral presentations.

Scoring Each performance indicator equals 20 points (20 × 5 = 100 points).
Excellent (16–20)   **Good** (10–15)   **Fair** (4–9)   **Poor** (0–3)

Chapter 20

Chapter 20 Print Advertisements

 Study Skills
Improving Vocabulary

Directions Read the tips on improving vocabulary. Then match each term in the left column with the correct phrase in the right column. Write the letter of the phrase in the blank by the term.

Improving Vocabulary
• When matching terms and definitions, start by reading a definition. Then look for the term that matches the definitions. That way, you will save time by reading the longer definitions only once.

_____ 1. ad layout

_____ 2. advertising agencies

_____ 3. advertising proof

_____ 4. alliteration

_____ 5. clip art

_____ 6. copy

_____ 7. headline

_____ 8. illustration

_____ 9. print advertisement

_____ 10. pun

_____ 11. signature

_____ 12. slogan

_____ 13. typeface

a. Companies that work with business clients to develop advertising campaigns

b. The words that get the readers' attention, arouse their interest, and lead them to read the rest of the ad

c. Computer-generated images that are placed in a print advertisement

d. A headline writing technique that involves the humorous use of a word that suggests two or more meanings

e. The distinctive identification symbol or logo for a business

f. A catchphrase or small group of words that are combined in a special way to present an advertising message

g. A rough draft that shows the general arrangement and appearance of a finished ad

h. This usually includes a headline, copy, illustrations, and a signature

i. The selling message contained in a written advertisement

j. This shows exactly how an ad will appear when printed

k. The photograph or drawing used in a print advertisement

l. The style of printing type used in a print advertisement.

m. A headline writing technique that involves repeating initial consonant sounds

n. The creation and coordination of a series of advertisements around a particular theme to promote a product

Chapter 20 Print Advertisements

Study Skills
Test Preparation

Directions Study the Test-Prep Tips and think about how you can use them to improve your test scores. Then categorize each ad element as a headline, copy, illustration, or signature.

Test-Prep Tips
• Before a test, make sure you understand the general concepts about your topic.
• Learn the details after you learn the main ideas.

_____ **1** Intrepid The New Dodge
A DIVISION OF THE CHRYSLER CORPORATION

_____ **2.** "A nagging cough with congestion. Or a cough with a painful sore throat. Take new Drixoral Liquid Caps. You can't buy a more powerful liquid cap for long-lasting cough relief."

_____ **3.** "Introducing the New Ford Explorer."

_____ **4.** ENTERPRISE RENT-A-CAR

_____ **5.** A painting of Nestle Sweet Success Healthy Shake on a brick wall.

_____ **6.** There is a difference™ IBM.

_____ **7.** "COROLLA. Where promises are kept. And new ones made every day."

_____ **8.** "The fear of choosing the wrong fund, of losing money. How to conquer it? First, choose an amount of money that doesn't make you nervous. Start small. Invest monthly. At Janus Funds, you can open an account for as little as $50 a month."

_____ **9.** "Milk. What a surprise!"

_____ **10.** A photo of an International truck

_____ **11.** "A great deal on a new Nissan. That's the bottom line." (Nissan)

_____ **12.** ▲DELTA AIR LINES
————— YOU'LL LOVE THE WAY WE FLY™ —————

_____ **13.** "FIRST AGAIN." (Prodigy)

_____ **14.** A picture of a clear blue sky. (Lufthansa)

_____ **15.** "Sound this big from a radio?" (Bose)

_____ **16.** Mobil

Chapter 20

Chapter 20 Print Advertisements

✎ Study Skills
Practice Test

Directions Take the practice test. Circle the letter of the best answer to the question or the phrase that best completes the sentence.

1. Which is most often true of an effective headline?
   a. It makes use of synonyms.
   b. It is brief.
   c. It uses unfamiliar words for impact.
   d. It details how the product meets the customer's need.

2. Which is NOT a characteristic of good ad copy?
   a. It is conversational.
   b. It appeals to the senses.
   c. It uses descriptive adjectives and action words.
   d. It includes a call to action written in the first person.

3. The headline "Functional, Fashionable, Formidable. . ." is an example of
   a. a play on words.
   b. a paradox.
   c. a pun.
   d. alliteration.

4. Effective ads most often include
   a. a focal point and lines of force.
   b. the most dominant item at the bottom.
   c. sans serif type and two colors.
   d. a signature at the top.

5. Which color might be used to communicate passion, excitement and power?
   a. red
   b. dark blue
   c. blue and green
   d. purple and yellow

6. Two-color ads are usually printed in
   a. vivid colors.
   b. black and another color.
   c. dark blue and another color.
   d. black and white.

Chapter 21 Channels of Distribution

Note Taking
Main Ideas and Supporting Details

Directions As you read, write key words and short phrases in the Cues column. Write notes, facts, and main ideas in the Note Taking column. Then summarize the section in the Summary box.

Cues	Note Taking
• Distribution	• Distribution
• Distribution Planning	• Distribution Planning

Summary

Chapter 21 Channels of Distribution

 Academic Integration: Mathematics
Analyzing Channels of Distribution

Evaluating Sales The Paresi Company makes cookies and candies. The company uses several channels of distribution. Paresi products are sold through company stores, direct mail catalogs, specialty stores, and online. The printout shows the channels used and sales for each channel. The company wants its money directed to the channels with the strongest sales.

	A	B	C	D	E	F	G
1		Previous Year Sales	Previous Year Percentage of Total	Last Year Sales	Last Year Percentage of Total	This Year Sales	This Year Percentage of Total
2	Chapter 21 Channels of Distribution						
3	Company stores	$1,848,900		$1,760,800		$2,084,600	
4	Mail order	$1,680,400		$2,988,600		$3,140,900	
5	Specialty stores	$1,200,780		$1,480,900		$1,690,200	
6	Electronic Marketplace	$400,250		$785,100		$1,248,300	
7	TOTAL BUYERS						

Directions Follow these steps to complete the spreadsheet and evaluate sales. Then answer the questions below about the completed spreadsheet.

• Open your spreadsheet software program on your computer.
• Create a spreadsheet like the above using your spreadsheet application.
• First, enter a formula to calculate total sales for each year.
• Next, calculate the sales for company stores as a percentage of total sales for each year. Copy these formulas to all remaining rows.
• Save your work. Print out a copy of your work if your teacher has instructed you to do so.

1. Which is the most important channel of distribution for the company?

_____

2. Which channel has most increased in importance in the last three years?

_____

3. How would you allocate advertising dollars to each channel of distribution?

_____

_____

_____

Chapter 21 Channels of Distribution

Real-World Application
Distribution Planning

Directions The following news briefs on Tupperware are related to distribution planning. Read them and answer the questions that follow.

Tupperware and the Home Shopping Network Tupperware Corporation, a $1.1 billion multinational company, is one of the world's leading direct sellers and the major supplier of food storage containers, with products reaching consumers in more than 100 countries. Tupperware's core distribution policy makes use of an independent sales force and a home-party format for selling.

Tupperware's sales consultants get paid a 35 percent commission on sales, plus other bonuses and benefits. They are required to purchase a sample kit when they first get started, which costs $20 or $65, depending on the products in the kit.

In May 1999, Tupperware entered into an agreement with the Home Shopping Network to air television specials to sell Tupperware products. The Home Shopping Network program features specials from home shopping parties across America during each broadcast. The Home Shopping Network is the pioneer in electronic retailing. It has 24-hour programming reaching more than 70 million households.

1. According to the news brief, what is Tupperware's core distribution policy?

    _____

2. How would you classify Tupperware's independent sales force?

    _____

    _____

Tupperware's Sales Consultants and the Internet The Tupperware Corporation has a special program for its 75,000 U.S. sales agents to bring them low-cost Internet access. My.tupperware.com is a Web site specifically designed for use by Tupperware's sales consultants. Special software permits them to personalize Web sites with product information and promote Tupperware parties. Online sales go through Tupperware's main Web site, but consultants earn sales credit and commission on all sales that originate from each personal Web site.

3. How does Tupperware's service my.tupperware.com help its sales consultants?

    _____

    _____

    _____

Chapter 21 Channels of Distribution

 Real-World Application
Recommending Channels of Distribution

Directions For each of the following scenarios, identify the current channel of distribution being used. Then recommend a channel of distribution or multiple channels for the product. Indicate the intensity of distribution desired for the product. Provide rationale for both recommendations.

Scenario #1 A manufacturer of home health care products has just developed a new home blood pressure monitoring machine. At present the company sells the majority of its other consumer health care products through mass merchandisers, like Kmart and Wal-Mart, as well as through drugstore chains, like CVS, Rite Aid, and Genovese. Over the years, solid relationships have been established with these retailers.

1. What is the current channel of distribution being used by this company for its consumer health products?

   _____

2. What channel(s) of distribution do you recommend for the new home blood pressure machine? Why?

   _____

   _____

   _____

3. What intensity of distribution do you recommend: intensive, selective, or exclusive? Why?

   _____

   _____

Scenario #2 A small importer of bags of all sizes and purposes is seeking national exposure. Some of the bags are designed for laptop computers, while other bags are designed to keep food warm and are marketed to food catering and food delivery businesses, such as pizza restaurants. Duffel bags are designed for use as promotional gifts for clients or as employee prizes for outstanding performance. All bags are unique in that they are designed specifically for the client, and, in many cases, include the client's logo. Currently the owner does all the business-to-business selling himself. The owner would like to increase sales while controlling his selling expenses.

4. What channel of distribution is being used currently by this importer of specialty bags?

   _____

Chapter 21 Channels of Distribution

 **DECA Connection**
Distributor

Role Play Imagine that you are an employee of Sky Millwork. Your company is a local distributor of XYZ Windows. A new Home Depot is slated to open in your territory in the next few months. As the person who has direct contact with most of your company's customers, you have heard firsthand how worried your customers are about their new competitor and its clout and bargaining power. Several of your customers have asked if your company will be selling to the new Home Depot. You feel obligated to share these concerns with your supervisor (judge).

Directions Write a memo to your supervisor (judge) explaining the current customers' concerns regarding the new Home Depot. Request a meeting to discuss this issue. Suggest a plan that will allow Sky Millwork to benefit from Home Depot's reputation by selling them XYZ products, but at the same time, will not ruin your company's relationship with current, loyal customers.

Organize your thoughts around the performance indicators noted below. Use these indicators to jot down your ideas during the preparation period. Time your preparation period to last 15 minutes and your role-play presentation to last a maximum of ten minutes. After your role play, use the performance indicators to evaluate your efforts.

Assessment You will be evaluated on how well you meet the following performance indicators:

Score:

_____ Explain the nature of channels of distribution.

_____ Evaluate channel members.

_____ Explain the nature of channel strategies.

_____ Explain the nature of channel member relationships.

_____ Write informational messages.

Scoring Each performance indicator equals 20 points ($20 \times 5 = 100$ points).
Excellent (16–20)   **Good** (10–15)   **Fair** (4–9)   **Poor** (0–3)

Chapter 21 Channels of Distribution

 ## Study Skills
Meanings and Spellings

Directions Use the following tips to help improve your vocabulary. Then match each definition with the correct term from the Word Bank.

Spelling Longer Words
• When learning to spell a longer word, use a dictionary to find out how the word is broken into syllables. Copy the word syllable by syllable into your notebook at least three times.
• Look at the word and pronounce each syllable. Then try to write the word from memory.

Word Bank		
agents	brick-and-mortar retailers	direct distribution
drop shippers	e-marketplace	exclusive distribution
indirect distribution	integrated distribution	intensive distribution
rack jobbers	selective distribution	wholesalers

_____ 1. This involves no intermediaries.

_____ 2. Intermediaries who do not own the goods they sell

_____ 3. An online shopping location

_____ 4. This involves one or more intermediaries.

_____ 5. Those who buy large quantities of goods from manufacturers and store the goods to resell them to other businesses

_____ 6. This involves protected territories for product distribution in a given geographic area.

_____ 7. Those who sell goods to consumers through their own stores

_____ 8. This involves use of a limited number of outlets in an area to sell product.

_____ 9. This involves use of all suitable outlets to sell a product.

_____ 10. Wholesalers that manage inventory and merchandising for retailers

_____ 11. Wholesalers that own the goods they sell but do not physically handle the actual product

_____ 12. When a manufacturer acts as wholesalers and retailers for its products

Chapter 21 Channels of Distribution

Study Skills
Test Preparation

Directions Study the Test-Prep Tip and think about how you can use it to improve your test scores. Write a paragraph to answer each of the following questions about the main ideas in Chapter 21.

Test-Prep Tip
• Before answering a question that asks you to write a paragraph, consider how you will organize your paragraph. For example, you might present a statement and then follow it with supporting details. You might tell how two things are alike and different, describe a sequence of events, or list possible solutions to a problem. Good organization is important and will help you get a better grade.

1. What is the channel of distribution of a product?

_____

_____

_____

_____

2. What are the two major types of merchant intermediaries involved in distribution?

_____

_____

_____

_____

3. What are the three levels of distribution intensity?

_____

_____

_____

_____

_____

_____

Chapter 21

Chapter 21 Channels of Distribution

Study Skills
Practice Test

Directions Circle the letters of ALL choices that accurately complete the sentence or answer the question.

1. Intermediaries provide value to producers because they
   a. provide expertise in areas producers do not have, such as displaying and merchandising products.
   b. reduce the number of contacts required to reach the final consumer.
   c. may have contacts and ongoing relationships with potential customers the producers do not have.
   d. may reduce a company's selling expenses.

2. Intermediaries that take ownership of goods are classified as
   a. agents.   c. manufacturers' agents.
   b. brokers.   d. merchant intermediaries.

3. Non-store retailing operations include
   a. automatic retailing (vending machines).   c. TV home shopping.
   b. direct mail and catalogs.   d. online retailing.

4. Industrial goods can be marketed
   a. by agents.   c. using direct distribution.
   b. by distributors.   d. using indirect distribution.

5. A retail stationery store that sells its products to consumers for their personal use and to businesses for use in their operations would be considered
   a. a retailer in the consumer market.
   b. an industrial distributor in the industrial market.
   c. a producer in any market
   d. a user of multiple channels of distribution.

6. For a small manufacturer that wants to sell its products in a new marketplace, the most economical decision would be to
   a. hire a direct sales force who could be trained to sell the manufacturer's products.
   b. hire independent sales agents to sell its products.
   c. maintain complete control over its sales functions.
   d. relinquish some control over how sales are made to keep costs down.

7. A franchised operation is an example of what type of distribution policy?
   a. intensive
   b. selective
   c. exclusive
   d. integrated

Chapter 22 Physical Distribution

Note Taking
Main Ideas and Supporting Details

Directions As you read, write key words and short phrases in the Cues column.
Write notes, facts, and main ideas in the Note Taking column. Then summarize
the section in the Summary box.

Cues	Note Taking
• Transportation Systems And Services	• Transportation Systems and Services
• Inventory Storage	• Inventory Storage

Summary

Chapter 22 Physical Distribution

 Academic Integration: Mathematics
Analyzing Distribution Costs

Expanding Distribution The Nugen Company has central distribution centers in five regions of the country. The company uses its own trucks to transport goods from the distribution centers to stores. The company is expanding its distribution facilities in three of the regions to meet increased demand. The spreadsheet below shows the additional shipping needs for each of the three regions. Each company truck can haul 55,000 pounds of goods per load. The number of trips that can be made by a truck during a week varies by region and is shown in the spreadsheet.

	A	B	C	D	E
1	Chapter 22 Physical Distribution				
2		Shipping Needs Per Week (in Pounds)	Number of Pounds Per Truck	Number of trips Per Week	Number of Trucks Needed
3	Region A	2,000,000	55,000	2	
4	Region B	1,500,000	55,000	3	
5	Region B	2,750,000	55,000	2	
6				Total Trucks	

Directions Follow these steps to complete the spreadsheet and to determine the number of trucks the company needs to buy to handle the additional shipments. Then answer the questions on the next page about the completed spreadsheet.
- Turn on your computer and open your spreadsheet software program.
- Create a spreadsheet like the one above using your spreadsheet application.
- Calculate the number of trucks needed for each region based on the shipment weights and the trips per week. Then calculate the total number of trucks needed. Enter the appropriate formula for each calculation.
- Complete the calculations, and then save your work.
- Print out a copy of your work if your teacher has instructed you to do so.

Chapter 22 Physical Distribution

Academic Integration: Mathematics
Analyzing Distribution Costs (continued)

1. How many trucks are needed for all regions to handle the extra shipping? Which region needs the most trucks?

_____

_____

_____

2. If each truck costs $120,000 to operate per year, what is the total annual operating cost of the added trucks?

_____

_____

_____

3. Suppose that 30 percent of the additional shipping needs could be handled by train at a total cost of $2,200,000. Would you recommend shipping only by truck or also by rail shipments. Why or why not?

_____

_____

_____

_____

_____

_____

_____

_____

_____

_____

_____

_____

_____

Chapter 22

Chapter 22 Physical Distribution

 Real-World Application
Transportation Options

Directions Write the preferred form of transportation when shipping each product in the circumstances described (air carrier, motor carrier, pipeline, railroad, or waterway).

_____ 1. Oil shipping from an oil field in Oklahoma to a refinery in Houston, Texas

_____ 2. Iron ore transportation from Duluth, Minnesota, to the steel mills of Gary, Indiana

_____ 3. Cut flowers transported from Hawaii to the mainland

_____ 4. Gasoline transported from a refinery to a local service station

_____ 5. Corn transported from a farm to a local grain elevator

_____ 6. Beef transported from a meatpacker to a supermarket

_____ 7. An overnight letter transported from Phoenix, Arizona to New York City

_____ 8. Furniture transported from a distribution center to a store

_____ 9. Natural gas transported from Alaska to Vancouver, British Columbia

_____ 10. Merchandise shipped from a warehouse to a discount store

_____ 11. Coal transported from a mine in Pennsylvania to a power plant in Detroit, Michigan

_____ 12. Lumber transported from Seattle, Washington, to Tokyo, Japan

_____ 13. Farm equipment manufactured in Canada transported to a warehouse in Wisconsin

_____ 14. Vaccine transported from Atlanta, Georgia, to Los Angeles, California

_____ 15. Sugar transported from the port of New Orleans, Louisiana to Europe

_____ 16. Lobsters transported from Maine to a restaurant in San Francisco

_____ 17. Gasoline shipped from a Texas oil refinery to Chicago, Illinois

_____ 18. Steel transported from Gary, Indiana, to Dallas, Texas

_____ 19. Grain transported from Milwaukee, Wisconsin, to Cleveland, Ohio

_____ 20. Limestone shipped from a quarry off Lake Huron to Detroit, Michigan

Chapter 22 Physical Distribution

 Real-World Application
Case Study

Directions Read the case study below. Then answer the questions that follow.

A New Way to Buy Baseball Cards

Once a staple of dime-store counters, baseball cards are moving to the Internet. The largest maker of baseball cards, The Topps Company, Inc., has announced plans to sell a new line of premium, extra glossy baseball cards through its Web site.

Topps will continue to sell its trading cards in stores and stadiums, its principle distribution system. The new "etopps" cards will be deluxe cards available exclusively through the company's Web site during Initial Player Offerings. The deluxe cards will be sold individually for $3 to $12. The company will either send them directly to the customer or hold them in the customer's portfolio so the cards can later be sold through eBay.com, the Internet auction site. Collectors could buy a Mark McGwire card for about $3, for example, then sell it a few months later on eBay without ever actually seeing the card themselves. eBay is expected to resell one to five percent of every new etopps card Topps sells on topps.com.

Topps began selling baseball cards in 1951 and now controls 37 percent of the trading card market. While Topps does not believe the move to selling deluxe, limited-edition cards on the Internet will alienate distributors or young collectors, other trading card companies have so far not followed Topps' lead. Critics say distributing deluxe cards over the Internet does nothing to address the business's real problem—primarily that today's kids are not as interested in collecting baseball cards as their parents were. Whether Topps will be able to attract buyers to single cards when they are accustomed to buying packs is yet to be seen.

1. What are some potential risks for Topps by adding another distribution channel for its cards?

_____

_____

_____

2. Unlike its competitors, Topps is pursuing an online distribution strategy. Speculate on the company's rationale for this move.

_____

_____

_____

Chapter 22 Physical Distribution

 **DECA Connection**
Distribution Planner

Role Play Imagine that you are the assistant manager of a retail outlet located on the site of the Big B Ranch in Montana. The Big B Ranch is unique because it raises buffalo and sells the meat to specialty stores and restaurants. The ranch specializes in buffalo steaks, ribs, and hamburger (bulk and patty).

The retail store also sells the product directly to consumers who visit the ranch, but retail sales are limited to a fairly small geographic area. Buffalo meat is very nutritious, tasty, and low in fat and cholesterol compared with beef. The business market for the product is very specialized and focused on quality restaurants and independent grocery stores.

The ranch has its own private carrier to deliver its products to area restaurants and stores. Because of limited distribution, it is difficult for potential consumers to purchase the products. Past experience has indicated that many people prefer buffalo to beef after they have had an opportunity to try it. The ranch owner (judge) believes that with proper advertising and better distribution, more consumers would try the products.

Directions The ranch owner (judge) has asked you to develop a marketing and distribution plan for selling the product to consumers through the Internet. You are to present your ideas to the owner (judge). As you prepare your ideas, be sure to consider how the product would be marketed, distributed, and what type of transportation carrier you would use for local, in-state (outside of the local area), and out-of-state deliveries.

Organize your thoughts around the performance indicators noted on the next page. Use these indicators to jot down your ideas during the preparation period. Time your preparation period to last 15 minutes and your role-play presentation to last a maximum of ten minutes. After your role play, use the performance indicators to evaluate your efforts.

Chapter 22 Physical Distribution

 DECA Connection
Distribution Planner *(continued)*

Assessment You will be evaluated on how well you meet the following performance indicators:

Score:

_____ Describe the use of technology in the distribution function.

_____ Explain the relationship between customer service and distribution.

_____ Explain shipping processes.

_____ Select advertising media.

_____ Demonstrate orderly and systematic behavior.

Scoring Each performance indicator equals 20 points (20 × 5 = 100 points).
Excellent (16–20)   **Good** (10–15)   **Fair** (4–9)   **Poor** (0–3)

Chapter 22 Physical Distribution

 Study Skills
Improving Comprehension

Directions Use the following tips to help improve your comprehension. Then, for each series of items, circle the one that does not belong. Write a sentence or two on the line to explain your choice.

Improving Comprehension
Comprehension is the capacity to understand something fully. One way to make sure you are understanding what you read is to monitor your comprehension as you go. While you read, ask yourself these questions: • Can I put the ideas into my own words? • Do I need to look up any words? • Do I understand how the new information fits with what I previously learned? • Do I need to read a section over again? • Can I predict what will happen next?

1. common carrier   contract carrier   private carrier   public carrier

_____

2. fishyback service   international transportation   physical distribution   piggyback service

_____

3. air carrier   express delivery   freight forwarder   U.S. Postal Service

_____

4. pipelines   storage   transportation   waterway

_____

5. air carriers   distribution center   pipeline   waterway

_____

6. U.S. Postal Service   storage   express delivery   freight forwarder

_____

7. waterway   international waters   railroad   seaports

_____

8. air carriers   air bill   airports   pipelines

_____

Chapter 22 Physical Distribution

 ## Study Skills
Test Preparation

Directions Study the Test-Prep Tips and think about how you can use them to improve your test scores. Then write a term from the box on the line next to each phrase to tell which form of transportation it describes.

Test-Prep Tips
• Read directions and questions carefully.
• Ask yourself what they are specifically asking you to do.
• Be sure to address each aspect of the question in your answer.

Forms of Transportation				
air carrier	motor carrier	pipeline	railroad	waterway

_____ **1.** This form of transportation can handle larg quantities at relatively low cost and is rarely affected by weather.

_____ **2.** This is the cheapest way to transport freight but also the slowest.

_____ **3.** This form of transportation carries approximately two percent of the ton-miles of freight moved in the United States.

_____ **4.** This form of transportation is used for virtually all intracity shipping.

_____ **5.** This is the most expensive form of transportation but also the fastest.

_____ **6.** This form of transportation handles nearly 87 percent of the shipments weighing less than 1,000 pounds.

_____ **7.** This form of transportation moves nearly six percent of the total intercity ton-miles of freight.

_____ **8.** This is the oldest form of transportation of large quantities.

Chapter 22

Chapter 22 Physical Distribution

 Study Skills
Practice Test

Directions Circle the letters of ALL choices that accurately complete the
sentence or answer the question.

1. Carriers that are free from direct regulation of rates and operating procedures are
   referred to as _____?
   a. private carriers
   b. common carriers
   c. exempt carriers
   d. contract carriers

2. What are some of the disadvantages of using air transportation?
   a. very expensive
   b. delays due to inclement weather
   c. delays due to customs inspections
   d. delays due to mechanical problems

3. Express delivery companies like DHL and FedEx can ship packages by _____?
   a. air
   b. truck
   c. train
   d. ship

4. A warehouse that is designed to speed delivery of goods and to minimize storage costs is
   called a _____?
   a. public warehouse
   b. private warehouse
   c. bonded warehouse
   d. distribution center

5. What are some of the costs associated with product storage?
   a. cost of space
   b. cost of equipment
   c. pre-shipment charges
   d. cost of personnel

6. What are some of the additional services provided in most public warehouses?
   a. shipment consolidation
   b. receiving
   c. order filling
   d. inspecting

Chapter 23 Purchasing

 Note Taking
Main Ideas and Supporting Details

Directions As you read, write key words and short phrases in the Cues column. Write notes, facts, and main ideas in the Note Taking column. Then summarize the section in the Summary box.

Cues	Note Taking
• The Role of the Buyer	• The Role of the Buyer
• The Purchasing Function	• The Purchasing Function

Summary

Chapter 23

Chapter 23 Purchasing

Academic Integration: Mathematics
Database Application

Supplier Information The Brewster Corporation is updating its database of the suppliers from which it purchases items used to operate the business. Several of the company's suppliers have added online services and have e-mail addresses. The printout below shows a list of suppliers used by the Brewster Corporation.

	A	B	C	D	E	F	G
	Company	**Address**	**City/State/ZIP**	**Telephone**	**Fax**	**Terms**	**Shipping**
1							
2	Chapter 23 Purchasing						
3	Practical Business Solutions	914 South Lane Center	Dallas, TX 75212	(555) 982-4478	(555) 982-4479	2/15, n/30, EOM	FOB Destination
4	McAvoy Plastics & Coatings, Inc.	648 Industrial Drive	Lansing, MI 48932	(555) 278-4401	(555) 278-4405	Net 30	FOB Destination
5	Bryant Equipment Corp.	1229 St. Paul Street	Springfield, MA 01105	(555) 688-4501	(555) 688-7802	2/10 n/30	FOB FFP

Directions Follow these steps to update the Brewster Corporation's database. Then answer the questions that follow.
- Open your database software program on your computer.
- Create a database like the one above.
- Create a new field called "e-mail address" and place it after the fax telephone number. Add a fictional e-mail address for each company.
- Save your data. Print out a copy of your work if your teacher has instructed you to do so.

1. How does adding a field in a database change the information that can be retrieved?

_____

_____

_____

Activity

Can you have either too much or too little information in a database? On a separate sheet of paper explain why each situation might cause difficulty for someone searching a database for information.

_____

_____

_____

Chapter 23 Purchasing

 Real World Application
Purchasing Math

Doing the Math Assume you are a gift store manager and you are completing the merchandise plan entries for the month of December. Last year's December sales totaled $112,000. You are projecting a 3 percent increase in sales for this year. During the month of December, you usually maintain a 3:1 stock-to-sales ratio. Last year's reductions were $7,000. This year you hope to reduce that amount by 5 percent. Assume an EOM stock figure for December of $250,000.

Directions Use the information above to review the calculation for a merchandise plan. Following each element, write the formula used to obtain that figure.

1. Planned sales   _____
    Previous sales   _____
    Desired increase   _____
    Calculation of planned sales   _____
                                                    _____

2. Beginning-of-the-month stock   _____
    Stock-to-sales ratio   _____
    Planned sales   _____
    Calculation of BOM   _____

3. Planned reductions   _____
    Last year's reductions   _____
    Desired decrease   _____
    Calculation of planned reductions   _____

4. Planned purchases   _____
                                                    _____
    Planned sales   _____
    EOM stock   _____
    Planned reductions   _____
    BOM stock   _____
    Calculation of planned purchases   _____
                                                    _____

5. Planned purchases at cost with
    55 percent markup on retail.   _____
    Planned purchases at retail
    Cost equivalent percentage
        (100-MU% retail)   _____
    Planned purchases at cost   _____

Chapter 23 Purchasing

 Real-World Application
Working with Vendors

Directions Compare and contrast the deals offered by suppliers X, Y, and Z, and decide with which you would do business. Provide a rational for your selection by reviewing the criteria buyers use in selecting supply sources. The product is men's cotton/polyester blend shirts to which you will add your own private label.

Vendor X Vendor X has been your source of supply for the past ten years and is located in the United States. Resource file data indicates that Vendor X has recently been bought out by a large corporation, and since then deliveries have been $5.85 per shirt with FOB factory freight prepaid and dating terms 3/10, net 45.

Vendor Y Vendor Y is a potential new source of supply and is located abroad (China). A visit to the manufacturing facility revealed that Vendor Y has the production capabilities to deliver the quantities needed at significantly lower prices than Vendor X and Vendor Z. Deliveries will take longer, so purchasing must be done earlier. Vendor Y offers FOB destination charges reversed and ROG dating of 2/10, net 30. The price will be $0.25 per shirt, and shipping costs have been projected to be $0.50 per shirt, based on shipping by boat. Hidden costs include frequent trips abroad to monitor the manufacturing process for quality-control purposes.

Vendor Z Vendor Z is a potential new source of supply. It is in the United States and has the capacity to make frequent deliveries. It has its own delivery trucks and an excellent reputation for servicing its customers. Its production facilities are smaller than those of Vendor X and Vendor Y, but worker productivity appears to be higher. Vendor Z offers FOB destination (no charge for shipping) and dating terms of 2/20, net 30. The price per shirt with the quantity discount is $6.50.

Note: All three vendors offer UPC labeling and will take care of your private labeling and packaging requirements but will not agree to consignment or memorandum buying arrangements.

_____

_____

_____

_____

_____

_____

_____

_____

_____

Chapter 23 Purchasing

 **DECA Connection**
Online Purchasing Consultant

Role Play Imagine you are the employee of a locally-owned restaurant. The owner (judge) is not knowledgeable about computers. Since you have worked in all areas of the restaurant, including ordering and checking in supplies, the owner wants your input about the benefits and risks of purchasing online.

B2B purchases online are expected to double in each of the next three years. If estimates are correct, the cost of traditional purchasing using paper forms runs around $100 per purchase order, while the same process online typically costs around $5. Checking on orders is faster because computerized data can be accessed quickly and easily.

Directions Role-play a meeting with your employer. Discuss the pros and cons of buying online versus buying in the traditional manner with the owner (judge).

Organize your thoughts around the performance indicators noted below. Use these performance indicators to jot down your ideas during the preparation period. Time your preparation period to last 15 minutes and your role-play presentation to last a maximum of ten minutes. After your role play, use the performance indicators to evaluate your efforts.

Assessment You will be evaluated on how well you meet the following performance indicators:

Score:

_____   Explain the nature and scope of purchasing.

_____   Explain types of business risk.

_____   Explain the nature of risk management.

_____   Review performance of vendors.

_____   Identify factors affecting a business's profit.

Scoring Each performance indicator equals 20 points (20 × 5 = 100 points).
Excellent (16–20)   **Good** (10–15)   **Fair** (4–9)   **Poor** (0–3)

Chapter 23 Purchasing

 Study Skills
Improving Comprehension

Directions Use the following tips to help improve your study habits. Then review Chapter 23 and your class notes to answer the questions that follow. If the statement is true, circle **T**. If the statement is false, circle **F** and rewrite the statement so that is it true.

Using Class Notes
• Before class, review the notes you have taken for the class already. In that way, you will be ready to take in new information.
• Take notes during class. Jot down main ideas in a column on the left side of your paper. Note details next to related main ideas in a column to the right.
• Rewrite your notes after class to make them more complete and accurate.

1. Wholesale and retail buyers purchase goods for resale.   T   F

   _____

2. Open-to-buy estimates planned purchases for a six-month period.   T   F

   _____

3. When companies post what they want to buy on the Internet and   T   F
   suppliers bid for the contract, this is called "reverse auction."

   _____

4. Centralized buying is buying for all branches in a chain store   T   F
   operation at a central location.

   _____

5. Organizational buyers are customers who request items not   T   F
   carried in the store.

   _____

   _____

6. Memorandum buying is an arrangement by which goods are paid   T   F
   for only after they are purchased by the consumer.

   _____

   _____

7. Resident buying offices are the retailers' representatives in   T   F
   the central market.

   _____

Chapter 23 Purchasing

 Study Skills
Test Preparation

Directions Study the Test-Prep Tips and think about how you can use them to improve your test scores. Write a sentence or two to answer each of the following questions about the main ideas in Chapter 23.

Test-Prep Tips
• When taking a timed test, start by reviewing the test questions so you will know how much you have to accomplish in the time allowed.
• Decide how much time you will spend on each item so you will be sure to finish.

1. What steps can a buyer take when choosing to use a new supplier?

_____

_____

2. What are some pros and cons of conducting business on the Internet?

_____

_____

_____

_____

_____

_____

3. What is the main responsibility of a buyer?

_____

_____

4. What are the three types of purchasing situations?

_____

_____

_____

5. What type of goods do government buyers purchase?

_____

_____

Chapter 23

Chapter 23 Purchasing

Study Skills
Practice Test

Directions Take the practice test. Circle the letters of ALL the choices that accurately complete each of the following sentences.

1. A purchasing agent for a manufacturing business is involved with
   a. production planning.
   b. the preparation and/or implementation of a master production schedule.
   c. materials requirement planning.
   d. buying goods for resale.

2. Business people who buy goods for resale include
   a. industrial buyers.
   b. production planners.
   c. retail buyers.
   d. wholesale buyers.

3. In manufacturing and service businesses, the people responsible for purchasing are called
   a. purchasing managers.
   b. industrial buyers.
   c. procurement managers.
   d. wholesale buyers.

4. Criteria that buyers use to select supply sources include
   a. production capabilities.
   b. previous experience with a vendor.
   c. product offerings and terms (price, discounts, dating, etc.).
   d. service offered.

5. When projecting planned sales on a six-month merchandise plan, the firm's sales goal for the current year is derived from a study of
   a. last year's sales.
   b. current market conditions.
   c. current economic conditions.
   d. analysis of the competition.

6. On a merchandise plan, planned retail reductions take into account reductions in the selling price, as well as shortages of merchandise caused by
   a. defective merchandise returned to the vendor.
   b. clerical mistakes.
   c. employee pilferage.
   d. customer shoplifting.

Chapter 24 Stock Handling and Inventory Control

Note Taking
Main Ideas and Supporting Details

Directions As you read, write key words and short phrases in the Cues column. Write notes, facts, and main ideas in the Note Taking column. Then summarize the section in the Summary box.

Cues	Note Taking
• The Stock Handling Process	• The Stock Handling Process
• Inventory Control	• Inventory Control

Summary

Chapter 24 Stock Handling and Inventory Control

Academic Integration: Mathematics
Database Application

Supplier Information Inventory management is the process of buying and storing merchandise for sale while controlling costs for ordering, shipping, handling, and storage. As inventory manager, you place orders for new merchandise at the end of each week. With the aid of a spreadsheet, you track the daily sales of each item in the department to determine how much to order.

Inventory and sales information for five products in your department are shown in the spreadsheet below. Based on past sales records, you have estimated the "planned Weekly Stock Level." This is the level that you need at the beginning of each week. Your computer has also generated information on the beginning inventory level and sales for each item for the past six days.

Use a spreadsheet to calculate the ending inventory for each product. Then calculate the number of each product that you must order to bring your inventory back up to the "Planned Weekly Stock Level."

	A	B	C	D	E	F	G	H	I	J	K
1	Chapter 24 Stock Handling and Inventory Control										
2	Stock Number	Planned Weekly Stock Level	Beginning Inventory	Day 1 Sales	Day 2 Sales	Day 3 Sales	Day 4 Sales	Day 5 Sales	Day 6 Sales	Ending	Amount to Order
3	17345	55	65	5	6	3	9	5	4		
4	35567	105	104	12	10	4	20	3	3		
5	97365	25	25	2	14	6	0	2	1		
6	55677	60	62	4	5	3	0	0	4		
7	9785	40	38	1	0	0	3	5	7		

Directions Follow these steps to create a spreadsheet to calculate the ending inventory. Then answer the questions on the next page.
- Open your spreadsheet software program on your computer.
- Create a spreadsheet like the one above.
- Enter a formula to calculate the current Ending Inventory for Stock Number 17345.

- Copy the formula to appropriate cells in all remaining rows.
- Enter the formula to calculate Amount to Order for Stock Number 17345. Copy the formula to appropriate cells in all remaining rows.

- After completing your calculations, save your work.
- Print out a copy of your work if your teacher has instructed you to do so.

Chapter 24 Stock Handling and Inventory Control

Academic Integration: Mathematics
Database Application *(continued)*

1. List the Ending Inventory levels for each of the five products.

_____

_____

_____

2. At the end of the week, how many of each item must be ordered, based on Planned Weekly Stock Levels?

_____

_____

_____

3. How are the Planned Weekly Stock Levels determined?

_____

_____

_____

_____

_____

4. Does using these calculations to place orders for merchandise ensure that the business will not run out of product next week?

_____

_____

_____

5. Does an ending inventory of 0 at the end of week indicate that the manager made an excellent buying decision?

_____

_____

_____

Chapter 24

Chapter 24 Stock Handling and Inventory Control

Real-World Application
Case Study

Apple Reaches Out to Retailers During most of the 1990s, Apple Inc. sold its computers only through its own Web site, CompUSA, and through a few other specialty retailers.

That distribution was a conscious choice by the computer maker and was in reaction to inventory problems and the expense of maintaining relationships with retail stores. Retail outlets that did carry Apple products had trouble keeping them in stock. They complained that the company's policies were too rigid. At one point Apple mandated that dealers had to sell at least $500,000 worth of product to carry Apple.

Later, toward the end of the 1990s, retail stores were willing to work with Apple again, because, in addition to the popular iMac, Apple introduced Powerbook laptops and G4 desktops that were attracting new customers. The company had solved its inventory problems, so it was able to keep retailers stocked. Plus, Apple computers looked good in displays. National retailer Sears Roebuck & Co. began selling Apple computers. However, another retailer, Best Buy, refused to carry all of the iMac product line, so Apple pulled its products from Best Buy stores for a time.

Getting into more retail establishments seemed to be working for Apple. But it was not the solution they needed to gain market share. In 2001, Apple decided to open a chain of its own retail stores. They were able to put the stores in high traffic areas, merchandise them, and market them in whatever ways they wanted to attract new customers. The Apple Stores became the solution to all their problems giving them the control they needed in order to sell their products efficiently and become a market leader.

Directions Answer the questions that follow about the case study above.

1. What are some of the costs involved with maintaining effective dealer networks for a computer company such as Apple?

_____

_____

_____

_____

_____

_____

Chapter 24 Stock Handling and Inventory Control

Real-World Application
Case Study (continued)

2. What did Apple do to alienate many retailers from carrying its products before the new strategy was implemented?

_____

_____

_____

_____

_____

_____

_____

3. Why do you think Apple's decision to open its own stores was so successful?

_____

_____

_____

_____

_____

_____

_____

4. What were some key factors for Apple in helping them decide to open the Apple Stores?

_____

_____

_____

_____

_____

_____

Chapter 24

Name _____ Date _____ Class _____

Chapter 24 Stock Handling and Inventory Control

Real-World Application
Completing Inventory Forms

Directions Assume you are responsible for doing inventory in the stationery department of a school store. Complete the inventory form below, by filling in the heading and calculating the necessary extensions (total retail value for each item and for the entire stationery inventory).

School Store_____

INVENTORY FORM

Date _____   Counted by ———————————

Page _____   Check by ———————————

Description of Merchandise	Units on Hand	Unit Price	Total Retail Value
refrigerator magnets	45	45	
5" x 8" note cards	25	.79	
filler notebook paper	38	1.19	
erasers	60	.29	
pencils	115	.15	
medium-point pens	45	.39	
fine-point pens	51	.39	
computer paper (250 ct.)	10	10.59	
typewriter ribbons	20	1.98	
posterboard (white)	15	.59	
posterboard (colored)	10	.79	
protractors	5	2.19	
rulers (6")	6	.39	
rulers (12")	12	.79	
pocket portfolios	12	.79	
Total Retail Value			

Chapter 24 Stock Handling and Inventory Control

 DECA Connection
Supermarket Assistant Manager

Role Play Imagine you are the assistant manager of a large supermarket that has over 27,000 individual stock keeping units. The store uses point-of-sale terminals for all selling transactions. Your store is located in a state that does not require all stock keeping units to be individually price marked. However, the state does require that shelf labels and signs accurately reflect the price of each item to be sold. Your state also penalized a store for overcharging. Because of a busy weekend and some newly hired stockpersons, shelf prices and signs were not changed to accurately reflect the prices on several sale items. Accordingly, an irate but regular customer (judge) has approached you complaining about being overcharged and loudly alleges in front of several customers that your store has a reputation for overcharging customers. This is not a correct allegation, since your store genuinely tries to be fair and honest with its pricing practices. The customer's sales receipt indicated that there has been an overcharge of $3.59 on four sales items.

The manager has asked you to handle the disgruntled customer (judge) in a manner that will not embarrass the customer and do further damage to the store's reputation.

Directions Role-play a conversation with the customer in which you resolve the situation to the satisfaction of the customer and gain a commitment from the customer to continue shopping at your store.

Organize your thoughts around the performance indicators noted below. Use these performance indicators to jot down your ideas during the preparation period. Time your preparation period to last 15 minutes and your role-play presentation to last a maximum of ten minutes. After your role play, use the performance indicators to evaluate your efforts.

Assessment You will be evaluated on how well you meet the following performance indicators:

Score:

_____ Handle customer/client complaints.

_____ Demonstrate problem-solving skills.

_____ Interpret business policies to customer/clients.

_____ Explain the nature of positive customer/client relations.

_____ Describe the role of business ethics in pricing.

Scoring Each performance indicator equals 20 points (20 × 5 = 100 points).
Excellent (16–20)   **Good** (10–15)   **Fair** (4–9)   **Poor** (0–3)

Chapter 24 Stock Handling and Inventory Control

Study Skills
Studying at Home

Directions Use the following tips to help improve your study habits. Then, review Chapter 24 using the tips to answer the questions that follow. If the statement is true, circle **T**. If the statement is false, circle **F** and rewrite the statement so that is it true.

Your Study Area
• Organize a study area to promote your ability to concentrate and avoid distractions. • Make sure your study area is well-lit and has good ventilation. • Locate your work area as far away from stereos, TVs, and loud noises as possible.

1. Perpetual inventory systems track inventory on a constant basis. T F

   _____

2. A stock plan used to monitor staple items is called a basis stock list. T F

   _____

3. Never-out list is when the seller or manufacturer puts the price on T F
   the merchandise before it is delivered to a retailer.

   _____

   _____

4. Inventory turnover is the number of times the average inventory is sold and T F
   replaced in a given time period.

   _____

5. Dollar control is the planning and monitoring of the total inventory investment. T F

   _____

6. Real-time inventory is a stock plan used to monitor fashionable items. T F

   _____

7. Each item or a group of related items is called receiving record. T F

   _____

8. Inventory management is a system in which suppliers deliver parts and materials T F
   just before they are needed for use.

   _____

   _____

Chapter 24 Stock Handling and Inventory Control

Study Skills
Test Preparation

Directions Study the Test-Prep Tips and think about how you can use them to improve your scores on open-book tests. Then write a sentence or two to answer each of the questions about the main ideas in Chapter 24. Refer to your book if you need to.

Test-Prep Tips
• When taking an open-book test, answer the easy questions that you are confident about first.
• Then go back and work on the answers to questions you need the book to answer.

1. What items might be found on a receiving record?

_____

_____

_____

2. Explain the blind-check method. Is this the most accurate checking method?

_____

_____

_____

3. What is inventory and what does it include?

_____

_____

_____

4. How are Retail businesses expected to maintain their inventory?

_____

_____

_____

5. What are the steps in the stock handling process?

_____

_____

_____

Chapter 24

Chapter 24 Stock Handling and Inventory Control

Study Skills
Practice Test

Directions Take the practice test. Circle the letters of ALL the choices that accurately complete each of the following sentences.

1. What are the different methods of checking in merchandise?
   - **a.** blind-check
   - **b.** direct-check
   - **c.** spot-check
   - **d.** inventory-check

2. What are the various forms used when receiving in goods?
   - **a.** dock
   - **b.** quality
   - **c.** invoice
   - **d.** receiving record

3. What are the different technologies and computerized methods for tracking merchandise?
   - **a.** UPC
   - **b.** stock shrinkage
   - **c.** SCM
   - **d.** electronic data exchange

4. A model stock list is
   - **a.** a stock plan used to monitor fashionable items.
   - **b.** a stock plan that is modeled after previous ones.
   - **c.** a never-out list.
   - **d.** a just-in-time list.

5. All of these terms except _____ relate to dollar control of inventory.
   - **a.** dollar control
   - **b.** sales
   - **c.** unit control
   - **d.** stock shortages

6. A perpetual inventory system
   - **a.** tracks items once a month.
   - **b.** tracks inventory on a continual basis.
   - **c.** controls all inventory systems.
   - **d.** periodically computes inventory levels.

Chapter 25 Price Planning

 Note Taking
Main Ideas and Supporting Details

Directions As you read, write key words and short phrases in the Cues column. Write notes, facts, and main ideas in the Note Taking column. Then summarize the section in the Summary box.

Cues	Note Taking
• Price Planning Considerations	• Price Planning Considerations
• Factors Involved in Price Planning	• Factors Involved in Price Planning

Summary

Chapter 25

Name _____ Date _____ Class _____

Chapter 25 Price Planning

Academic Integration: Mathematics
Spreadsheet Application

Price Planning Breakdown The Martinez Company makes equipment for racket sports. The marketing manager has asked you to analyze the cost of manufacturing and selling this new tennis racket the company has developed. Determine the units that must be sold to break even at three different manufacturing volumes. The unit manufacturing costs decrease as the number of units manufactured increases. See the printout below for the cost for each manufacturing level. The sales expense for this new racket is estimated at 3 percent of the selling price of $79.50. Marketing expenses will average 4 percent of the selling price.

	A	B	C	D	E	F	G
1		Unit Manufacturing Cost	Sales Expense	Marketing Expenses	Total Unit Cost	Total Cost	Breakeven point
2	Chapter 25 Price Planning						
3	20,000	28.50					
4	30,000	27.35					
5	40,000	27.00					

Directions Follow these steps to create a spreadsheet and determine break-even points. Then answer the questions that follow.
- Turn on your computer and open your spreadsheet software program.
- Create a spreadsheet like the one above.
- Enter a formula to calculate the sales expense.

- Enter the formula to calculate the marketing expense.

- Enter a formula to calculate the total unit cost for each manufacturing level (add columns B, C, and D), then enter a formula to find the total cost for each level.

- Enter a formula to calculate the break-even points.

- Print out a copy of your work if your teacher has instructed you to do so.

  1. What is the total unit cost at each level of manufacturing?

  _____

  _____

Chapter 25 Price Planning

Real-World Application
Maintaining Profitability

Newspaper Cost-Cutting Measure Due to lower than average advertising revenues and increasing paper costs, newspapers are cutting the length of their newspapers instead of increasing their prices. The *Dallas Morning News* reduced the amount of space designed for stock tables, sports results, television listings, and comics. Other newspapers across the nation facing the same problem have elected to cut some of their comic strips, which caused a fury among dedicated followers. To avoid offending these followers, some newspapers have shrunk the size of comic strips so that they fit into a smaller space, while others have conducted surveys to determine which comic strips to cut. The results of the survey, however, have been skewed toward older readers who prefer long-time favorites and who are still the mainstay for newspaper readership.

   In some cases, comic strips that have been cut have been reinstated due to popular demand. *The Salt Lake Tribune* cut its weekday comic section from three pages to two pages and, in doing so, retired comic strips *Judge Parker* and *Mary Worth*. Readers responded with e-mails, phone calls, and faxes asking for those comic strips to be restored. A few weeks later the two comic strips were restored and a newer one was cut instead. Some syndicated comic strips can cost several hundred dollars a week per strip. Newsprint prices increased 10 percent from 2003 to 2004, and those increases are expected to continue.

Directions Answer the questions that follow about the article above.

1. What two major factors have impacted newspapers' profits?

   _____

   _____

2. How have newspapers responded to their current financial situation?

   _____

   _____

3. Why do you think newspapers did not increase prices, given their financial situation?

   _____

   _____

Chapter 25

Chapter 25 Price Planning

Real-World Application
Understanding Antitrust Legislation

New York—A coalition of auto parts retailers and warehouse distributors filed an antitrust suit against Wal-Mart Stores and Sam's Club, Bentonville, Arkansas; Auto-Zone, Memphis, Tennessee; Advanced Auto, Roanoke, Virginia; and 13 auto parts manufacturers. The coalition said the manufacturers that sell engage in monopolistic pricing practices and claim those manufacturers named in the suit sell parts to Wal-Mart, Sam's Club, Auto-Zone and other defendants named at substantially lower per-unit prices than [to] other distributors. Those actions, according to the suit, violate both the Robinson-Patman Act and the [Clayton] Antitrust Act. The plaintiffs claim they are unable to compete because of the price discrimination, and will be driven out of business. The suit also alleges the defendant auto parts manufacturers have failed to comply with the Sarbanes-Oxley corporate governance statute by not reporting they are selling below cost to their largest customers. (Source: Supermarketnews.com, October 29, 2004)

Directions Answer the questions that follow about the article above.

1. What three laws are the plaintiffs using as the basis for their suit against the auto parts manufacturers and large retailers that sell auto parts? Note the purpose of each law.

_____

_____

_____

_____

_____

Activity

Write a paragraph on another sheet of paper to answer the following questions. If you were a lawyer for a defendant in this case, how would you argue for your client? Who do you think will win—plaintiffs or the defendants? Why?

_____

_____

_____

_____

_____

_____

Chapter 25 Price Planning

DECA Connection
Assistant Manager

Role Play Imaging that you are the assistant manager of an independent coffee cafe. For a special promotion you planned for the store's anniversary, you were going to slash prices on cups of coffee and bags of coffee beans due to a price cut you were told you would receive from your wholesale supplier. Today you received a fax from your coffee supplier that rescinded the 10 percent cut because of bad weather in Brazil, where one-third of the world's coffee is produced. In a trade paper, you learned that Starbucks, a competitor, is increasing its coffee prices by about seven cents a cup in order to defray operating expenses. You are not sure if Starbucks will be increasing its profits even more in anticipation of higher coffee prices in the near future.

Directions The owner of the store (judge) is meeting with you to discuss the upcoming anniversary promotion. With all the information you now have, you must decide what to do about coffee prices and the special promotion.

Assessment You will be evaluated on how well you meet the following performance indicators:

Score:

_____ Handle customer/client complaints.

_____ Demonstrate problem-solving skills.

_____ Interpret business policies to customer/clients.

_____ Explain the nature of positive customer/client relations.

_____ Describe the role of business ethics in pricing.

Scoring Each performance indicator equals 20 points (20 × 5 = 100 points).
Excellent (16–20)   **Good** (10–15)   **Fair** (4–9)   **Poor** (0–3)

Chapter 25

Chapter 25 Price Planning

 Study Skills
Improving Vocabulary

Directions Use the following tips to help improve your vocabulary. Then review the vocabulary and key terms in Chapter 25, using the tips as you answer the questions that follow. If the statement is true, circle T. If the statement is false, circle F and rewrite the statement so that is it true.

Improving Vocabulary
• When improving vocabulary or learning key terms it is important to make sense of the term and internalize it.
• Try to continually use the new term in your everyday vocabulary.

1. A marketer's relative standing/rank in relation to competitors is their market position.   T   F

   _____

2. Price fixing is a demand that is affected by a change in price.   T   F

   _____

   _____

3. Return on investment is a calculation used to determine the relative profitability of a product.   T   F

   _____

4. An item priced at or below cost to draw customers into a store is a loss leader.   T   F

   _____

5. A break-even point is a firm's percentage of the total sales volume generated by all competitors in a given market.   T   F

   _____

   _____

6. Bait and switch advertising refers to charging different prices to similar customers in similar situations.   T   F

   _____

   _____

7. Price is the value of money (or its equivalent) placed on a good or service.   T   F

   _____

8. Inelastic demand is demand that is barely, if at all, affected by a change in price.   T   F

   _____

Chapter 25 Price Planning

Study Skills
Test Preparation

Directions Study the Test-Prep Tips and think about how you can use them to improve your test scores. Write a sentence or two to answer each of the following questions about the main ideas in Chapter 25.

Test-Prep Tips
• When studying from a textbook, develop questions in your mind as you go. Try to identify the who, what, when, where, why, and how of the subject at hand.
• Read the chapter summaries in the textbook. They usually do a good job reviewing the important points.

1. What does price establish for a company?

_____

_____

_____

2. What are the goals of pricing?

_____

_____

_____

3. Explain inelastic demand.

_____

_____

_____

4. What is the law of supply and demand?

_____

_____

_____

5. What are the four factors that affect pricing?

_____

_____

_____

Chapter 25

Chapter 25 Price Planning

 Study Skills
Practice Test

Directions Take the practice test. Circle the letter of the choice that accurately completes each of the following sentences.

1. The prices a business charges its customers for its products are important because they establish and maintain a firm's
   a. image, competitive edge, and profits.
   b. ability to control competition.
   c. costs and expenses.
   d. ability to manipulate elastic and inelastic consumer demand.

2. Assume your firm's sales increased from $3 million last year to $10 million this year. However, the market leader still enjoys a 40 percent share of the $200 million widget market. The other four competitors had sales this year of $35 million, $38 million, $12 million, and $7 million, respectively. For this year, your firm's market position would be
   a. 1.5 percent.   c. last.
   b. five percent.   d. fifth.

3. If you sell a product for $18.98 and it costs you $16.50 to make and market it, your return on investment for that product would be
   a. 13 percent.   c. 87 percent.
   b. 15 percent.   d. 115 percent.

4. To maintain a firm's profits in the face of rising costs and expenses or declining sales, businesses might do all of the following except
   a. reduce the size of the product to maintain or lower the price.
   b. decrease the price by reducing the number of product features.
   c. improve product quality and increase the number of features to justify a higher price.
   d. maintain prices while increasing product size and/or features.

5. A manufacturer plans to produce 300,000 dolls that will be sold to wholesalers and retailers for $15 each. Unit costs and expenses associated with making and distributing one doll are $12. The point at which this manufacturer will break even is
   a. 375,000 dolls.   c. 240,000 dolls.
   b. 200,000 dolls.   d. 100,000 dolls.

6. When a person is at a vacation resort where the only food service available is affiliated with the resort, prices will most likely be higher than normal because
   a. the food service would be classified as luxury.
   b. the law of diminishing marginal utility says so.
   c. all consumers are brand loyal.
   d. the demand is inelastic because of the lack of substitutes.

Chapter 26 Pricing Strategies

 ### Note Taking
Main Ideas and Supporting Details

Directions As you read, write key words and short phrases in the Cues column.
Write notes, facts, and main ideas in the Note Taking column. Then summarize
the section in the Summary box.

Cues	Note Taking
• Basic Pricing Policies	• Basic Pricing Policies
• Strategies in the Pricing Process	• Strategies in the Pricing Process

Summary

Chapter 26 Pricing Strategies

 ## Academic Integration: Mathematics
Using and Analyzing a Spreadsheet

Determining Price The Sun Protection Company has conducted research asking customers the maximum price they would pay for a new sunblock cream with an SPF of 40. The number of customers saying they would buy the product at each price is shown in the spreadsheet below. The company plans to sell its new sunblock in one city first to test market acceptance. Assume that the research group represents 5 percent of the total market of potential buyers in the test city.

	A	B	C	D
1	Price	Number of Customers	Total Market	Estimated Retail Sales
2	$3.99	500	10,000	
3	$4.49	1,100		
4	$4.99	800		
5	$5.49	600		
6	$5.99	200		
7	Total			

Directions Follow these steps to complete the spreadsheet. Then answer the questions that follow.

- Turn on your computer and open your spreadsheet software program.
- Create a spreadsheet like the one here using your spreadsheet application.
- Enter a formula to calculate the total market at each price (assuming the research group to be five percent of the total market).
- Enter a formula to calculate the total for the "Total Market" column.
- Enter a formula to calculate the estimated retail sales at each price level.

- Perform all calculations.
- Save your work. Print out a copy of your work if you have been instructed to do so.

1. Which price would get the largest market share?

   _____

2. What is the number of total potential buyers when all prices are included?

   _____

3. Assume that Sun Protection's major competitor sells its sunblock cream for $4.39. Recommend a price for Sun Protection's new sunblock. Explain your reasons.

   _____

Chapter 26 Pricing Strategies

Real-World Application
Policy Analysis

Directions Read the article below, and then answer the questions that follow.

Costco—A Warehouse Retailer with Low Prices

With a combination of low markups, bare bones design, and a wide merchandise mix, the warehouse retailer Costco is able to offer customers low prices daily. Costco stores are the epitome of no frills. They are warehouses with merchandise stacked to the rafters.

While Costco carries only a few brands and sizes, it offers an impressive range of products, from groceries to household products, from clothes, books, and music to furniture and even luxury items. Fresh food accounts for 10 percent of Costco's annual sales. Costco customers can get their photos processed in the hour it takes to pick up fresh salmon, Waterford crystal, and motor oil. Customers can also get an eye exam and have glasses made, and at some locations they can fill up with gas that is up to 25 cents a gallon cheaper than retail gas stations.

Costco relies on a predictable pricing strategy. It keeps markups between 10 and 14 percent above cost, well below the minimum 25 percent for most retailers. And Costco avoids selling items at cost to attract customers, instead relying on a low markup to ensure that prices on all items stay low. In addition, Costco charges all its customers a membership fee: $45 for business owners and the general public, and $100 for executive memberships with added features.

Costco does not have as many stores as Sam's Club, a major competitor. There are about 300 Costcos compared with around 530 Sam's Clubs (a subsidiary of Wal-Mart). Another competitor is BJ's Wholesale Club, with around 150 locations. Regardless of number of locations, Costco manages to generate greater annual sales per store, $112 million, which is significantly higher than the $63 million per store for Sam's Club and $46 million for BJ's Wholesale Club.

1. How does Costco demonstrate cost-oriented, demand-oriented, and competition-oriented pricing?

_____

_____

_____

_____

_____

Chapter 26

Chapter 26 Pricing Strategies

 Real-World Application
Policy Analysis (continued)

2. Is Costco's pricing policy more representative of a one-price policy or a flexible-price policy? Explain your answer.

_____

_____

_____

_____

_____

_____

_____

3. How is Costco able to keep its prices so low and still be profitable?

_____

_____

_____

_____

_____

_____

_____

4. Why do you think Costco's annual sales per store exceed those of its competitors?

_____

_____

_____

_____

_____

_____

Chapter 26 Pricing Strategies

Real-World Application
Steps to Pricing a Product

Directions Use the six steps in setting a price to demonstrate how a luggage manufacturer would price a newly designed piece of luggage.

Product Description The case has wheels and a retractable handle for pulling. It is 14 ¹/₂ inches wide by 9 inches deep by 22 inches high and weighs 9 pounds empty. This new model is approved as carry-on luggage for airline flights. It can be made of a heavy-duty polyester fabric or a water resistant tapestry fabric with leather trim.

1. **Determine pricing objectives** Do you want to generate a certain sales volume, take away market share from competitors, or establish a prestigious or value-oriented image?

   _____

   _____

   _____

   _____

2. **Study costs** It costs $43.50 to make and market this piece of luggage. The company would like to get a return on investment on this new design of 10–20 percent. Determine the floor, mid-range, and ceiling prices (plus 10, 15, and 20 percent, respectively) that would be charged to retailers. Then, assuming that the retailers would charge customers at least double their cost, determine what the retail prices would be for this item.

   _____

   _____

   _____

   _____

3. **Estimate demand** Who will be your final target market, and what will that group be willing to pay? This design is similar to the type of luggage flight attendants use. Research indicates that it is fast becoming the luggage of choice for female business travelers and other people who do not like waiting for their luggage in airline terminals.

   _____

   _____

   _____

Chapter 26 Pricing Strategies

🌐 Real-World Application
Steps to Pricing a Product (continued)

4. Study competition With whom will you compete?

_____

_____

_____

_____

_____

5. Decide on a pricing strategy Will it be skimming, going-rate, or penetration? Why?

_____

_____

_____

_____

_____

6. Set price
   a. What will be the suggested retail price for the luggage?

_____

_____

_____

_____

   b. What is the price you will charge retailers for this luggage?

_____

_____

_____

_____

_____

Chapter 26 Pricing Strategies

DECA Connection
Assistant Buyer

Role Play Imagine you are the assistant buyer for fragrances in an upscale department store. You are always on the lookout for new product ideas. After seeing advertisements for French perfume and other toiletries for dogs in *Elle* and *Vogue*, two fashion magazines, you decide to conduct a little research. You learn that a celebrity is about to launch her own doggie perfume. Research indicates that the French perfume for dogs is retailing for $38 in other upscale department stores. Your store's customary markup based on cost for high-end toiletries is between 60 percent and 100 percent, depending on the brand. The celebrity's doggie perfume will cost the store $22.50.

Directions Write a memo to your buyer (judge) detailing your discovery of doggie perfume and toiletries and providing a suggested retail price for the celebrity's doggie perfume. You need to take cost, demand, and competition into account when providing your rationale. You should also provide a pricing strategy for the new, innovative product, as well as strategies to sell more than one product in the line. Explain any psychological pricing ideas you have, as well as any ideas about promotional pricing to launch this new line.

Organize your thoughts around the performance indicators noted below. Use these indicators to jot down your ideas during the preparation period. Time your preparation period to last 15 minutes and your role-play presentation to last a maximum of ten minutes. After your role play, use the performance indicators to evaluate your efforts.

Assessment You will be evaluated on how well you meet the following performance indicators:

Score:

_____ Select an approach for setting a base price.

_____ Identify strategies for pricing new products.

_____ Select product mix pricing strategies.

_____ Use psychological pricing to adjust base prices.

_____ Select promotional pricing strategies used to adjust base prices.

Scoring Each performance indicator equals 20 points (20 × 5 = 100 points).
Excellent (16–20)   **Good** (10–15)   **Fair** (4–9)   **Poor** (0–3)

Chapter 26 Pricing Strategies

Chapter 26

Study Skills
Learning New Vocabulary

Directions Use the following tips to help improve your vocabulary. Then match each definition with the correct term from the Word Bank. (Not all terms will be used.)

Learning New Vocabulary
• When performing a matching exercise, match the easiest, most recognizable words first. Then the amount of choices left may make finding the remaining pairs much easier.
• Think about synonyms and antonyms to new vocabulary or to key words in their definitions. How closely do the synonyms or antonyms relate to the key term?
• Once you learn a new word, try to use it right away—verbally in a conversation or on paper in a sentence.

Word Bank		
bundle pricing	cost-plus pricing	discount pricing
EDLP flexible-price	policy markup	pricing
penetration pricing prestige	pricing promotional	pricing
seasonal discounts	skimming pricing	trade discounts

_____ 1. The price of a new product is set very high to capitalize on the high demand during its introductory period.

_____ 2. Prices are reduced for a short period of time.

_____ 3. The seller offers reductions from the usual price.

_____ 4. These are offered to buyers who are willing to buy in advance of the customary buying season.

_____ 5. The initial price for a new product is set very low in order to encourage as many people as possible to buy it.

_____ 6. A company sets prices consistently low with no intention of offering discounts in the future.

_____ 7. Prices are higher than average to suggest status and an upscale image to the consumer.

_____ 8. Some manufacturers quote prices to wholesalers and retailers in this way.

_____ 9. Arriving at a price by adding a dollar amount to the cost of an item.

_____ 10. This permits customers to bargain for merchandise.

Chapter 26 Pricing Strategies

 Study Skills
Test Preparation

Directions Study the Test-Prep Tips and think about how you can use them to improve your test scores. Then circle the letter of the option that best answers each question about the main ideas in Chapter 26.

Test-Prep Tips
• When answering multiple-choice questions, ask yourself if each option is true or false. This may help you find the best answer if you are not sure.
• Read the question first, then read all the answer choices before choosing your answer. Eliminate answers you know are not correct.

1. When might penetration pricing be used to sell a product?
   a. when a product is first introduced onto the market
   b. in its growth stage
   c. in its maturity phase
   d. when a product is on the decline, to generate interest again

2. Where can you see an example of flexible-price policy?
   a. grocery stores
   b. hardware stores
   c. online auction sites, such as e-Bay
   d. online e-tailers where one can order the same items as in their brick-and-mortar stores plus some specialty products, such as target.com or borders.com

3. What kind of policy does a store have that prices all of its sweaters at $50, $75, and $100?
   a. bundle
   b. EDLP
   c. price-lining
   d. discount pricing

4. Which is not a type of promotional pricing?
   a. EDLP
   b. rebates
   c. bundle
   d. prestige

5. Which activity might some businesses do to suggest a bargain and help increase sales volume?
   a. price items in multiples, like 3 for $1
   b. use prestige pricing
   c. set prices that end in even numbers, like $30
   d. price just above round amount, like $31

6. Which is a special type of promotional discount that goes directly to buyers when they sell back an old model of the product they are purchasing?
   a. rebate
   b. trade-in allowance
   c. loss leader
   d. special deal

Chapter 26 Pricing Strategies

 Study Skills
Practice Test

Directions Circle the letter of the word or phrase that best completes each of the following sentences.

1. Cost-plus pricing is used primarily by
   a. consumers.
   b. manufacturers.
   c. retailers.
   d. wholesalers.

2. The consumer's perceived value of an item is the basis for
   a. competition-oriented pricing.
   b. cost-oriented pricing.
   c. demand-oriented pricing.
   d. markup-oriented pricing.

3. Skimming pricing permits marketers to
   a. cover the research and development costs incurred in designing the product.
   b. enjoy a bargain image.
   c. lure customers away from higher-priced brands.
   d. raise their product's price in the future without affecting customer loyalty.

4. A retail department store that has price tags on all of its merchandise is practicing a
   a. flexible-price policy.
   b. penetration pricing policy.
   c. skimming pricing policy.
   d. one-price policy.

5. The main goal of marketers is to keep products in the
   a. decline stage.
   b. growth stage.
   c. introduction stage.
   d. maturity stage.

6. A marketer who wants to project a quality image would price a sweater at
   a. $153.50.
   b. $149.99.
   c. $150.
   d. $147.59.

Chapter 27 Pricing Math

Note Taking
Main Ideas and Supporting Details

Directions As you read, write key words and short phrases in the Cues column. Write notes, facts, and main ideas in the Note Taking column. Then summarize the section in the Summary box.

Cues	Note Taking
• Calculating Prices	• Calculating Prices
• Calculating Discounts	• Calculating Discounts

Summary

Chapter 27 Pricing Math

Academic Integration: Mathematics
Spreadsheet Application

Calculating Markup Your company sells the eight products shown in the printout below. For some of the products, the cost and desired markup are known, and you must calculate the selling price. For other products, the planned selling price is known, and you must calculate cost based on the desired markup. If the cost and selling price are both known, you will need to calculate the markup. Calculate the markup percentage on retail for all the products.

	A	B	C	D	E
1	Item	Cost	Markup	Selling Price	Markup Percentage
2	Chapter 27 Pricing Math				
3	1	$10.45	$10.49		
4	2	$72.16		$145.47	
5	3		$0.71	$1.46	
6	4	$4.35		$8.70	
7	5	$83.12	$82.88		
8	6	$13.17		$25.75	
9	7	$0.49		$1.00	
10	8	$2.69	$2.56		

Directions Follow these steps to create a spreadsheet. Then answer the questions below.

Spreadsheet Directions
- Start your spreadsheet software program.
- Create a spreadsheet like the one above using your spreadsheet application.
- Calculate the following:
    - Find the selling price by adding cost and markup.
    - Find the cost by subtracting markup from selling price.
    - Find the markup by subtracting cost from selling price.
    - Find the markup percentage on retail by dividing markup by the selling price.
- After completing your calculations, save your work.
- Print out a copy of your work if your teacher has instructed you to do so.

1. Which product shows the highest dollar markup? Which product shows the lowest?

_____

2. Which product shows the highest markup percentage? Which product shows the lowest?

_____

Chapter 27 Pricing Math

 Real-World Application
Pricing

Directions Solve the following pricing math problems. Record your answers in the spaces provided.

1. Determine the retail price for a calculator that a business wants to mark up $3.49 above its cost of $6.50.

   _____

2. Determine the markup percentage based on both retail and cost for a hand-held hair dryer that sells in the store for $17.95 and costs the business $10.77.

   _____

   _____

3. Use the markup equivalents table to determine the markup percentage based on cost and the retail price for a child's bicycle that cost the business $43.99 and has a markup on retail of $33^1/3$ percent.

   _____

   _____

4. Use the retail box to determine the retail price and markup in dollars for a coffee machine that costs a business $15.78. The retail markup percentage used by the firm is

   _____

   _____

5. Sally's Dinettes has an invoice dated March 10 that totals $65,429 for an order of tables and chairs it purchased from George's Manufacturing. George's terms are 3/15, net 60. How much will Sally's Dinettes pay for that order if the check is mailed on March 16?

   _____

6. The Shop Vac Wet/Dry Vacuum is purchased by a wholesaler with trade discounts of 45 percent and 10 percent off the list price of $70. Determine the wholesaler's cost.

   _____

   _____

7. Baseballs are on special for the week. During the promotion, customers can buy three baseballs for $26.99. What is the retail price for a customer who wants to buy two baseballs?

   _____

Chapter 27 Pricing Math

 Real-World Application
Retail Pricing

Directions The school store has purchased 72 T-shirts and 72 pairs of boxer
shorts with the school's mascot and name on them. The cost was $5.75 each.
Choose two possible retail prices, and then calculate the unit dollar markup
and markup percentage based on the retail price for each. Then compare each
price's profitability by calculating the gross profit for each, assuming all items
sell. Based on everything you know about cost-, demand-, and competition-
oriented pricing strategies, settle on a realistic price for the new items and provide rationale for your answer. The school store would like a total gross profit
of $600, assuming all 144 items sell at that price.

A		B	
Suggested Retail Price		Suggested Retail Price	
Cost	$5.75	Cost	$5.75
Markup in Dollars		Markup in Dollars	
Markup % (retail)		Markup % (retail)	
Gross Profit		Gross Profit	

1. **Determine pricing objectives** Do you want to generate a profit? What is the retail price
   you selected? Write a rationale for your choice.

   _____

   _____

   _____

   _____

2. What if you had to mark down 40 items at the end of the season by 25 percent? Would
   you still make the required $600 gross profit? Show your calculations.

   _____

   _____

   _____

   _____

Chapter 27 Pricing Math

DECA Connection
Fundraiser

Role Play Imagine that you are the fundraising chairperson for your DECA chapter. A local electronics wholesaler is willing to sell your DECA chapter new, brand-name electronics for a fundraiser. The selected products are discontinued models, all of which are under full warranty. This wholesaler also has a Web site where its products are displayed with suggested retail prices. He is offering to sell DECA these discontinued items at 40 percent off the suggested retail prices. It is up to DECA members to decide how much to mark up the goods in order to make a profit from the fundraiser. A few of the items and their suggested retail prices are as follows: Digital Video Camcorder $799.95; Portable CD Player $49.95; Cordless Digital Phone $59.95; Portable DVD Player $1,299.95; Digital Ready DVD Player $249.95; Wizard Organizer $39.95; and Microwave Half Pint Size $99.95. The wholesaler is willing to let you return any unopened boxed items for full credit. However, you must purchase all products that will be used for display purposes because they will no longer be classified as "new" after the DECA electronics sale. You need a pricing plan for the sale of those displayed products at the end of the sale.

Directions Prepare a report to share with the DECA treasurer (judge) that details the cost, markup, and suggested sale price for this fundraiser. The treasurer needs to know how you will present this proposal.

Organize your thoughts around the performance indicators noted below. Use these performance indicators to jot down your ideas during the preparation period. Time your preparation to last 15 minutes and your role play presentation to last a maximum of ten minutes. After your role-play, use the performance indicators to evaluate your efforts.

Assessment You will be evaluated on how well you meet the following performance indicators:

Score:

_____ Explain the nature and scope of the pricing function.

_____ Explain the use of technology in the pricing function.

_____ Determine the cost of a product.

_____ Determine discounts and allowances used to adjust base prices.

_____ Set prices.

Scoring Each performance indicator equals 20 points (20 × 5 = 100 points).
Excellent (16–20)   **Good** (10–15)   **Fair** (4–9)   **Poor** (0–3)

Chapter 27 Pricing Math

Study Skills
Note Taking

Directions Use the following tips to help improve your study habits. Then review Chapter 27 using the tips as you complete the statements that follow. Fill in the blanks with the correct term from Chapter 27.

Taking Notes from a Textbook
• As you read from your textbook, take down notes on key material. This will help you to better comprehend what you have read. • Study your notes regularly to keep the information fresh in your mind.

1. The difference between sales revenue and the cost of goods sold is called

   _____ profit.

2. To determine the percentage markup based on cost, you would divide

   _____ by the cost of the item.

3. You can use a visual device, known as the _____ box, to help you when

   calculating the retail price of an item for which you know only cost and percentage

   markup on retail.

4. To determine net profit before taxes, _____ must be deducted from

   gross profit.

5. Cash, seasonal, and promotional are types of _____ .

6. To encourage employees to buy the products a business resells or manufactures, employ-

   ees are often granted a(n) _____ discount.

7. _____ discounts are based on manufacturers' list prices.

8. The difference between an item's final sale price and its cost is called the

   _____ markup.

9. A quantity discount that is dependent on reaching a minimum amount of purchases over

   an extended period of time is called a _____ quantity discount.

Chapter 27 Pricing Math

Study Skills
Test Preparation

Directions Study the Test-Prep Tips and think about how you can use them to improve your test scores. Write a sentence or two to answer each of the following questions about the main ideas in Chapter 27.

Test-Prep Tips
• Read the question carefully and make sure your answer addresses all parts of it. Short answer questions often have several parts.
• When taking a short answer test, try not to leave any question unanswered. Even if you are not confident about your answer, instructors often give partial credit.

1. What does gross profit mean?

_____

_____

2. What is the maintained markup?

_____

_____

3. What three steps are used by retailers to calculate the percentage markup on cost?

_____

_____

4. Why is it important to know how to calculate discounts and the resulting net amounts?

_____

_____

5. When might a manufacturer give a promotional discount to a business?

_____

_____

6. Why do sellers offer seasonal discounts to their customers?

_____

_____

Chapter 27

Chapter 27 Pricing Math

Study Skills
Practice Test

Directions Circle the letter of the word or phrase that completes each of the following questions.

1. For a business to be successful, its markup (like its gross profit) must be
   a. high enough to cover expenses and provide the profit sought.
   b. low.
   c. lower than its costs.
   d. the same as its costs.

2. The formula for calculating retail price is
   a. cost − markup = retail price.
   b. cost + markup = retail price.
   c. retail price = cost − markup = final retail price.
   d. retail price = markup − cost.

3. Most retailers choose to express their markup percentage on retail prices because
   a. future markdowns and discounts are calculated on a retail basis.
   b. manufacturers express their markup percentages in retail terms.
   c. profits are generally calculated on the cost of goods sold.
   d. markup on retail sounds like a higher percentage when compared with markup based on cost.

4. Maintained markup is
   a. always the same as the initial markup.
   b. always different from the initial markup.
   c. calculated when the initial retail price is different from the final sale price.
   d. generally calculated when sales tax is added to the purchase price.

5. A $50,000 invoice has payment terms of 2/10, net 30. If the buyer takes advantage of the discount, the net amount payable will be
   a. $40,000.   c. $49,000.
   b. $45,000.   d. $49,900.

6. A manufacturer offers a 5 percent cumulative quantity discount for total purchases that equal or exceed $10,000 in one calendar year (January 1 through December 31). The one business that would be permitted the discount is
   a. Dana Dimples, which purchased goods worth $3,000 in January, $2,500 in February, and $4,300 in April.
   b. Lia Look-Alikes, which purchased goods worth $3,000 in January, $4,000 in March, and $6,000 in December.
   c. Lauren's Laughs, which purchased goods worth $9,000 in August.
   d. Charlie's Champs, which purchased goods worth $9,979 in June and $2,000 on January 15 of the following year.

Chapter 28 Marketing Research

Note Taking
Main Ideas and Supporting Details

Directions As you read, write key words and short phrases in the Cues column. Write notes, facts, and main ideas in the Note Taking column. Then summarize the section in the Summary box.

Cues	Note Taking
• Marketing Information Systems	• Marketing Information Systems
• Types, Trends, and Limitations of Marketing Research	• Types, Trends, and Limitations of Marketing Research

Summary

Chapter 28

Name _____ Date _____ Class _____

Chapter 28 Marketing Research

 Academic Intergration: Social Studies
Using and Analyzing a Questionnaire

Evaluating Customer Responses The Olympic Health Club recently conducted a marketing research survey to find out about customers' opinions of the health club. The customers' responses were all recorded in a database. Customers responded to the two questions noted in the key. On the printout below, you will find the customers' responses.

Key

1. How would you rate the exercise facilities in this health club?
   A. Excellent   **B.** Above Average   **C.** Average   **D.** Below Average   **E.** Poor

2. Which category includes your age?
   A. 21 and under   **B.** 22–35   **C.** 36–45   **D.** 46–55   **E.** 55+

Customer	Age Category	Question #1 Response
1	A	A
2	B	A
3	A	B
4	A	A
5	E	A
6	D	D
7	E	E
8	A	B
9	B	A
10	A	C
11	E	B
12	D	A
13	A	A
14	B	A
15	C	A

Directions Follow these steps to create a database. Then answer the questions that follow.

- Open your database software program on your computer.
- Create a database like the one here using your database application.
- Sort the responses for Question 1 by type of response. The database will sort these responses alphabetically.
- Save your sorted database.
- Save your work. Print out a copy of your work if you have been instructed to do so.

Chapter 28

Chapter 28 Marketing Research

Social Studies
Using and Analyzing a Questionnaire *(continued)*

1. Did the customers who responded "excellent" to Question 1 fall into any type of age pattern? How many customers responded "excellent"?

   _____

   _____

   _____

   _____

2. Did the customers who responded "below average" or "poor" fall into any type of age or gender pattern? How many customers responded with these answers?

   _____

   _____

   _____

   _____

3. Assuming that these 15 customers represent the typical customers at Olympic Health Club, what is a characteristic of the majority of the customers of the health club?

   _____

   _____

   _____

   _____

4. Based on these responses, what recommendations would you make to the owner of Olympic Health Club?

   _____

   _____

   _____

   _____

   _____

   _____

   _____

Chapter 28

Chapter 28 Marketing Research

🌐 Real-World Application
Analyzing a Market Research Database

Directions Review the database chart on the next page, prepared by a company specializing in compiling mailing lists. Then answer the questions below.

1. What are some ways companies can compile such large amounts of information?

   _____

   _____

   _____

2. The company that compiles this database uses an Affluence Model to score and categorize every household in the United States according to its net worth (defined as assets minus liabilities), real estate values, financial holdings, business equity, attitudes/consumption, and occupational characteristics. What are the advantages of this model?

   _____

   _____

   _____

3. What types of companies would be interested in marketing their products to America's most wealthy?

   _____

   _____

4. What five states have the largest number of aircraft owners? How many aircraft owners are in the database altogether?

   _____

   _____

5. What state has the largest number of attorneys in the database? The smallest?

   _____

   _____

6. What category under America's Most Wealthy has the highest number of people in the database? What category has the smallest number of people in the database?

   _____

   _____

Chapter 28 Marketing Research

🌐 Real-World Application
Analyzing a Market Research Database (continued)

	Highest Salaried Executive	Social Register	Prominent Medical Specialists	Attorneys	Wealthy at Home	Prominent Americans	Yacht Owners 30%	Wealthy Women	Corp. Presidents Manufacturing	Aircraft Owners
					America's Most Wealthy					
AL	593	211	6,679	5,842	18,658	1,941	535	1,767	4,937	2,763
AK	44	10	770	1,764	21,791	283	513	1,543	90	6,525
AZ	435	200	7,778	6,960	26,608	2,659	245	2,825	2,847	5,136
AR	304	6	3,672	4,451	9,388	791	99	873	2,393	2,351
CA	3,957	1,988	67,089	78,001	219,136	32,118	11,486	23,367	18,787	29,323
CO	713	238	7,341	11,242	27,686	2,996	150	3,298	4,289	4,173
CT	2,843	1,686	9,573	8,808	36,392	9,645	554	4,017	6,187	1,983
DE	156	136	1,419	1,271	6,833	681	394	529	5,294	2,119
DC	133	684	4,370	12,839	6,718	3,701	209	1,517	80	310
FL	1,874	1,420	26,722	28,747	153,176	10,467	7087	11,945	14,817	12,658
GA	1,137	194	11,112	13,737	36,183	4,987	720	3,792	8,129	4,960
HI	163	37	2,619	2,835	7,609	739	198	796	1,987	578
ID	150	20	1,432	1,680	6,914	435	64	615	1,194	1,893
IL	4,173	729	25,632	36,629	67,496	14,722	2046	8,001	21,167	7,043
IN	1,406	18	9,161	11,009	25,868	3,255	388	2,778	9,890	3,806
IA	624	8	5,202	6,526	14,035	1,550	240	1,644	5,064	2,586
KS	703	6	4,823	5,673	14,751	1,839	63	1,672	3,247	3,322
KY	552	60	6,426	8,063	12,529	1,476	431	1,464	4,240	1,681
LA	518	144	8,224	12,954	24,876	1,692	1,368	1,919	2,746	2,672
ME	277	295	2,537	2,336	13,409	1,146	915	1,172	1,856	1,216
MD	1,183	1,187	14,677	9,742	60,115	10,639	3,689	8,276	4,610	2,706
MA	2,758	2,323	20,006	15,437	54,532	11,823	3,304	6,243	6,690	3,141
MI	1,921	98	21,183	17,479	80,103	7,364	4,630	6,490	15,104	6,675
MN	1,261	41	9,691	12,263	31,392	3,076	738	3,269	8,306	4,617
MI	265	46	3,472	5,234	10,922	799	370	996	2,569	1,832
MO	1,234	476	11,504	12,556	25,535	4,226	343	3,071	8,301	4,272
MT	75	22	1,305	1,788	5,868	361	21	579	1,479	1,823
NE	415	10	3,086	3,283	8,179	911	35	938	1,665	1,749
NV	118	19	1,797	2,280	10,271	575	179	834	2,239	2,426
NH	413	258	2,189	2,154	11,438	1,350	385	1,192	2,090	1,471
NJ	4,054	894	19,870	15,637	64,166	26,358	2,018	6,695	6,937	3,572
NM	123	74	2,929	3,173	8,763	1,119	16	1,159	1,531	2,243
NY	5,990	4,460	56,690	46,472	126,743	38,723	5,434	16,981	8,962	6,352
NC	1,229	180	12,321	9,830	42,632	3,876	880	4,761	5,360	4,878
ND	94	1	1,263	911	4,605	271	12	436	576	1,150
OH	3,585	581	23,811	27,482	69,729	8,736	2,457	6,880	19,959	7,295
OK	559	17	5,839	10,073	17,526	1,512	100	1,884	4,359	3,906
OR	360	76	6,230	6,307	24,495	1,478	928	2,215	6,513	5,127
PA	3,773	3,168	31,929	20,543	70,831	13,469	1,592	8,463	19,145	5,969
RI	397	236	2,634	1,820	8,160	1,273	0	769	2,344	361
SC	473	235	5,902	4,802	22,453	1,855	416	2,986	3,020	1,875
SD	87	1	1,098	973	4,143	278	14	450	915	1,042
TN	822	108	9,787	10,661	22,483	2,579	574	2,528	4,998	3,348
TX	3,447	453	30,091	35,291	104,069	13,701	1,759	10,448	18,787	16,434
UT	265	13	3,284	3,331	9,781	769	64	792	2,408	1,481
VT	171	192	1,376	1,289	5,233	784	133	598	1,277	501
VA	1,352	692	12,491	21,219	48,121	11,375	1,684	4,542	3,405	3,363
WA	632	114	10,139	11,475	57,827	2,773	3,422	4,228	3,756	6,542
WV	240	10	3,779	2,987	5,695	611	80	717	2,199	981
WI	1,526	57	9,753	9,671	31,308	3,302	805	3,076	9,997	4,053
WY	64	32	671	939	3,261	336	6	350	558	802
TOTALS	59,641	24,164	557,701	588,482	1,804,132	273,531	65,490	188,763	309,444	209,467
	$50/M	$45/M	$50/M	$50/M	$60/M	$45/M	$50/M	$60/M	$55/M	$50/M

Chapter 28

Chapter 28 Marketing Research

 Real-World Application
Analyzing Market Research Methods

Directions Read the case study below, then answer the questions that follow.

Prepaid Phone Cards as Market Research In industries as disparate as consumer goods, automotive, hospitality, pharmaceutical, and healthcare, pre-paid phone cards have been used successfully to conduct marketing research. The Health Communication Research Institute provides prepaid phone cards to patients in Sacramento when they leave a doctor's office or hospital. When patients first use the card, they are connected to an automated service that asks five or six questions and records the responses. After responding, each patient is rewarded with 30 minutes of free long-distance service.

Several companies have done similar research, compiling short surveys, which are recorded by a professional announcer on an automated system. Questions can cover customer satisfaction, use of service, or even a customer's percep-tion of a product. The automated service conducts the interview, then sorts the results, delivering them either graphically as bar graphs or textually. Some companies deliver the results in a printed report, others provide a secure Web site on which businesses view the results in real time.

A marketing research campaign using prepaid phone cards is significantly cheaper to operate than other marketing research methods. According to the marketing research firm Market Facts Inc., direct mail campaigns cost approxi-mately $10 per person, telemarketing interviews can cost $20 per person, and focus groups can cost $200 to $250 per person. By contrast, an automated voice survey with as many as 10 questions offering a prepaid phone card reward can be as little as $5 per person, and sometimes less.

According to recent research, an interactive phone survey with an immediate reward nets a 25 percent response rate, compared with a ten percent response rate for telemarketing and a 2 percent response rate for direct mail, when both offer compensation for a response.

1. What are some other ways marketing researchers could reward people for completing marketing surveys, besides phone cards?

_____

_____

_____

_____

Chapter 28 Marketing Research

Real-World Application
Analyzing Market Research Methods *(continued)*

2. How have interactive telephone surveys changed the way survey results are collected and reported?

_____

_____

_____

_____

3. Why do you think the survey response rates for interactive phone surveys are better than traditional telemarketing and direct mail response rates?

_____

_____

_____

_____

_____

4. What are some advantages of automated voice surveys compared with other methods of collecting marketing research?

_____

_____

_____

_____

_____

_____

_____

_____

Chapter 28

Chapter 28 Marketing Research

DECA Connection
Marketing Research Consultant

Role Play Imagine you are an employee of a bed and breakfast lodging estab-lishment. The B&B has recently completed remodeling and restoring a large 1850s farmhouse in a beautiful and historically significant part of New England. Because of the large expenditures for remodeling and landscaping, the B&B has limited resources for conducting marketing research.

You strongly believe in the importance of marketing research to learn about the demographics of your customers, their interests, and their overall satisfaction with their stay at your bed and breakfast. However, the owner (judge) is more concerned about the overall appearance of the building and grounds. The owner believes that word of mouth alone will sell the business and that a marketing information database and marketing research itself is too costly and unnecessary.

Directions Role-play a meeting with the owner (judge) to convince him or her about the overall importance of marketing research and the need for a market-ing research database of past guests to help the business grow and prosper. You must also identify for the owner the type of marketing research that you would use to collect information about customer satisfaction about their stay. Remem-ber that you are on a very limited budget and your marketing research efforts must be effective, but cost a minimum amount.

Organize your thoughts around the performance indicators noted below. Use these indicators to jot down your ideas during the preparation period. Time your preparation period to last 15 minutes and your role-play presentation to last a maximum of ten minutes. After your role play, use the performance indicators to evaluate your efforts.

Assessment You will be evaluated on how well you meet the following perfor-mance indicators:
- Discuss the need for marketing information.
- Develop a marketing information system.
- Explain the nature of marketing research in a marketing information system.
- Identify information monitored for marketing decision making.
- Persuade others.

Chapter 28 Marketing Research

DECA Connection
Marketing Research Consultant (continued)

Discuss the need for marketing information.   **Score** _____

_____

_____

Develop a marketing information system.   **Score** _____

_____

_____

Explain the nature of marketing research in a marketing information system. **Score** _____

_____

_____

Identify information monitored for marketing decision making.   **Score** _____

_____

_____

Persuade others.   **Score** _____

_____

_____

Scoring Each performance indicator equals 20 points (20 × 5 = 100 points).
Excellent (16–20)   **Good** (10–15)   **Fair** (4–9)   **Poor** (0–3)

Chapter 28 Marketing Research

Study Skills
Learning New Vocabulary

Directions Use the following tip to help improve your vocabulary. Then complete each sentence by writing a key term from the box in the blank. (Two terms will not be used.)

Learning New Vocabulary
• Use familiar word parts to help you figure out unfamiliar vocabulary. Any part of the word may help—prefixes, suffixes, roots, etc. For example, the term *quantitative research* may not look familiar, but you know what *research* is and the word *quantitative* sounds somewhat like the word *quantity*. What do you think the term means now?

attitude research	marketing information system	product research
database	marketing research	qualitative research
market intelligence	media research	quantitative research

1. Research that answers questions of "how many" and how much" is known as

   _____.

2. In order to conduct marketing research, businesses need a _____

   that regularly generates, stores, analyzes, and distributes marketing information.

3. A _____ is a collection (or file) of related information about a specific

   topic.

4. The type of research that tries to answer questions about "why" or "how" is called

   _____.

5. _____ is concerned with the size, location, and/or makeup of the market

   for a particular product or service.

6. Research that is designed to obtain information on how people feel about certain products, services, or ideas is called _____.

7. Satisfaction surveys are used to gather information about existing products and services

   and are examples of techniques used in _____.

Chapter 28 Marketing Research

Study Skills
Test Preparation

Directions Study the Test-Prep Tips and think about how you can use them to improve your test scores. Write a sentence or two to answer each of the following questions about the main ideas in Chapter 28.

Test-Prep Tips
• Budget your time. Make sure you have sufficient time to study so that you are well prepared for the test.
• Real learning occurs through studying that takes place over a period of time. Relate the information you are learning to what you already know, and you will be better able to understand and retain it. For example, you may have already taken part in market research by responding to surveys.

1. How would you define market research?

_____

_____

2. How might a soap company track the sales of its liquid soap in a one-year period? What other information might they keep track of as they collect this information?

_____

_____

3. What is are some advantages of using a database when doing market research?

_____

4. How would a manufacturer of ATVs (all-terrain vehicles) predict the number of customers that would buy their newest model of ATVs?

_____

_____

_____

5. What are some limitations to market research?

_____

_____

_____

Chapter 28

Chapter 28 Marketing Research

Study Skills
Practice Test

Directions Take the practice test. Circle the letter of the option that best answers the question.

1. If you were designing a product's packaging, what kind of research would you do?
   a. attitude
   b. opinion
   c. product
   d. media

2. Which is not media research, but a different type?
   a. A radio station asks listeners to keep a listening diary to send in.
   b. An appliance company surveys customers to determine demographics and attitudes.
   c. A magazine includes a poll with each new subscription to determine most effective advertising message for a particular advertiser.
   d. A car company offers a large rebate one month to increase sales penetration of a new series of automobile.

3. Which is an example of attitude research?
   a. product samples in the mail
   b. opinion surveys by a campaigning politician
   c. a hotel's customer satisfaction survey
   d. a Web site recording the number of clicks on an ad banner

4. What scenario does not show product research?
   a. A video rental store has a "two-for-one" price special on Tuesdays to increase rentals.
   b. A laundry detergent company sends out mass-mailing of coupons for their new product.
   c. A ketchup company releases a purple ketchup in one city for a limited time.
   d. A fast-food burger joint test markets pizzas in select stores in the Midwest.

5. Companies began embedding advertisements in video games after what kind of research told them that less young men of a certain age were watching TV (thus seeing less of their ads)?
   a. attitude
   b. opinion
   c. product
   d. media

6. Which is not a marketing research company?
   a. Gallup
   b. Forbes
   c. Nielson
   d. Arbitron

Chapter 29 Conducting Marketing Research

Note Taking
Main Ideas and Supporting Details

Directions As you read, write key words and short phrases in the Cues column. Write notes, facts, and main ideas in the Note Taking column. Then summarize the section in the Summary box.

Cues	Note Taking
• The Marketing Research Process	• The Marketing Research Process
• The Marketing Survey	• The Marketing Survey

Summary

Chapter 29 Conducting Marketing Research

Academic Integration: Social Studies
Database Software

Marketing Research FMB-Maynard Allen Bank recently surveyed customers to learn whether they were satisfied with the quality of service they received in their local branch. This market research was stored in a database. Here is a sampling of the questions:

Question 1:   In general, how satisfied are you with the service provided at the FMB branch office you visit most often?

    A. Very Satisfied   **D.** Somewhat Dissatisfied
    B. Somewhat Satisfied   **E.** Very Dissatisfied
    C. Neither Satisfied Nor Dissatisfied

Question 2:   Check one: _____ Male _____ Female

Question 3:   Please indicate your age category.

    A. 21 and under   **D.** 46–55
    B. 22–35   **E.** over 55
    C. 36–45

On the printout below you will find the responses to these questions that were entered into the database.

Customer	Question 1	Question 2	Question 3
1	A	M	B
2	D	F	A
3	E	M	C
4	E	M	C
5	A	F	B
6	D	M	C
7	E	M	C

Directions Follow these steps to create a database, and then answer the questions.
- Open your spreadsheet software program on your computer.
- Create a database like the one on page 259 using your database application.
- Sort the responses based on each of the three questions.
- Save your work. Print it if your teacher has instructed you to do so.

1. As a market researcher hired to help the bank review its customer service, would you suggest that the bank make changes based on these responses?

_____

_____

2. Were any age groups more or less satisfied with the quality of service than others?

_____

_____

Chapter 29

Chapter 29 Conducting Marketing Research

Real-World Application
Survey

Directions A restaurant at a resort location conducted a customer satisfaction survey over the summer season in an effort to provide the best possible dining experience for its patrons. The results of the survey are summarized in the table below. Study it and answer the questions that follow.

1.	Was your reservation in order?	95% Yes	5% No		
2.	Cleanliness	65% Excellent	20% Good	15% Fair	
3.	Food Quality	75% Excellent	20% Good	5% Fair	0% Poor
4.	Beverage Quality	70% Excellent	20% Good	10% Fair	0% Poor
5.	Friendliness of Staff	50% Excellent	30% Good	10% Fair	10% Poor
6.	Were you served in a timely manner?	40% Excellent	20% Good	30% Fair	10% Poor
7.	Overall Value	50% Excellent	30% Good	15% Fair	5% Poor
8.	Would you return?	75% Yes	25% No		
9.	Any recommendatons or comments?				
10.	How can you be reached?				
Name					
Address					
City			State		Zip
Telephone					
E-mail					

1. What questions on the survey would you classify as forced-choice questions and which questions would you classify as open-ended?

    _____

2. Given the responses to Questions 1–4, what conclusion would you draw?

    _____

    _____

    _____

3. Why do you think the restaurant would want the names and addresses of its patrons?

    _____

    _____

    _____

    _____

Chapter 29

Chapter 29 Conducting Marketing Research

 Real-World Application
The Market Research Process

Directions Michael Diego, owner of Michael's Catering, has been comparing his profit reports with last year's reports and has noticed a dip in revenue. He has decided to conduct a comprehensive marketing research project to determine why his business is generating less revenue. Read each of the following scenarios and determine which step of the marketing research process Michael and his staff are conducting.

1. After conducting post-catering interviews, and reading through the questionnaires that were distributed, Michael has determined that many of his customers were unhappy with the service they received during their catered event. Also, he has found that a high percentage of guests were unhappy with the service charges included in the invoice.

   _____

2. Michael's staff has now completed their month-long training program and is prepared to put their new skills into action. They have a big catering event with a new customer coming up this weekend. With the new service standards in place, Michael is confident that his staff will provide excellent service and make the new customer very happy.

   _____

3. Michael and his staff want to know if their food quality, service, and pricing are meeting the needs of their customers.

   _____

4. Michael has reviewed the results of the questionnaires distributed and interviews conducted and is now planning to improve the service provided by his staff. He has decided to arrange a training session to be held on Saturday mornings for the next four weeks. At the sessions he will cover all aspects of food preparation and service. Further, he has decided to reduce his service charges from 25 percent to 20 percent.

   _____

5. Michael has designed a questionnaire to distribute at his next five catering events. With his questionnaire he hopes to obtain data from his customers that will help him determine if they are satisfied with his product and service. Further, he has decided to conduct post-catering interviews with his customers to get their feedback on his product and service.

   _____

Chapter 29

Chapter 29 Conducting Marketing Research

DECA Connection
Marketing Research Consultant

Role Play Imagine that you are a marketing researcher for a nationally recognized hotel/resort chain. The chain wants to build a database and study individuals who would likely vacation at a luxury resort and hotel complex. Your company is also interested in the following information: the time of year that individuals would most likely take a vacation of four or more days; favored geographical locations of planned vacations; amenities and activities favored; transportation methods used to get to a vacation resort; number of vacations taken per year; number of weekend trips taken per year; hotel chains that potential customers would consider; how individuals pay for their vacations; and whether respondents would like additional information about vacation packages. Your company also wants ideas on how to encourage responses to the study.

Directions Your supervisor (judge) has asked you to design a survey questionnaire that will provide the needed information. You must also recommend a plan to encourage high responses to the survey. Your survey must include a section for the name and address of the respondent and can have no more than ten questions. You will meet with your supervisor to discuss your ideas for the survey.

Organize your thoughts around the performance indicators noted below. Use these performance indicators to jot down your ideas during the preparation period. Time your preparation to last 15 minutes and your role-play presentation to last a maximum of ten minutes. After your role play, use the performance indicators to evaluate your efforts.

Assessment You will be evaluated on how well you meet the following performance indicators:

Score:

_____ Identify information monitored for marketing decision making.

_____ Collect marketing information from others.

_____ Write marketing reports.

_____ Explain the nature of marketing research in a marketing information system.

_____ Make oral presentations.

Scoring Each performance indicator equals 20 points (20 × 5 = 100 points).
Excellent (16–20)   **Good** (10–15)   **Fair** (4–9)   **Poor** (0–3)

Chapter 29

Chapter 29 Conducting Marketing Research

Study Skills
Quality Study Time

Directions Use the following tips to help improve your concentration when you study. Then review Chapter 29 using the tips as you answer the questions that follow. If the statement is true, circle **T**. If the statement is false, circle **F** and rewrite the statement so that it is true.

Time and Place
• Find a place to study where you will be free from distractions such as television or radio.   • Study when you are most awake and energetic. If you are a morning person, study in the morning. Or if you concentrate best in the afternoon, study at that time.

1. Primary data are data that have already been collected for some purpose other   T   F
   than the current study.

   _____

   _____

2. The observation method is a research technique in which the actions of people   T   F
   are watched and recorded either by cameras or by observers.

   _____

3. Data analysis is a powerful form of research that combines natural observation   T   F
   with personal interviews to get people to explain buying behavior.

   _____

   _____

4. Problem definition is a research technique in which information is gathered   T   F
   from people through the use of surveys or questionnaires.

   _____

   _____

5. A sample is a part of the target population that represents is accurately.   T   F

   _____

6. The experimental method is a research technique in which a researcher   T   F
   observes the results of changing one or more marketing variables while keeping
   all other variables constant under controlled conditions.

   _____

Chapter 29 Conducting Marketing Research

 Study Skills
Test Preparation

Directions Study the Test-Prep Tips and think about how you can use them
to improve your test scores. Write a sentence or two in response to each of the
following questions or statements about the main ideas in Chapter 29.

Test-Prep Tips
• Study your past tests to familiarize yourself with the different ways in which your teacher organizes his or her tests. This will help you prepare for your next test.
• Always ask your teacher to explain any information you do not understand before the test day.

1. What are the five steps in the marketing research process?

   _____

   _____

2. What is the greatest advantage of secondary data?

   _____

   _____

   _____

3. What is data mining?

   _____

   _____

4. Explain reliability as it pertains to research questionnaires.

   _____

   _____

5. Why do many market researchers prefer forced-choice questions over open-ended
   questions?

   _____

   _____

6. Why are general demographic questions usually grouped at the end of a questionnaire?

   _____

Chapter 29

Chapter 29 Conducting Marketing Research

Study Skills
Practice Test

Directions Demonstrate your knowledge of primary and secondary data research techniques by classifying each of the following situations as either primary (P) or secondary (S) research.

_____ 1. Black & Decker sends out a survey to past purchasers of its portable drill.

_____ 2. An aspiring entrepreneur studies the U.S. census data to obtain information on single heads of households in Phoenix, Arizona.

_____ 3. Jewel/Osco Supermarkets conducts a focus group regarding customer attitudes toward its meat department.

_____ 4. Gantos Fashions examines operating ratios available from Dun & Bradstreet for apparel stores of its size.

_____ 5. A local Ace Hardware store owner purchases demographic data regarding population, housing, education, and income from CACI Marketing Systems, a business information company.

_____ 6. Taco Bell records the number of used ticket stubs turned in from a hockey game promotional tie-in.

_____ 7. A local mall conducts personal interviews with customers.

_____ 8. McDonald's gives out a free breakfast sandwich for each customer questionnaire that is turned in by March 31.

_____ 9. Quebec's maple syrup makers conduct a taste test of various flavored syrups to market in different countries.

_____ 10. To determine the popularity of its talk shows, a radio station has listeners complete listening diaries.

_____ 11. When forecasting this year's summer sales, a heating and air conditioning firm reviews last year's sales for the months of June to August.

_____ 12. When developing new toys, Fun House Toys creates a room for observing children playing with toy prototypes.

_____ 13. An independent floral shop uses the Internet to search for commercial directories and potential suppliers.

_____ 14. Post uses a syndicated service to track its retail cereal sales by brand.

_____ 15. Coca-Cola uses an interactive telephone survey to obtain information about a new product.

Chapter 29

Chapter 30 Product Planning

Note Taking
Main Ideas and Supporting Details

Directions As you read, write key words and short phrases in the Cues column. Write notes, facts, and main ideas in the Note Taking column. Then summarize the section in the Summary box.

Cues	Note Taking
• Product Planning, Mix, and Development	• Product Planning, Mix, and Development
• Sustaining Product Sales	• Sustaining Product Sales

Summary

Chapter 30

Chapter 30 Product Planning

Academic Integration: English Language Arts
Creating a Presentation

Expanding a Product Line   The McCallum Foods Corporation is developing a new candy to add to its successful line of peanut and chocolate candies. Nutty Chewy Bits will be peanuts coated with caramel and milk chocolate. As part of the product development process, McCallum Foods has hired you to help determine how Nutty Chewy Bits will build on the company's image and appeal to new markets, as well as how it should position the product.

First, identify how this new candy will build on the company's image, increase sales, and appeal to new markets. Then determine where Nutty Chewy Bits will fit within the product mix of the stores where McCallum hopes to sell the candy, and how the company should best position the product. Then prepare a presentation, presenting your ideas about adding Nutty Chewy Bits to the McCallum Foods product line. Be as specific as possible. Beginning with a title screen, create a series of screens to present your ideas to the head of McCallum Foods. You should include at least one screen to describe how Nutty Chewy Bits will build on the company's image, one screen on the product mix, and at least one screen on proposed product placement.

Directions Follow these steps to complete the presentation. Then answer the questions below.

- Turn on your computer and open your presentation software program.
- Follow your software's instructions to create a title screen. Save your file as CH30PROB.
- Develop a minimum of four more screens based on the information you have compiled about the proposed launch of Nutty Chewy Bits. Include clip art or other appropriate art and graphics to illustrate your ideas.
- Save your work. Print out a copy of your screens if you have been instructed to do so.

Screen 1	Screen 2	Screen 3	Screen 4
Title Screen	Build on Company's Image Increase Sales Appeal to New Markets	Product Mix	Product Positioning

Chapter 30 Product Planning

Academic Integration: English Language Arts
Creating a Presentation *(continued)*

1. Which is the most important step of the product line expansion process?

   _____

   _____

   _____

   _____

2. If the company follows all your product planning advice, will Nutty Chewy Bits be guaranteed a successful launch? Explain.

   _____

   _____

   _____

   _____

Activity
Exchange a copy of your slide presentation with a classmate. Check whether your classmate's ideas are concisely and clearly written. Suggest any additional ideas.

Chapter 30

Chapter 30 Product Planning

Real-World Application
Product Expansion

Directions Try your hand at developing new product strategies. In the first column below, list five well-known products. In the second column, describe a possible product expansion. In the third column, suggest a possible product modification. Your ideas for product expansion and modification should be original and not currently being used.

Product	Product Expansion	Product Modification
Example: Palm Tungsten personal digital assistant (PDA).	Add another type of PDA with more power and memory.	Create a PDA with built-in cell phone and MP3 with portable keyboard.

Chapter 30 Product Planning

Real-World Application
Case Study

Directions Read the case study below. Then answer the questions that follow.

Repositioning an Established Product Line

During World War II, Procter & Gamble developed a moisturizer to treat burns. That moisturizer later took on a new life. In 1962, it was tinted a light pink, named Oil of Olay, and marketed to women. In the 1990s, P&G expanded the Oil of Olay line to include other skin-care products and cosmetics. But the company realized that it needed to update the product line to attract younger buyers. After product research found that young women avoid any product that seems like it would be oily, company executives decided to remove the word oil from the name. Oil of Olay became simply the Olay line of beauty products. Along with the new name came new packaging and a new logo.

After research showed that women do not like having wet washcloths by their sinks, P&G expanded the Olay line to include disposable paper washcloths called Olay Daily Facials. Using information gathered through market research, the company developed a new advertising campaign to promote desired features of the product, using TV commercials, outdoor ads, and in-store and direct mail samples. P&G hoped the newly repositioned line would boost the sales of the old, established Olay line by keeping the existing customer base and attracting new customers.

1. What techniques did P&G use to reposition its Olay product line?

_____

_____

2. What type of research do you think P&G might have done to evaluate customer acceptance of the product?

_____

_____

3. Why might P&G have involved different divisions in the development of Daily Facials?

_____

_____

_____

Chapter 30

Chapter 30 Product Planning

DECA Connection
Product Planner

Role Play Imagine you are an employee in the marketing department of Sheldon Sound Systems, an established electronics manufacturer. One of your company's product lines is audio players and speakers. The company makes models in several sizes. Bookshelf speakers were introduced in 1996. Sales of those speakers have grown steadily. However, in recent years, younger consumers have begun to view the company as stodgy and old-fashioned. The company has seen its sales drop among Generation Y consumers, the 70 million people born between 1977 and 1997. The company is concerned because this market is nearly as large as the baby boom generation (born between 1946 and 1964) and three times the size of Generation X (born between 1965 and 1976). The industry trend moving toward smaller and more technologically advanced products.

Directions Your task is to identify the steps and strategies that you would use to change the image of the Sheldon product line. Your supervisor (judge) has asked you to recommend strategies to reposition the Sheldon product line to better meet the needs of a generation of potential customers who want advanced technology and more portability built into their products. Your suggested strategies must aim to create an image that appeals to the desired target market. Your strategies could involve positioning by price, quality, features, benefits, or unique characteristics. You will present your ideas to your supervisor.

Organize your thoughts around the performance indicators noted below. Use these indicators to jot down your ideas during the preparation period. Time your preparation period to last 15 minutes and your role-play presentation to last a maximum of ten minutes. After your role play, use the performance indicators to evaluate your efforts.

Assessment You will be evaluated on how well you meet the following performance indicators:
- Explain the concept of marketing strategies.
- Explain the concepts of market and market identification.
- Develop strategies to position a product/business.
- Explain the nature of marketing plans.
- Develop a marketing plan.

Scoring Each performance indicator equals 20 points (20 × 5 = 100 points).
Excellent (16–20)   **Good** (10–15)   **Fair** (4–9)   **Poor** (0–3)

Chapter 30 Product Planning

DECA Connection
Product Planner *(continued)*

Explain the concept of marketing strategies.   **Score** _____

_____

_____

_____

_____

Explain the concepts of market and market identification.   **Score** _____

_____

_____

_____

_____

Develop strategies to position a product/business.   **Score** _____

_____

_____

_____

_____

Explain the nature of marketing plans.   **Score** _____

_____

_____

_____

_____

Develop a marketing plan.   **Score** _____

_____

_____

_____

_____

Chapter 30

Chapter 30 Product Planning

Study Skills
Learning New Vocabulary

Directions Use the following tips to help improve your vocabulary. Then complete puzzle on this page by using keys terms found in the chapter. Then read down the column of circle entries to discover the Mystery Phrase.

Learning New Vocabulary
• Often key terms contain individual words that are quite familiar separately, but seem to lose their meaning when paired. First try to puzzle out the meaning of term by using what you know about the words already. Then check the book definition. Figuring out the meaning yourself will help you remember the meaning better. • Discuss new vocabulary and concepts with your parents and other people you know who have worked in business, such as a friend who has worked in a store. Ask business-people you know if they have experienced such events as product planning.

CLUES

1. Computer-generated diagram showing retailers how and where products within a category should be displayed ◯ _ _ _ _ _ _ _ _

2. A specific model, brand, or size of a product within a product line
_ ◯ _ _ _ _ _ _ _ _

3. Dropping a product _ _ _ _ _ _ _ ◯ _

4. The number of items offered within each product line
_ _ _ _ _ _ _ ◯ _ _ _

5. Evaluating a new product measures this
_ ◯ _ _ _ _ _ _ _ _ _ _ _ _ _ _ _

6. Introduction, growth, maturity, and decline _ _ _ _ _ _ _ ◯ _ _

7. The number of different product lines a business manufactures or sells
_ _ _ _ _ _ ◯ _ _ _ _ _

8. The effort a business makes to identify, place, and sell its products
◯ _ _ _ _ _ _ _ _ _ _ _ _ _ _ _

9. An example is all the different canned soups made by Campbell's
_ _ _ _ _ _ ◯ _ _ _

10. A process for marketing and selling products that treats each product group as an individual business unit
_ _ _ _ _ _ _ _ _ ◯ _ _ _ _ _ _

11. The first step in new product development
_ _ ◯ _ _ _ _ _ _ _ _ _

Mystery Phrase: _____

Chapter 30 Product Planning

Study Skills
Test Preparation

Directions Study the Test-Prep Tips and think about how you can use them to improve your test scores. Then answer each question about the main ideas in Chapter 30.

Test-Prep Tips
• Keep your parents informed about your test schedule. They can help you with your study schedule, provide encouragement, and keep you motivated.
• When answering essay questions, make sure that you support generalizations with evidence. Back up your ideas with names, places, and dates. Answer even short essay question with accurate explanations backed up by facts.

1. At what stage would management need to make a decision about how long to continue supporting a product? What would happen at the end of this cycle?

   _____

   _____

2. During the growth cycle of a product, what are businesses focused on for that product?

   _____

   _____

3. What kinds of marketing strategies do companies use to introduce a new product into a market?

   _____

   _____

4. At what stage of a product's life cycle would most of the target market already own the product? What should the manufacturer do next to ensure continued sales?

   _____

   _____

   _____

   _____

   _____

   _____

Chapter 30

Chapter 30 Product Planning

 **Test Taking**
Practice Test

Directions Circle the letter of the word or phrase that best answers the question.

1. During the growth stage, what best shows the success of a product?
   a. sales level off
   b. sales and profits rise
   c. competitors offer new products too
   d. manufacturers modernize the product

2. At which part of a product's life cycle is promotion the most important?
   a. decline
   b. growth
   c. introduction
   d. maturity

3. Why might a business delete a product from its line?
   a. because the profits from the product are smaller than its costs
   b. because a competitor creates a similar product
   c. because the product is in its mature stage
   d. because the company thinks the product may need to be repositioned

4. What is the term that means all the different items that a company makes or sells?
   a. product line   c. product depth
   b. product width   d. product mix

5. Which statement is generally not true about a product at the introduction stage?
   a. This is the least profitable time for the product.
   b. The major goal is to draw attention to the product now.
   c. Companies spend more advertising dollars fighting off the competition at this stage.
   d. Companies work on building sales by increasing product awareness in this stage.

6. Which is an example of product modification?
   a. the deletion of an unprofitable product
   b. the introduction of a better cell phone/MP3 player combination
   c. the bundling of a popular TV, phone, GPS, and satellite radio services
   d. a business surveying existing customers to see how they can improve services

Chapter 30

Chapter 31 Branding, Packaging, and Labeling

Note Taking
Main Ideas and Supporting Details

Directions As you read, write key words and short phases in the Cues column. Write notes, facts, and main ideas in the Note Taking column. Then summarize the section in the Summary box.

Cues	Note Taking
• Branding Elements and Strategies	• Branding Elements and Strategies
• Packaging and Labeling	• Packaging and Labeling

Summary

Chapter 31

Chapter 31 Branding, Packaging, and Labeling

Chapter 31

 ## Academic Integration: Mathematics
Analyzing Survey Results

Building Brand Recognition A fruit drink manufacturer recently conducted a survey asking consumers which brands they recognized. The results of the survey are shown in the spreadsheet below. The manufacturer has been test marketing a new brand drink for this market. The marketing manager wants to determine whether the advertising and product promotion have resulted in significant gains in brand recognition. The name of the product is Fruition.

	A	B	C
1	**Brand**	**Number of Customers Recognizing Brand**	**Percentage of Total (Sample = 3,980)**
2	Chapter 31 Branding, Packaging, and Labeling		
3	Fruitbreak	1,020	
4	A Taste of Fruit	950	
5	Mountain Springs	3,790	
6	Fruit Spa	3,810	
7	Fruition	250	
8	Jucier	1,780	

Directions Follow these steps to analyze the database. Then answer the questions that follow.

- Turn on your computer and open your spreadsheet software program.
- Create a spreadsheet like the one above using your spreadsheet application.
- Enter a formula to calculate the percentage of the total for each brand. The total number of consumers in the survey was 3,980.

- Use the percentages calculated to create a bar chart showing the percentage of brand recognition for each brand.
- Save your work. Print out a copy of your work if your teacher has instructed you to do so.

1. Which brand has the highest percentage of brand recognition?

_____

2. Which brand has the lowest percentage of brand recognition?

_____

 ### Activity
On another sheet of paper, write a paragraph telling what you think the low brand recognition for Fruition means in terms of advertising and market promotion. Explain the reasons for your conclusions.

Chapter 31 Branding, Packaging, and Labeling

Real-World Application
Branding

Directions Read the case study below. Then answer the questions that follow.

Dodge sees NASCAR Building Brand and Sales

After years off the race track, Dodge returned to the NASCAR circuit in 2001. Dodge, a division of Chrysler, raced in one of the series of the National Association for Stock Car Auto Racing (NASCAR). In addition, the 3,000 Dodge dealers of North America sponsored a two-car racing team.

With the most loyal fans of any sport in America, NASCAR is growing quickly. Attendance grew steadily and significantly throughout the 1990s, and NASCAR races reliably attract more television viewers than baseball or basketball games. NASCAR fan loyalty is double the fan loyalty for pro football, baseball, and basketball. Fans love NASCAR's down-to-earth drivers, in addition to the excitement of racing. NASCAR racing features American-made sedans outfitted for the racetrack. They look very different from the single-seat, open-wheeled race cars of Indy and Formula One racing. Several manufacturers race their sedans in NASCAR: General Motors races the Pontiac Grand Prix and Chevrolet Monte Carlo; the Ford Motor Company competes with its Taurus; Dodge added the Intrepid R/T sedan to the track.

Dodge also hoped to make money from branded merchandise sold at NASCAR retail outlets, online stores, during NASCAR events, and at Dodge dealerships. NASCAR merchandise includes clothing, flags, key chains, license plates, decals, and other race-related items. Some top NASCAR teams generate as much as $10 million in annual profits from merchandise sales. While Dodge and Dodge dealers are no doubt pleased with the percentage of sales they receive, the main goal of the new racing program is enhancing Dodge's brand image.

1. Why are the Dodge dealers willing to sponsor a Dodge car in NASCAR races?

_____

2. Even though top NASCAR teams generate profits from merchandise sales, what is the main reason for a car manufacturer to get involved with a racing series?

_____

_____

3. Why does Dodge think sponsoring a NASCAR team will pay off?

_____

_____

Chapter 31 Branding, Packaging, and Labeling

Real-World Application
Labeling

Directions Create your own brand for a product. Give your product a brand name, brand mark, trade name, trade character, and trademark. In the space below, draw a package and label for your product. Make sure the brand name, brand mark, trade name, trade character, and trademark are clearly identified. Below the drawing, note any appropriate information, such as a product guarantee, directions for use, safety instructions, ingredients, date of manufacture, and manufacturer's name and address.

Chapter 31 Branding, Packaging, and Labeling

 DECA Connection
Sports Marketing

Role Play Imagine that you are an employee of a sports marketing consulting firm that performs a variety of integrated branding services for local and national sports teams. Your company provides branding services such as brand valuation, brand research, strategies, naming, and corporate identification for sports teams. Your firm has also helped financial institutions and manufacturers negotiate contracts with sports teams to place their corporate brand on new sports arenas in different communities. Through corporate branding of sports arenas, team owners receive additional revenue and corporate sponsors receive tremendous promotional value by being associated with a popular sports team.

Directions A shopping mall developer has approached your firm to explore the feasibility of having a newly developed mall named after a local sports team. Your company has been asked to prepare a proposal. Your supervisor (judge) has asked you to develop the possible branding elements that would be necessary for a shopping mall naming proposal. You will present your ideas to your supervisor.

Organize your thoughts around the performance indicators noted above. Use these performance indicators to jot down your ideas during the preparation period. Time your preparation period to last 15 minutes and your role-play presentation to last a maximum of ten minutes. After your role play, use the performance indicators to evaluate your efforts.

Assessment You will be evaluated on how well you meet the following performance indicators:

Score:

_____ Explain the nature of branding.

_____ Develop strategies to position a product/business.

_____ Describe factors used by marketers to position products/businesses.

_____ Demonstrate orderly and systematic behavior.

_____ Make oral presentations.

Scoring Each performance indicator equals 20 points (20 × 5 = 100 points).
Excellent (16–20)   **Good** (10–15)   **Fair** (4–9)   **Poor** (0–3)

Chapter 31 Branding, Packaging, and Labeling

Study Skills
Study Partners

Directions Use the following tips to help improve your study habits. Then review Chapter 31 using the tips as you complete the statements that follow. Write the correct term from the chapter to complete each statement.

Studying with a Partner
• Studying with one or two of your classmates can be beneficial to you as well as your study partners. Remember two or three minds are better than one!
• Choose study partners who are serious about studying, and who you get along with to get the most out of your study time.

1. A _____ is a type of brand mark with human form or characteristics.

2. _____ incorporates a technology that keeps foods fresh without refrigeration for extended periods.

3. A _____ strategy combines one or more brands in the manufacture of a product or in the deliver of service.

4. Packaging different products and services together is known as _____.

5. _____ are packages with preformed plastic molds surrounding individual items arranged on a backing.

6. Many brands incorporate a unique symbol, coloring, lettering, or other design elements known as a _____.

7. A _____ is an information tag, wrapper, seal, or imprinted message that is attached to a product or its package.

8. A _____ states the quality of the product.

9. A _____, also called a product brand, is a word, group of words, letters, or numbers that represent a product or service.

10. _____ are owned and initiated by national manufacturers or by companies that provide services.

Chapter 31 Branding, Packaging, and Labeling

 Study Skills
Test Preparation

Directions Study the Test-Prep Tips and think about how you can use them to improve your test scores. Then answer the questions by circling the letter of the correct answer choice.

Test-Prep Tips
• Creating a visual framework for the content that you are studying will help you to understand it better.
• Use outlines, maps, word webs, and graphic organizers when studying for a test.

1. What are some characteristics of an effective brand name?

   _____

   _____

2. Why is the use of branding important in product planning?

   _____

   _____

3. How can mixed-brand strategy be advantageous to a business?

   _____

   _____

   _____

4. Why is attractive packaging important to a company?

   _____

   _____

5. What are three types of contemporary packaging?

   _____

   _____

6. As determined by the Nutrition Labeling and Education Act of 1990, what must food product labels clearly state?

   _____

   _____

Chapter 31

Chapter 31 Branding, Packaging, and Labeling

 Test Taking
Practice Test

Directions Read the statements listed below and classify each statement as typical of national, private distributor, or generic brands.

_____ 1. Brand owned and initiated by producers

_____ 2. These products are promoted by stressing quality.

_____ 3. Brand owned and initiated by wholesalers and retailers

_____ 4. This type of brand is priced 30 to 50 percent lower than nationally advertised brands.

_____ 5. This type of product is generally sold in supermarkets and discount stores.

_____ 6. Brands that are popular with retailers because of high gross margins

_____ 7. These are often viewed as "no frills" products.

_____ 8. This type of brand appeals to customers who want the quality and performance of manufacturers' brands but at lower price.

_____ 9. Popular brands that attract customers to stores that carry them

_____ 10. This type of brand helps to promote store loyalty.

_____ 11. Products that do not carry a company identity

_____ 12. Products that cost less because they are not usually advertised or promoted

_____ 13. Products with this type of brand often become so popular that they rival manufacturers' brands.

_____ 14. Customers who want consistent quality, dependable product performance, and status often desire this type of brand.

_____ 15. Brands that shift balance of power in distribution channel to retailer

_____ 16. These brands have higher advertising costs because there is less support from the manufacturer.

Chapter 32 Extended Product Features

Note Taking
Main Ideas and Supporting Details

Directions As you read, write key words and short phases in the Cues column. Write notes, facts, and main ideas in the Note Taking column. Then summarize the section in the Summary box.

Cues	Note Taking
• Warranties	• Warranties
• Credit	• Credit

Summary

Chapter 32

Chapter 32 Extended Product Features

 Academic Integration: Mathematics
Spreadsheet Analysis

The Cost of Credit The Ticket Broker serves as a sales agent for concert promoters and community organizations. The company earns its revenue from a percentage of the price of each ticket sold. It also charges a handling fee of $1.50 per ticket, which is 5 percent of the average ticket price of $30. The majority of tickets sold by the Ticket Broker are sold on credit. The company accepts Visa and MasterCard and pays a service fee of 2.5 percent. It also accepts American Express and Discover, paying service fees of 2.8 percent for those transactions. Both cash and credit ticket sales are shown below.

Directions Follow these steps to complete the spreadsheet.
- Turn on your computer and open your spreadsheet software program.
- Create a spreadsheet like the one above using your spreadsheet application.
- Enter a formula to calculate the total sales for each type of event.
- Enter a formula to calculate the total cash sales for all events, total Visa and MasterCard sales, total American Express and Discover sales, and total sales.
- Enter a formula to calculate the servicing cost of the credit card sales.

- After completing all calculations, save your work. Print out a copy of your work if you have been instructed to do so. Answer the questions about the completed sheet.

	A	B	C	D	E
1	**Event**	**Cash Sales**	**Visa & MasterCard Sales**	**AmEx & Discover Sales**	**Total**
2	Pop music concerts	$1,500,000	$5,670,000	$1,25,000	
3	Touring Broadway plays	$200,000	$22,000	$2,885,000	
4	Ballet/Opera	$300,000	$16,000	$900,000	
5	Classical music concerts	$400,000	$12,000	$1,240,000	
6	Sports events	$890,000	$4,000	$2,080,000	
7	Total				
8	Credit service fees				

1. What is the amount of total cash sales?

_____

2. What is the amount of total sales for pop music concerts?

_____

3. Why do retailers accept credit cards for customer purchases if the practice costs them money?

_____

Chapter 32 Extended Product Features

Real-World Application
Reading a Warranty

Directions Read the warranty below. Then use it to answer the questions on the next page.

Bush's Written Warranty to You

In order to provide you with timely assistance, please thoroughly inspect your furniture for missing or defective parts immediately after opening the carton. To receive a replacement or missing part under this warranty, call our Consumer Service Department. Please have your model, part, and lot numbers found in the instruction booklet available for your reference. You will also need your sales receipt or other proof of purchase. Replacement part(s) will be shipped to you at no charge. All Bush furniture is warranted to the original purchaser at the time of purchase and for a period of six years thereafter.

We warrant to you, the original purchaser, that our furniture and all its parts and components are free of defects in material or workmanship. "Defects," as used in this warranty, is defined as any imperfections, which impair the use of the product.

Our warranty is expressly limited to the replacement of furniture parts and components. For six years after the date of purchase, Bush Industries will replace any part described on the enclosed Parts List that is defective in material or workmanship.

This warranty applies under conditions of normal use. Our furniture products are not intended for outdoor use. The warranty does not cover: 1) defects caused by improper assembly or disassembly; 2) defects occurring after purchase due to product modification, intentional damage, accident, misuse, abuse, negligence, or exposure to the elements; and, 3) labor or assembly costs.

IMPLIED WARRANTIES, INCLUDING THE WARRANTY OF MERCHANTABILITY, SHALL NOT EXTEND BEYOND THE DURATION OF THE WRITTEN WARRANTY STATED ABOVE, AND IN NO EVENT SHALL BUSH INDUSTRIES BE LIABLE FOR INCIDENTAL OR CONSEQUENTIAL DAMAGES RESULTING FROM USE OF THE PRODUCT. Some states do not allow a limitation on how long an implied warranty lasts or the exclusion or limitation of incidental or consequential damages, so the above limitation and exclusion may not apply to you.

IMPORTANT REMINDER: Please fill out and return your Product Registration Card promptly. Although not required, it will help us serve you even better in the future.

THIS WARRANTY GIVES YOU SPECIFIC LEGAL RIGHTS. YOU MAY ALSO HAVE OTHER RIGHTS, WHICH MAY VARY FROM STATE TO STATE.

— — — — — — — — —Part No. A45351 — — 1/97–1.5MM — —

Please retain this portion of the card for your records. You may need to refer to this information in case of warranty claim or for insurance purposes.

Date purchase _____   Model # _____

Dealer Name _____

Product Purchased _____

BUSH INDUSTRIES, INC.   One Madison Drive   Jamestown, NY 14702

Chapter 32 Extended Product Features

Real-World Application
Reading a Warranty *(continued)*

1. Would you classify this warranty to be a full or limited warranty? Provide your rationale.

2. What procedures must the customer follow to make a claim under this warranty?

3. If the warranty conditions are met, what is the length of time that the company will warrant the product?

4. Are there any limitations to the implied warranty period?

5. The warranty applies under conditions of normal use. What conditions does the warranty not cover?

Chapter 32 Extended Product Features

Real-World Application
Comparing Credit Cards

Directions Read the following chart, and then answer the questions that follow.

Institution Credit Card Plan	Annual Type of Percentage Rate (APR)	Pricing (V/F)	Grace Period	Annual Fee
Security Bank Visa	13.74	Variable	30 days	$18
Simmons First Visa	8.50	Fixed	25 days	$35
Travelers Bank MasterCard/Visa	16.00	Variable	25 days	$0
Union Bank MasterCard	19.80	Fixed	25 days	$15

1. Which of the banks has the best grace period and how can you tell?

   _____

2. Why do you think having a grace period is important to customers?

   _____

   _____

3. Which of the banks has the most favorable annual fee arrangement and why?

   _____

4. Which bank has the least favorable interest rate and why?

   _____

5. How do banks receive their income from credit cards?

   _____

   _____

6. Why does the government pass legislation regulating credit?

   _____

   _____

Chapter 32 Extended Product Features

DECA Connection
Sales Associate

Role Play Imagine you are a sales associate in an appliance store. The store sells nationally known and advertised appliances. Management encourages employees to sell extended service contracts with every appliance purchase. An extended service contract has the following features: 1) all parts and repairs provided (minus a $20 deductible) for every operating problem; 2) fast, convenient service scheduling; 3) factory-trained service experts; and 4) unlimited repairs for the entire term of the contract. Management believes that the top-quality service available through their extended service contract maximizes years of enjoyment on appliances, is very affordable, and offers great protection in the event of needed repairs. The store charges $25 per hour for repairs that are not covered by warranty or an extended service contract.

A customer (judge) has just purchased a $300 nationally branded microwave oven. The oven comes with a limited manufacturer's warranty on parts and repairs for one year. The store's extended service contract rates for parts and repairs when purchased at time of sale are as follows: one year $29.95; two years $59.90; and three years $89.85. The customer seems unwilling to spend additional money for an extended service contract.

Directions Your task is to convince the customer of the need, value, and importance of obtaining an extended service policy for a new appliance. Convince the customer to purchase the policy even though the microwave is high quality.

Organize your thoughts around the performance indicators noted below. Use these indicators to jot down your ideas during the preparation period. Time your preparation period to last 15 minutes and your role-play presentation to last a maximum of ten minutes. After your role play, use the performance indicators to evaluate your efforts.

Assessment You will be evaluated on how well you meet the following performance indicators:

Score:
- Explain warranties and guarantees.
- Handle customer inquiries.
- Sell a good/service/idea to individuals.
- Facilitate the customer buying decision.
- Explain the role of customer service as a component of selling relationships.

Scoring Each performance indicator equals 20 points (20 × 5 = 100 points).
Excellent (16–20)   **Good** (10–15)   **Fair** (4–9)   **Poor** (0–3)

Chapter 32

Chapter 32 Extended Product Features

DECA Connection
Sales Associate *(continued)*

Explain warranties and guarantees.   **Score** _____

_____

_____

_____

_____

Handle customer inquiries.   **Score** _____

_____

_____

_____

_____

Sell a good/service/idea to individuals.   **Score** _____

_____

_____

_____

_____

Facilitate the customer buying decision.   **Score** _____

_____

_____

_____

_____

Explain the role of customer service as a component of selling relationships. **Score** _____

_____

_____

_____

_____

Chapter 32

Chapter 32 Extended Product Features

 Study Skills
Learning New Vocabulary

Directions Use the following tips to help improve your vocabulary. Then complete each sentence with the correct term. (Not all terms will be used.)

Learning New Vocabulary
• To learn new vocabulary that is very technical, use the List/Group/Label strategy. List key words. Then group the terms into as many different categories as you can, and then label each separate group. What do the terms have in common and how are they different? What other words might you add to the groups? What other groupings could you make?
• Use a highlighter in your notes or underline the key terms in your notes to more easily find them. Consider adding a section with just vocabulary.

credit	warranty of fitness	regular accounts
implied warranty	disclaimer	full warranty
warranty limited	warranty	revolving accounts
budget accounts	warranty of merchantability	assurance
installment accounts	express warranty	marketing

1. A promise from a seller that a product which is sold is fit for its intended purpose is an example of a _____.

2. An _____ is one that is explicitly stated in writing or spoken word, to induce a customer to buy.

3. A warranty that exists automatically by state law whenever a purchase takes place is called an _____.

4. Under a _____, if a product is found to be defective within the warranty period, it will be repaired or replaced at no cost to the purchaser.

5. A _____ is used to limit damages to be recovered by a customer.

6. It is not uncommon for a _____ to specify that the manufacturer will pay for replacement parts but charge the customer for labor or shipping.

7. _____ is an arrangement whereby businesses or individuals can obtain products or money in exchange for a promise to pay later.

8. _____ are normally used for large purchases and require a down payment and a separate contract for each purchase.

9. With _____, a minimum payment is usually a certain percentage of the balance owed or a minimum dollar amount.

10. Under _____, the customer is not required to pay an interest charge as long as the amount owed is paid within the interest-free time period.

Chapter 32 Extended Product Features

 Study Skills
Test Preparation

Directions Study the Test-Prep Tips and think about how you can use them to improve your test scores. Then answer each question about the main ideas in Chapter 32.

Test-Prep Tips
• At the beginning of a test, review it quickly to see what kinds of questions are on the test. You may find multiple choice, matching, true or false, short answer, extended response, and essay questions. If possible, note how much each section is worth. Divide your time accordingly, so that you can do your best on all sections.
• Concentration can reduce anxiety when you are taking a test. Do not worry about how good a student you are or whether you should have studied more. Pay close attention to one question at a time.

1. How does an express warranty differ from an implied warranty?

_____

_____

2. How does a full warranty differ from a limited warranty?

_____

_____

_____

3. Why are warranty disclaimers used by businesses?

_____

_____

4. How does a warranty differ from a guarantee?

_____

_____

5. How does a warranty of merchantability differ from a warranty of fitness for a particular purpose?

_____

_____

_____

Chapter 32 Extended Product Features

 Test Taking
Practice Test

Directions Circle the letter of the word or phrase that best answers the question.

1. What is another term for a regular credit account?
   a. revolving
   b. 30-day
   c. installment
   d. budget

2. What does a customer have to pay for if he or she has to use a limited warranty?
   a. nothing
   b. replacement parts
   c. paint
   d. labor or shipping

3. What is not true about an extended service contract?
   a. Customers pay an extra fee for the service.
   b. It prolongs the warranty's protection.
   c. It often covers only parts and repairs.
   d. They always extend the warranty by two years.

4. Which type of warranty advises the customer that the product is suitable for a particular use?
   a. implied
   b. merchantability
   c. fitness
   d. express

5. Which is not a way to protect the manufacturer from paying out too much from warranties?
   a. disclaimers
   b. limited warranties
   c. full warranties
   d. conditions

6. How does taking credit cards help businesses such as stores?
   a. Customers may choose to shop there rather than a place that does not take credit cards.
   b. Customers use budget accounts.
   c. Businesses also offer extended service contracts.
   d. Businesses make money when customers pay their regular accounts on time.

Chapter 33 Entrepreneurial Concepts

 Note Taking
Main Ideas and Supporting Details

Directions As you read, write key words and short phrases in the Cues column.
Write notes, facts, and main ideas in the Note Taking column. Then summarize
the section in the Summary box.

Cues	Note Taking
• Entrepreneurship	• Entrepreneurship
• Logistics of Business Ownership	• Logistics of Business Ownership

Summary

Chapter 33

Chapter 33 Entrepreneurial Concepts

 Academic Integration: English Language Arts
Using Presentation Software

Entrepreneurial Paths Lots of businesses in your neighborhood are operated by entrepreneurs—from the flower shop to your local McDonald's—but those entrepreneurs did not all take the same path to owning their own businesses. Some started their businesses from scratch, while others purchased a business from someone else or took over a family business. Still others purchased a franchise.

Directions Identify a successful entrepreneur and find out everything you can about the path he or she took to success. If possible, interview a business owner in your neighborhood. Otherwise, read up on an entrepreneur in newspapers, magazines, or on the Internet. Find out the answers to questions such as these:

- Did this person start the business from scratch, buy an existing business, purchase a franchise, or take over a family business?
- How is the business organized: sole proprietorship, partnership, or corporation? Why did the entrepreneur choose that form of organization?
- What is the entrepreneur's background, and what does this person feel best prepared him or her for owning a business?
- What does the entrepreneur feel are the best and worst things about owning a business?

Now follow the directions below to create a slide show using presentation software that describes the entrepreneur's path to success. Then answer the question that follows.

- Start your presentation software program.
- Follow your software's instructions to create a title slide. Save your file as CH33PROB.
- Based on your interview or research, develop your slides to profile this entrepreneur.
- Prepare one slide for each of the following topics: title; entrepreneur's name; entrepreneur's education; entrepreneur's career path; type of business organization; pros of entrepreneurship; cons of entrepreneurship; and keys to success.
- Be sure to include clip art or other graphics when appropriate to illustrate your point.
- Print out a copy of your slides if your teacher has instructed you to do so.

1. Why is it important for potential entrepreneurs to understand the background and experience of other entrepreneurs?

_____

_____

_____

_____

_____

_____

Chapter 33 Entrepreneurial Concepts

 Real-World Application
Self-Assessment

Directions Are you the kind of person who can get a business started and make it run? The self-assessment questionnaire below was taken from U.S. Small Business Administration training materials. It is designed to determine whether you have the necessary entrepreneurial qualities. Under each question, check the letter that says what you feel or comes closest to it.

1. Are you a self-starter?
    a. I do things on my own. Nobody has to tell me to get going.
    b. If someone gets me started, I keep going all right.
    c. Easy does it. I don't put myself out until I have to.

2. How do you feel about other people?
    a. I like people. I can get along with just about anybody.
    b. I have plenty of friends—I don't need anyone else.
    c. Most people irritate me.

3. Can you take responsibility?
    a. I like to take charge of things and see them through.
    b. I'll take over if I have to, but I'd rather let someone else be responsible.
    c. There's always someone wanting to show how smart they are. I say let them.

4. How good an organizer are you?
    a. I like to have a plan before I start. I usually get things lined up in a group.
    b. I do all right unless things get too confused. Then I quit.
    c. You get all set and then something comes along and presents too many problems. So I just take things as they come.

5. Can you lead others?
    a. I can get most people to go along when I start something.
    b. I can give the orders if someone tells me what we should do.
    c. I let someone else get things moving. Then I go along if I feel like it.

Scoring Key

- If three or more of your checks were placed beside the letter **a**, you probably have what it takes to run a business.
- If three or more of your checks were placed beside the letter **b**, you are likely to have more trouble than you can handle by yourself. It would be better to find a partner who is strong on the points where you are weak.
- If three or more of your checks were placed beside the letter **c**, not even a good partner will be able to help you successfully run a business.
- If you do not have a majority of checks by any letter, you probably should start working for someone to gain valuable experience before you consider starting your own business.

(**Source**: SBA, Office of Management Assistance, *Small Business Management Training Instructors' Guide, Home-Based Business: The Basics of Doing Business from Your Home.* Washington, D.C., September 1984.)

Chapter 33 (side tab)

Chapter 33 Entrepreneurial Concepts

Real-World Application
Entrepreneurial Profile

Directions   Using books, autobiographies, biographies, periodicals, or the Internet, select an individual (living or not) who has been successful nationally in operating his or her own business. Develop a profile about the person. There are literally thousands of individuals whose stories you may investigate. A few examples are Henry Ford, Madame C. J. Walker, Calvin Klein, Orville Redenbacher, Oprah Winfrey, Bill Gates, and Levi Strauss. Then answer the questions that follow. After your profile is completed, be prepared to present a two- to three-minute oral report about the entrepreneur you investigated.

1. Who is the entrepreneur you investigated?

   _____

   _____

   _____

2. What is the name and nature of the business he/she started?

   _____

   _____

   _____

3. What is the history of the entrepreneur (i.e., place of birth, education, job history, family background, etc.)?

   _____

   _____

   _____

4. In your opinion, what personal traits did this person possess that made him/her so successful as an entrepreneur?

   _____

   _____

   _____

Chapter 33 Entrepreneurial Concepts

 DECA Connection
Interviewing

Role Play Assume the role of a student in a high school marketing class. You are very interested in using the skills you have developed in your marketing class to help you get a job with a company with entrepreneurial drive and spirit. A new online business has opened in your community and is seeking new employees with excellent personal skills, such as responsibility, initiative, good time-management behavior, and the abilities to problem-solve and work well with others. The company uses a job interviewing technique called targeted selection. Targeted selection defines a job on certain important dimensions and asks applicants to reflect on past performance and experiences to predict future effectiveness as an employee.

Directions You have decided to apply for the job and will interview with the entrepreneur (judge) who started the new business. The owner is asking the same questions of all applicants to measure their personal and interpersonal skills. You are to prepare answers for your interview with the entrepreneur.

Organize your thoughts around the performance indicators noted above. Use these performance indicators to jot down your ideas during the preparation period. Time your preparation period to last 15 minutes and your role-play presentation to last a maximum of ten minutes. After your role play, use the performance indicators to evaluate your efforts.

Assessment You will be evaluated on how well you meet the following performance indicators:

Score:

_____   Assess personal interests and skills needed for success in business.

_____   Analyze employer expectations in the business environment.

_____   Identify personality traits important to business.

_____   Participate as a team member.

_____   Demonstrate problem-solving skills.

Scoring Each performance indicator equals 20 points (20 × 5 = 100 points).
Excellent (16–20)   **Good** (10–15)   **Fair** (4–9)   **Poor** (0–3)

Chapter 33 Entrepreneurial Concepts

Study Skills
Reading Critically

Directions Use the following tips to help you read more critically. Then review Chapter 33 using the tips as you complete the statements that follow. Write the correct term from the chapter to complete each statement.

Critical Reading
• Learning to read critically will help you think independently and search for the truth when you read.
• When reading non-fiction, look at the author's credentials. Is the author an expert in his or her field?
• Think about why you may or may not agree with the conclusions reached by the author.

1. A _____ is a legal agreement between two or more people to be jointly responsible for the success or failure of a business.

2. _____ means that the personal assets of the owners cannot be taken if the company does not meet its financial obligations or if it gets into legal trouble.

3. A _____ is a business owned and operated by one person.

4. The owners of a corporation are the _____.

5. _____ is the process of starting and operating your won business.

6. A legal entity created by either a state or a federal statute authorizing individuals to operate an enterprise is called a _____.

7. A _____ is one that is incorporated under the laws of a state that differs from the one in which it does business

8. A _____ is a legal agreement to sell a parent company's product or services in a designated geographic area.

9. In a _____, each partner shares in the profits and losses.

10. In a _____, each limited partner is liable for any debts only up to the amount of his or her investment in the company.

Chapter 33

Chapter 33 Entrepreneurial Concepts

 Study Skills
Test Preparation

Directions Study the Test-Prep Tips and think about how you can use them to improve your test scores. Then answer the questions by circling the letter of the correct answer choice.

Test-Prep Tips
• When a test is near, pay close attention in class for clues as to what may be on the test.   • Come to class with some questions on your own; if you cannot answer them you will know you need to study further.

1. What are some advantages of entrepreneurship?

   _____

   _____

   _____

2. What are some disadvantages of entrepreneurship?

   _____

   _____

   _____

3. How do entrepreneurs and small to medium businesses affect the domestic and global economy?

   _____

   _____

   _____

4. What are the four ways to enter business?

   _____

   _____

5. Sole proprietorship is the most common form of business ownership. What are the advantages of this type of business ownership?

   _____

   _____

   _____

Chapter 33

Chapter 33 Entrepreneurial Concepts

Test Taking
Practice Test

Directions Decide whether each characteristic listed below describes a sole proprietorship, partnership, corporation, or limited liability company (LLC) and label it accordingly.

_____ **1.** The most common form of business ownership.

_____ **2.** The skills of the owners are combined in this type of business.

_____ **3.** This type of business can own assets and borrow money without directly involving the shareholders.

_____ **4.** There are two types of this business organization: general and limited

_____ **5.** The value of this type of business is divided into shares of stock.

_____ **6.** This allows the greatest freedom in making decisions.

_____ **7.** This is the easiest form of business organization to start.

_____ **8.** This type of business is generally taxed less than other forms of business.

_____ **9.** Actions of one owner are legally binding on the other owners in this type of business organization.

_____ **10.** Each owner has limited liability in this type of business organization.

_____ **11.** This type of business is a blend of characteristics of other types of businesses.

_____ **12.** Each owner has a voice in this type of business organization.

_____ **13.** This is the most complicated form of business ownership.

_____ **14.** In this type of business, governing bodies or boards hire directors to manage the affairs of the business.

_____ **15.** Raising outside capital is the most difficult in this type of business.

_____ **16.** Government regulations are the most complicated with this form of business organization.

_____ **17.** In this type of business the owners are called members.

_____ **18.** The owner is personally liable for the debts of the business.

Chapter 34 Risk Management

Note Taking
Main Ideas and Supporting Details

Directions As you read, write key words and short phrases in the Cues column.
Write notes, facts, and main ideas in the Note Taking column. Then summarize
the section in the Summary box

Cues	Note Taking
• Risk Management for Business	• Risk Management for Business
• Handling Business Risks	• Handling Business Risks
Summary	

Chapter 34 Risk Management

Academic Integration: English Language Arts
Using Presentation Software

Identifying Risks As a business owner, one of your primary goals is to make a profit. However, there is no guarantee that this will happen. Every business faces risks, from economic risks such as poor sales to unavoidable natural risks such as tornadoes. While a business cannot totally eliminate all the risks of doing business, marketers can reduce and manage risks through planning.

Imagine a business that you would like to start in the future. List at least three risks to the success of that business. Include economic risks, natural risks, and human risks. Then develop a plan for dealing with each risk. Will you prevent and control the risk by carefully screening employees? Will you transfer the risk by purchasing insurance? Or will you accept the risk as a part of doing business?

Create a presentation using presentation software describing the risks faced by your imaginary business and your plan for managing them. Each screen should list a risk, followed by the plan for dealing with it. Be specific. For example, if you plan to add security to your store to prevent theft, describe the types of security measures you will use. Include clip art and graphics when appropriate.

Directions Follow these steps to complete the presentation. Then answer the questions below.
- Open your presentation software program on your computer.
- Follow your software's instructions to create a title screen. Save your file as CH34PROB.
- Based on the information you have collected, create at least three more screens identifying risks to that business and your plan for managing them.
- Save your work. Print out a copy of your screens if you have been instructed to do so.

1. Why is it important to identify risks and develop risk management programs?

   _____

   _____

2. Why is it important for a marketing professional to have a risk management program?

   _____

   _____

3. Pay attention to your classmate's presentation. What risks were shared by businesses that seemed unrelated? What businesses had unique risks and what were they?

   _____

   _____

   _____

Chapter 34 Risk Management

Real-World Application
Assessing Risk

Directions Read the following story. Then use what you have learned to answer the questions that follow.

Training Day

Jacquelyn West reported early to her first day of work for Quick Print Graphics. The human resources manager, Jim Sinclair, summarized the company's extensive employee handbook, focusing on employment practices, employee benefits, and job expectations. The orientation ended with a tour of the production facilities. During the tour, Sinclair told West how the company—through its published policy—uses a four-step procedure to train new workers on job tasks:

Step 1: The immediate supervisor should be prepared to teach and should prepare a new employee to learn.

Step 2: The immediate supervisor should demonstrate and explain the tasks to be learned to a new employee.

Step 3: The new employee should demonstrate and explain each new task.

Step 4: The new employee should perform the new tasks on the job with supervision.

After explaining the steps involved with new worker training, Sinclair introduced West to Larry Ahler, her immediate supervisor, and left for other duties. Ahler told West that the company had just received a shipment of paper and that the truck had to be unloaded. "Just lift the cartons one at a time and place them in their designated bins," Ahler said. Ahler then excused himself to attend a meeting with a supplier. West began unloading the truck and, within an hour, injured her back and had to leave work. Because of her injury, West had to take sick leave for the rest of the week.

1. What type of risk is illustrated by this case? What is your rationale?

_____

2. What was probably the basic reason for West's injury?

_____

3. Why is it important for supervisors to demonstrate and explain new tasks to employees?

_____

_____

4. What other ways can companies prevent and control human risks?

_____

Chapter 34

Chapter 34 Risk Management

Real-World Application
Completing Tables

Workers' Comp Workers' compensation insurance is a type of insurance paid by employers to help employees who suffer job-related injuries and illnesses. The federal government requires businesses to carry workers' compensation insurance, but each state sets its own policies and procedures for administration. All occupations carry a specific industry code, and the insurance rates are based on every $100 of wages. Premiums are calculated on the estimated yearly payroll. Employers with small payrolls have to pay the minimum premium. One of your duties as an independent insurance agent is to write workers' compensation policies for advertising businesses in your community.

Directions Use the table below to calculate the premiums for the three types of businesses listed below the table. Then answer the questions that follow on the next page.

Basic Manual for Workers' Compensation and Employers' Liability Insurance Michigan Version								
Code No.	Rate	Min. Prem.	Code No.	Rate	Min. Prem.	Code No.	Rate	Min. Prem.
8803	0.29	229	9051	0.44	244	9156	2.45	445
8810	0.44	244	9052	3.60	560	9220	6.06	750
8820	0.27	227	9053	4.79	679	9402	11.04	750
8829	6.33	750	9058	2.79	479	9403	21.04	750
8831	2.17	417	9059	2.06	406	9410	1.88	388
8832	0.60	260	9060	3.02	502	9501	7.39	750
8833	2.53	453	9061	3.78	578	9519	4.31	631
8835	4.81	681	9063	1.59	359	9521	8.71	750
8837	5.55	750	9065	1.43	343	9522	5.31	731
8868	0.60	260	9093	2.89	489	9530	38.56	750
8869	0.27	227	9101	4.21	621	9558	18.77	750
8870	0.30	230	9102	3.03	503	9559	3.15	515
8901	0.51	251	9104	3.94	594	9586	0.98	298
9015	5.95	750	9108P	97.85	-	9620	1.03	303
9040	4.33	633	9145	3.09	509			

Code	Type of Business
9501	Advertising Display—installation or removal of advertising cards in or on vehicles
9521	Advertising Display Service—for stores
9558	Advertising Company—Outdoor

Chapter 34 Risk Management

 Real-World Application
Completing Tables *(continued)*

1. Which of these types of businesses has the highest workers' compensation rate? What is the rate charged per $100 of employee wages?

_____

2. Use the table to calculate annual premiums for companies listed below.

_____

_____

_____

Company	Code	Annual Payroll	Premium
Best Outdoor Signage	9558	$25,000	
John's Display Service	9521	$10,000	
Anderson's Advertising	9501	$55,000	
Design Team	9521	$6,600	
Model Printing Service	9558	$100,000	
The Place, Inc.	9521	$115,000	

3. Looking at the rate tables and your calculations, what might you think about the relationship of the type of business and the rate charged per hundred?

_____

_____

_____

4. Suppose The Place, Inc., underestimated its yearly payroll by $36,000. After a payroll audit by the insurance company, what would be the additional premium owed?

_____

5. Suppose Model Printing Service overestimated its yearly payroll by $8,000. What amount of credit would be owed to them from the insurance company?

_____

6. Why do you think the government mandated workers' compensation insurance?

_____

_____

Chapter 34

Chapter 34 Risk Management

 DECA Connection
Marketing Manager

Role Play Imagine you are a marketing manager for an independent manufac-tured housing company that has several sales outlets, a mobile home park, two installation companies, and a corporate home office. A young and resource-ful entrepreneur originally established the company as a single sales outlet. Because of the booming economy and low interest rates, sales of manufactured housing units have grown among first-time homebuyers and retirees building second homes on vacation properties. The company's sales staff has also grown from five employees to more than 50 employees in multiple locations.

You have noticed that managers at the sales outlets have been spending large amounts of time answering questions from new sales employees about company policies related to company practices, rules, and regulations. At the present time, there is no organized training and orientation program for the company. You have suggested to the owner (judge) a new program to provide a general orientation to the company, its policies, job expectations, employment practices, and general rules and regulations related to both customers and employees. Even though the owner believes that many duties are learned on the job, he has agreed to your suggestion and has asked for your input on what should be included in an orientation and training program.

Directions The owner (judge) wants you to identify in outline form the items that should be included in an orientation program that would be of interest to new employees and of benefit to the company. You are to present your ideas to the owner. Your presentation should also include how the company could ben-efit from an effective orientation and training program.

Organize your thoughts around the performance indicators noted below. Use these indicators to jot down your ideas during the preparation period. Time your preparation period to last 15 minutes and your role-play presentation to last a maximum of ten minutes. After your role play, use the performance indicators to evaluate your efforts.

Assessment You will be evaluated on how well you meet the following perfor-mance indicators:

Score:
- Orient new employees.
- Explain the role of training and human resource development.
- Explain the nature of risk management.
- Explain the types of business risk.
- Prepare simple written reports.

Chapter 34 Risk Management

 **DECA Connection**
Marketing Manager *(continued)*

Scoring Each performance indicator equals 20 points (20 × 5 = 100 points).
Excellent (16–20)   **Good** (10–15)   **Fair** (4–9)   **Poor** (0–3)

Orient new employees.   **Score** _____

_____

_____

_____

Explain the role of training and human resource development.   **Score** _____

_____

_____

_____

Explain the nature of risk management.   **Score** _____

_____

_____

_____

Explain the types of business risk.   **Score** _____

_____

_____

_____

Prepare simple written reports.   **Score** _____

_____

_____

_____

Chapter 34

Chapter 34 Risk Management

 Study Skills
Learning New Vocabulary

Directions Use the following tips to help improve your vocabulary. Then complete the puzzle by using keys terms found in the chapter. Then read down the column of circle entries to discover the Mystery Phrase.

Learning New Vocabulary
• Use the Preview and Review features as well as the figures to teach you about the key terms and concepts of a chapter. Skim photo and graphics captions for vocabulary. You already know that key terms will be in bold in the text—glance through the chapter to find where each word is introduced. You may also keep an eye out for key terms in headings.
• Familiarize yourself with how each key term is used in the chapter and how it relates to the other vocabulary. Which terms are related? Are any terms opposites?

1. The stealing of merchandise from a business. __Ⓞ__ __ __ __ __ __ __ __

2. An __ __ __Ⓞ__ __ __ __ __ policy is a contract between a business and an insurance company to cover a certain business risk.

3. This kind of risk results from changes in overall business conditions.

   __ __ __ __ __Ⓞ__ __

4. One way to transfer risk is through limiting __ __ __ __Ⓞ__ __ __ __ __ __.

5. Floods, tornadoes, and some fires are examples of this type of risk. Ⓞ__ __ __ __ __ __

6. These insure against losses that might occur when work or a contract is not finished on time or as agreed. __ __Ⓞ__ __ __ __ __ __ __ __ __ __ __ __ __ __ __

7. A type of bond that protects a business from employee dishonesty. __ __ __ __ __Ⓞ__ __

8. Insurance paid by employers to cover employees who suffer job-related injuries or illness and to protect employers from being sued by an employee injured on the job.

   __ __ __ __ __ __Ⓞ __ __ __ __ __ __ __ __ __

9. When it is impossible to prevent or transfer risks, businesses have __ __ __Ⓞ

   __ __ __ __ __ __ __ __.

10. A type of economic risk for businesses that depend on fashion or the latest trends to market goods and services is product __ __ __ __ __ __Ⓞ__ __ __ __ __.

Mystery Phrase: _____

How would you define the Mystery Phrase? _____

_____

Chapter 34 Risk Management

 Study Skills
Test Preparation

Directions Study the Test-Prep Tips and think about how you can use them to improve your test scores. Classify each of the following situations according to the risk it represents by writing **E** for economic, **H** for human, or **N** for natural.

Test-Prep Tips
• Concentration can reduce anxiety when you are taking a test. Do not worry about how good a student you are or whether you should have studied more. Pay close attention to one question at a time. • Look at completed homework and quizzes when studying for a test. Often you will find that most exam questions will be quite similar to problems you answered throughout the chapter. If you can answer questions on past assignments with confidence, chances are, you will do well on the test.

_____ **1.** A state's major employer moves its headquarters to another state, resulting in a loss of jobs.

_____ **2.** An earthquake in California leads to increased losses for an insurance company.

_____ **3.** Basketball shoes endorsed by professional players are no longer trendy among teenagers.

_____ **4.** Employees at a local restaurant improperly cook hamburgers, leading to customers being hospitalized.

_____ **5.** An inventory shortage occurs due to employee theft in the warehouse.

_____ **6.** Less snowfall last winter lead to fewer skiers and lost sales for Colorado ski resorts.

_____ **7.** Poor employee cash register training causes some customers to leave the stores because of long lines.

_____ **8.** A high unemployment rate causes a downturn in the retail sales sector for the year.

_____ **9.** An improperly designed tire breaks apart in certain situations and results in customer lawsuits against the corporation for deaths and injuries.

_____ **10.** A surplus of apartments causes apartment owners to lower rents.

_____ **11.** The Americans with Disabilities Act requires a local restaurant to modify its entranceways.

_____ **12.** A local manufacturer has to pay higher wages because there is a lack of skilled apprentices in the community.

Chapter 34

Chapter 34 Risk Management

Study Skills
Practice Test

Directions Circle the letter of the word or phrase that best answers the question.

1. If a company's computers got a virus, under which type of risk would that fall?
   a. economic
   b. natural
   c. human
   d. electronic

2. Which kind of fire is not caused by human risk?
   a. arson at a business
   b. wild fire caused by lightning
   c. apartment fire due to faulty wiring
   d. campfire that went out of control, and escalated when the fire department had too slow of a response time

3. What is the term used to describe how marketers can reduce risk?
   a. risk management
   b. business risk
   c. protection
   d. encoded firewall

4. What can generally not be insured?
   a. unsold merchandise
   b. the cost of inflation
   c. the honesty of one's employees
   d. the timing of when a job gets done

5. How are insurance companies protected from paying out too much from warranties?
   a. disclaimers
   b. limited warranties
   c. limits on the payout amounts
   d. all of the above

6. How can a business avoid risk altogether?
   a. by buying insurance
   b. by having a partner
   c. by not investing in risky investments
   d. There is no way to avoid risk completely in business.

Chapter 35 Developing a Business Plan

Note Taking
Main Ideas and Supporting Details

Directions As you read, write key words and short phrases in the Cues column. Write notes, facts, and main ideas in the Note Taking column. Then summarize the section in the Summary box

Cues	Note Taking
• The Business Plan	• The Business Plan
• The Marketing and Financial Plans	• The Marketing and Financial Plans

Summary

Chapter 35

Chapter 35 Developing a Business Plan

 Academic Integration: English Language Arts
Create a Presentation

Marketing Plan A business plan is a vital component of any new business because it will help you obtain financing, open your business, and successfully manage your business. An important part of any business plan is a marketing plan—a plan for pricing and promoting your products.

Imagine a business you would like to open and create a marketing plan for that business. Create a pricing policy that will produce a profit and be low enough to attract customers. Decide what promotional activities you will undertake to attract customers to your business. Be specific: What is your advertising budget? What type of advertising will you utilize?

Directions Develop a slide presentation to explain your marketing plan. Your slide presentation should include a title slide and at least three more slides explaining your pricing policy and promotional activities. Then answer the questions that follow.

- Start your presentation software program.
- Follow the directions for your software to create a title slide. Save the file as CH35PROB.
- Based on the marketing plan you have developed, create at least three more slides to describe and justify the marketing plan.
- Save your work. Print out a copy of your slides if your teacher has instructed you to do so.

1. How will your competitors' prices affect your pricing policy? When would a business be able to charge more or less than its competitors?

_____

_____

_____

_____

2. Compare your slide presentation with those of your classmates. Examine the presentations to see if their marketing plans were clearly explained. Describe the similarities and differences between the plans and presentations?

_____

_____

_____

_____

Chapter 35 Developing a Business Plan

Real-World Application
Trading Area Analysis

Directions Select a proposed or existing business in your community, and do a trading area analysis on it. Use the checklist that follows as a guide. For each numbered item, circle or highlight one of the options in parentheses. Then provide a rationale based on geographic, demographic, or economic data available for the area.

Trading Area Analysis Checklist

A. Location

_____

B. Economic Considerations
   1. Economic base (primarily farming, manufacturing, retail, or mixed)

   _____

   2. Economic trends (highly satisfactory, growing, stable, declining)

   _____

C. Population
   1. Income distribution (mostly wealthy, well-distributed, mostly middle income, poor)

   _____

   _____

D. Competition
   1. Number of competing stores (few, average, many, too many)

   _____

   2. Customer base (majority of customers shop in the area, out of the area)

   _____

E. General Attractiveness of Area
   1. General character of city or geographical area (homes neat and clean, mixed, shabby)

   _____

   2. Quality of facilities (good schools and churches, average, poor)

   _____

   _____

Chapter 35

Chapter 35 Developing a Business Plan

 ## Real-World Application
Case Study

Web-Site Design Service

Satish Dulam has been working part-time as a cooperative education student during his senior year. He works for a small commercial art and design agency in a fast-growing suburban area. Since he has taken computer applications courses and is very familiar with Web-page editing software, his employer allows him to design Web sites for existing clients. He has noticed that increasing numbers of local businesses are asking the agency for help in designing and improving their Web sites.

Satish feels that he can design Web pages faster and more creatively than many of his coworkers. So, he plans to begin a Web-site design service after graduation, working out of his parents' residence. In this way, he plans to keep his expenses down and work full-time as a Web-site designer.

Satish has completed a self-analysis of his skills, knowledge, and abilities and is convinced that he could successfully in operate his own business. In addition, he has checked and received the necessary zoning, licensing, and permit approvals for a home-based business. Because his parents were excited about his idea, they provided him with the capital to buy the necessary computer equipment and software, set up a portion of their home as an office, and began promoting his service.

Satish believes his service has great sales potential because of the increasing number of small businesses moving into the area. He is sure that he can provide a quality Web-site design service at competitive prices. However, he needs additional assistance with the development of his organization and marketing plans and has employed you as a professional business consultant to advise him.

1. Based upon the details in the case, what type of business organization should Satish initially establish and why?

_____

_____

2. Why is it important for Satish to prepare a job description for himself?

_____

_____

Chapter 35 Developing a Business Plan

DECA Connection
Business Plan

Role Play You have catered a few parties for family and friends. After receiving accolades on each occasion, you have decided that you could create a profitable catering business in your local area. You have decided to open your own business with a friend who shares your enthusiasm for cooking and entertaining. From your marketing class in high school, you know that starting your own business requires a business plan, complete with company objectives, suggested personnel, and planned financing.

Directions A family friend (judge) who works as a loan officer for a local bank has agreed to review your business plan with you. She has requested that you put your plan in writing and present it to her orally, as well.

Organize your thoughts around the performance indicators noted above. Use these performance indicators to jot down your ideas during the preparation period. Time your preparation period to last 15 minutes and your role-play presentation to last a maximum of ten minutes. After your role play, use the performance indicators to evaluate your efforts.

Score:

_____ Develop a business plan.

_____ Develop company objectives.

_____ Develop a personnel organization plan.

_____ Describe sources of financing for businesses.

_____ Determine the financing needed to start a business.

Assessment You will be evaluated on how well you meet the following performance indicators:

Scoring Each performance indicator equals 20 points (20 × 5 = 100 points).
Excellent (16–20)   **Good** (10–15)   **Fair** (4–9)   **Poor** (0–3)

Chapter 35

Chapter 35 Developing a Business Plan

 **Study Skills**
Improving Self Discipline

Directions Use the following tips to help improve your study habits. Then review Chapter 35 using the tips as you complete the statements that follow. Write the correct term from the chapter to complete each statement.

Self Discipline
• Learn how to schedule your priorities. Set small tasks at different times of the day. Do the tasks at the scheduled time. This will allow you to stay focused on your priorities. • Even though it may sound boring, you need to develop a routine. Stay with that routine. Practice the action at the scheduled time of day. • Do not let yourself get discouraged if you do not succeed at all your goals. Take them slowly. Give yourself positive feedback even if you do not get something accomplished.

1. Your _____ explores how you think the business should be run and demonstrates your understanding of your business's role in the marketplace.

2. _____ is a term used to describe borrowed funds that must be repaid.

3. _____ is something of value that you pledge as payment for a loan in case of default.

4. The geographical area from which a business draws customers is a

   _____.

5. A _____ is a cooperative association formed by labor unions or groups of employees for the benefit of its members.

6. Raising money from within your company or selling part of your interest is called using

   _____.

7. _____ is the process individuals use to decide what they will buy, where they will buy it, and from whom they will buy it.

8. A _____ is a proposal that outlines a strategy to turn an idea into reality.

9. _____ are written statements listing the requirements of a particular job.

10. An _____ is a diagram of departments and jobs with lines of authority clearly shown.

Chapter 35 Developing a Business Plan

 Study Skills
Test Preparation

Directions Study the Test-Prep Tips and think about how you can use them to improve your test scores. Then use what you have learned in Chapter 35 to answer the questions below.

Test-Prep Tips
• When it is time to take a test, get organized. Review early. This will give you an opportunity to realize what you do and do not know.
• Review a little every day. These short reviews will get you ready for the longer sessions right before the test.
• After a lecture review your notes as quickly as possible. This will help you identify areas that you did not understand and give you the opportunity to either talk with your teacher or look up the answers yourself.

1. What four components should be included in a business plan?

   _____

2. What does buying power index (BPI) measure?

   _____

   _____

3. What should be stated in the operations plan?

   _____

   _____

4. What information should be included in a job description? What is the purpose of a job description?

   _____

   _____

   _____

   _____

5. How can debt capital work to your advantage?

   _____

   _____

   _____

Chapter 35

Chapter 35 Developing a Business Plan

Test-Taking
Practice Test

Directions For each of the activities identified below, indicate in which section of the business plan—description and analysis (DA), organization and/or marketing plan (O/MP), or financial plan (FP)—you would discuss the activity.

_____ 1. Describe your plan and the products you will sell.

_____ 2. Detail promotional activities for the new business.

_____ 3. Describe sources of capital.

_____ 4. Describe a loan repayment plan.

_____ 5. Identify your business philosophy.

_____ 6. Describe your business's organization chart.

_____ 7. Identify the form of business ownership.

_____ 8. Describe your proposed pricing policies.

_____ 9. Explain your credit history.

_____ 10. Explain your proposed advertising plan.

_____ 11. Include your trading area analysis.

_____ 12. Identify your business location.

_____ 13. Explain your current and anticipated staffing needs.

_____ 14. Describe your previous training and experience.

_____ 15. Describe demographic, geographic, and economic data.

_____ 16. Where would you describe your potential suppliers?

_____ 17. Where would you describe your projected income?

_____ 18. Detail how to train, pay, and supervise employees.

_____ 19. Explain your balance sheet and income statement.

_____ 20. Include your self-analysis.

Chapter 35

Chapter 36 Financing the Business

Note Taking
Main Ideas and Supporting Details

Directions As you read, write key words and short phrases in the Cues column.
Write notes, facts, and main ideas in the Note Taking column. Then summarize
the section in the Summary box.

Cues	Note Taking
• Preparing Financial Documents	• Preparing Financial Documents
• Financial Aspect of a Business Plan	• Financial Aspect of a Business Plan

Summary

Chapter 36 Financing the Business

Academic Integration: Mathematics
Spreadsheet Analysis

Calculating Growth Trends Startup costs are the expenses that entrepreneurs have when they first set up their businesses. To identify startup costs, entrepreneurs review every aspect of their business plan and list everything that requires a cash outlay before the business opens. A dollar estimate should be made for each item. The startup expenses for a new business are listed and estimated on the printout shown below. Use a spreadsheet program to calculate a subtotal for each category as well as a total for all expenses.

Directions Follow the steps on the next page to complete the spreadsheet. Then answer the questions that follow.

	A	B	C
1	**FIXED ASSETS**	**Total Funds Required**	**Subtotals/Totals**
2	Chapter 36 Financing the Business		
3	Equipment	$11,500	
4	Fixtures	$25,400	
5	Furniture	$5,450	
6	Outdoor Signs	$560	
7	(Subtotal)		
8	PRE-PAID ITEMS AND DEPOSITS		
9	Rent Deposit	$500	
10	Utilities Deposit	$100	
11	Telephone Deposit	$200	
12	Insurance Payments	$850	
13	Taxes, Licenses, and Fees	$150	
14	(Subtotal)		
15	PRE-OPENING EXPENSES		
16	Advertising and Promotion	$1,500	
17	Training	$800	
18	Legal and Accounting Services	$2,000	
19	Subtotal)		
20	INVENTORY AND SUPPLIES		
21	Goods Purchased	$80,000	
22	Supplies	$2,600	
23	(Subtotal)		
24	WORKING CAPITAL		
25	Petty Cash	$200	
26	Projected Cash Deficits	$5,000	
27	3-Months Operating Expenses	$28,500	
28	(Subtotal)		
29	TOTAL		

Chapter 36 Financing the Business

Academic Integration: Mathematics
Spreadsheet Analysis (continued)

- Open your spreadsheet software program on your computer.
- Create a spreadsheet like the one on the previous page.
- In Column C, enter a formula to calculate the subtotal for categories listed. After calculating each subtotal, enter a formula for a total for all startup expenses.
- Save your work. Print out a copy of your screens if you have been instructed to do so.

1. Examine the data for each of the subtotals. Which category has the highest expenses? Which has the lowest?

   _____

   _____

   _____

2. What are the total startup expenses required for this business? Where can you find that information?

   _____

   _____

   _____

3. Many of these expenses are based on estimates. What will be the impact of underestimating specific expenses?

   _____

   _____

   _____

4. Will an entrepreneur be able to borrow funds to cover all these startup expenses?

   _____

   _____

   _____

   _____

   _____

Chapter 36 Financing the Business

Real-World Application
Projected Cash Flow Statement

Directions Study the following information on the recreational vehicle dealership and repair facility called Sports Unlimited. Then use it and the form on the next page to prepare balance sheets for the partnership for two consecutive years.

Year 1

As of July 31, 2—, the business had these assets: $65,000 in the bank, $800 in the till, and $50 in petty cash. Accounts receivable came to $26,300 and inventory to $1,950,000. The firm had prepaid a six-month insurance policy and license fees—a total of $11,000. The business site, three acres owned by the partners, was valued at $525,000. The dealership's building, also owned by the partnership, was appraised at $650,000. Equipment used in the business totaled $55,775; furniture and fixtures were worth $12,425. The business owned one delivery van valued at $28,000.

As of the same date, the business had these liabilities: accounts payable of $620,000; notes totaling $480,000 (one short-term note for $130,000 and another long-term note on the building for $350,000); and taxes payable of $32,800. Accrued payroll was $15,000. The partners owed $225,000 on the property.

Year 2

As of July 31, 2— the business had the following assets: $68,000 in the bank, $1,500 in the till, and $100 in petty cash. Accounts receivable came to $27,700 and inventory to $2,125,000. The business had prepaid insurance and licenses of $12,500. The business site was appraised at $538,000 and the building at $664,000. Equipment used in the business totaled $62,500; furniture and fixtures were worth $13,000. The business's delivery van depreciated to $20,000. It had added a pick-up truck worth $18,000.

As of the same date, the business had these liabilities: accounts payable of $630,000, notes totaling $330,000 (a new short-term note for $90,000 and the old long-term note on the building, now worth $340,000), and taxes payable of $40,500. Accrued payroll was $17,100. The partners owed $200,000 on the property.

Chapter 36 Financing the Business

Real-World Application
Projected Cash Flow Statement *(continued)*

Sports Unlimited Balance Sheet		
Current Assets	2—	2—
Cash		
Accounts receivable		
Inventory		
Fixed Assets		
Real estate and building		
Fixtures and equipment		
Vehicles		
Other Assets		
Licenses and insurance		
Goodwill		
TOTAL ASSETS		
Current Liabilities		
Notes payable (due within one year)		
Accounts payable		
Accrued expenses (payroll)		
Taxes owed		
Long-Term Liabilities		
Notes payable (due after one year)		
Other (property mortgage)		
TOTAL LIABILITIES		
NET WORTH (ASSETS minus LIABILITIES)		
TOTAL LIABILITIES plus NET WORTH should equal ASSETS.		

Name _____ Date _____ Class _____

Chapter 36 Financing the Business

 Real-World Application
Completing Tables

Directions Study the information provided below. Use it and the cash flow form to prepare a cash flow statement for the last six months of Year 1.

Cash Flow Statement Hanna Lukasik is completing a cash flow statement for the last half of her first year. Hanna entered her seventh month in July with $4,200 in the bank. She is projecting $5,000 in sales for July and an increase of $500 in sales receipts for each month thereafter. For the first 3 months, her supply costs (chemicals, styling products, etc.) will total $500 each month. Beginning in October her supply costs will increase to $600 for each remaining month. Part-time labor costs are $1,500 for the first 3 months and will then rise to $1,800 per month.

Overhead (electricity, gas, etc.) is projected to be $300 for each month. The owner will pay herself a salary of $2,500 for the first month and a $100 increase for each month thereafter. Since she owns the building, there is no rent. Insurance of $500 is paid in July and again in October. She will purchase a $2,500 computer during October. Advertising in the phone book costs $200 each month. Phone costs will be $150 for each of the first 3 months, and then $175 for each remaining month. Her personal income taxes are projected to be $350 for each of the first 3 months, then $400 for each remaining month.

Renata European Hair Studio & Spa Projected Cash Flow Statement Statement for the six months ending December 31, 2—						
Month	July	Aug	Sep.	Oct.	Nov.	Dec.
Total Cash Income						
Sales Receipts						
Expenses						
Materials						
Labor						
Overhead						
Salaries						
Rent						
Insurance						
Office Equipment						
Advertising						
Telephone						
Income Tax						
Total Expenses						
NET CASH FLOW						
Beginning Balance						
CASH SURPLUS						
Cash Deeds						

Chapter 36 Financing the Business

DECA Connection
Marketing Manager

Role Play Imagine you are assistant manager for your DECA school store. Your DECA Chapter has just voted to use some of the school store's profits to subsidize DECA members who become eligible to compete at this year's National DECA Conference. At this point in the year, it is important to see just how well the school store is doing and you have instituted a special school credit card for students with a "B" or better grade average. They have 30 days to pay for their credit charges. Therefore, the school store manager has asked that you prepare a profit and loss statement and analyze its operations to date.

Directions The school store manager (judge) wants you to prepare a profit and loss statement for the first three months of operation. Use the following figures in your calculations: Sales $15,600; sales returns $100; cost of goods sold $9,300; depreciation on the sales register $45 and on the fixtures $30; employee salaries $2,880; payroll taxes $432; promotion $775; and miscellaneous expenses $210. To analyze the profit and loss statement, calculate the operating ratios for cost of goods sold, gross profit, promotion, total expenses, and net profit from operations. Also be prepared to explain why the net profit does not reflect the actual cash available at any given time, especially when considering the money needed for the National DECA Conference competitors.

Organize your thoughts around the performance indicators noted below. Use these indicators to jot down your ideas during the preparation period. Time your preparation period to last 15 minutes and your role-play presentation to last a maximum of ten minutes. After your role play, use the performance indicators to evaluate your efforts.

Assessment You will be evaluated on how well you meet the following performance indicators.

Score:

_____ Describe the nature of business records.

_____ Prepare profit and loss statements.

_____ Calculate financial ratios.

_____ Describe the nature of profit and loss statements.

_____ Describe the nature of cash flow statements.

Scoring Each performance indicator equals 20 points (20 × 5 = 100 points).
Excellent (16–20)   **Good** (10–15)   **Fair** (4–9)   **Poor** (0–3)

Chapter 36

Chapter 36 Financing the Business

Study Skills
Learning New Vocabulary

Directions Use the following tips to help improve your vocabulary. Then match the correct term to each definition. Not all words will be used.

Learning New Vocabulary
• Generally, you need to see a new word five times before you can make it an active part of your vocabulary. Skim the chapter to find it. Write your own sentences using the word in context. Create a flashcard or sticky note with the word on it if you are having trouble with a particular key word. Make each new key word your own!
• When a key term is a homonym, such as *principal*, which sounds like *principle*, you need to find a way to spell it correctly. Form your own word picture, such as your money being the *principal* at a money school, while small payments around it are students and teachers. After all, the *principal* is always the last one to leave the school, just as the *principal* is the last part of the loan to be paid.

asset	interest	net worth
balance sheet	liability	personal financial statement
cash flow statement	net income	principal
gross sales	net sales	startup costs

1. The amount left after operating expenses are subtracted from gross profit.

   _____

2. This financial statement is often called a profit and loss statement. _____

3. A summary of your current financial condition. _____

4. Anything of monetary value that you own. _____

5. A monthly plan that shows when you anticipate cash coming into the business and when you expect to pay out cash. _____

6. The difference between the assets of a business and its liabilities. _____

7. The total of all sales for any period of time. _____

8. A debt that you owe. _____

9. A projection of how much money you will need for your new business's first year of operation. _____

10. The amount that you borrow. _____

Chapter 36 Financing the Business

 Study Skills
Test Preparation

Directions Study the Test-Prep Tips and think about how you can use them to improve your test scores. Then complete each sentence using the correct term or phrase from the list below. (Not all terms will be used.)

Test-Prep Tips
• Just before taking a test, try to avoid talking about it. Test anxiety can be contagious.
• When taking a test, do not use a mechanical pencil, pen, or correction fluid. Use a soft lead No. 2 pencil to mark your answers, and make sure you have a good eraser with you.
• Look for key words in test directions and questions such as: *choose, describe, explain, compare, identify, similar, except, not,* and *but.*

cost of goods sold	fixed expenses	net profit (or loss)
income statement	net income from operations	interest
variable expenses	net pay	gross sales
gross pay	total expenses	operating expenses

1. If your company sells only on a cash basis, then your _____ will be the total of your cash sales.

2. _____ are divided into variable and fixed expenses.

3. The total amount spent to produce or buy the merchandise to be sold is called the _____.

4. _____ change every month based upon the needs of the business.

5. The amount earned by an employee is that person's _____.

6. Costs which stay the same for a certain period of time are called _____.

7. _____ is found by subtracting total expenses from gross profit.

8. _____ is what an employee receives after deductions for taxes, insurance, and voluntary deductions.

9. The amount of money left over after federal, state, and local taxes are subtracted represents a business's _____.

10. If you borrow money to start a business, you will also have to pay _____.

Chapter 36 Financing the Business

 Study Skills
Practice Test

Directions Circle the letter of the word or phrase that best answers the question.

1. What is the primary goal for a new entrepreneur to prepare financial statements?
   a. to practice for the new business
   b. to determine a company's assets
   c. to prove that the new owners will not be dependent on their parents
   d. to determine the amount of money needed to borrow to startup and operate the new business

2. Why do entrepreneurs have to include their personal financial statements when discussing business plans and financial statements for their new businesses?
   a. they do not have to, the bank supplies all the money they need
   b. because they will need to invest their own money into the business
   c. to prove that they know how to earn and save money
   d. to show that they have lots of liability and few assets

3. Which would not be part of the start-up cost?
   a. income statements
   b. installation charges
   c. monthly rent
   d. advertising

4. Which shows how to find gross profit?
   a. net sales − total expenses
   b. total sales − total expenses
   c. net sales − cost of goods sold
   d. cost of goods + total sales

5. How would an entrepreneur know if he has a net profit after federal, state, and local taxes are subtracted?
   a. the net profit before taxes shows a profit
   b. the net profit before taxes shows a loss
   c. the net profit after taxes shows a profit
   d. the net profit after taxes shows a loss

6. If a lender wishes to rate how quickly a business could turn its assets into cash, what type of system would it use?
   a. balance sheet
   b. activity ratio
   c. cash flow statements
   d. profitability ratio

Chapter 37 Identifying Career Opportunities

Note Taking
Main Ideas and Supporting Details

Directions As you read, write key words and short phrases in the Cues column. Write notes, facts, and main ideas in the Note Taking column. Then summarize the section in the Summary box.

Cues	Note Taking
• Define Goals	• Define Goals
• Careers in Marketing	• Careers in Marketing

Summary

Chapter 37

Chapter 37 Identifying Career Opportunities

Academic Integration: Mathematics
Spreadsheet Analysis

Employment Trends The printout below shows employment figures in 2002 for all occupations. Projected employment figures for 2012 are also shown.

	A	B	C	D
1	Occupational Areas	Employment in 2002	Projected Employment in 2012	Projected Percentage Increase/Decrease
2	Chapter 37 Identifying Career Opportunities			
3	TOTAL, All Occupations	132,353,000	150,927,000	
4	All Executive & Managerial Occupations	13,542,000	15,866,000	
5	Advertising Services	291,000	324,000	
6	Travel & Tourism Marketing	156,000	179,000	
7	Food Marketing	249,000	294,000	
8	Restaurant Marketing	386,000	430,000	
9	Financial Services Marketing	343,000	498,000	
10	Business Services Marketing	800,000	946,000	
11	Fashion Merchandising	589,000	757,000	
12	Sports & Entertainment Marketing	207,000	202,000	
13	Retail Marketing	482,000	620,000	
14	Apparel and Accessories	271,000	315,000	
15	Vehicles & Petroleum Marketing	232,000	251,000	

Directions Follow these steps to analyze the spreadsheet. Then answer the questions that follow.
- Open your spreadsheet software program on your computer.
- Create a spreadsheet like the one above using your spreadsheet software.
- Enter a formula for All Occupations to calculate the projected percentage increase or decrease in the number of jobs between 2002 and 2012.

- Copy the formula to appropriate cells in all remaining rows. After completing your calculations, save your work to a new file.
- Print out a copy of your work if your teacher has instructed you to do so.

1. What is the projected percentage increase/decrease for All Occupations, 2002 and 2012?

   _____

2. Between 2002 and 2012, which occupations are projected or expected to increase?

   _____

   _____

   _____

Chapter 37 Identifying Career Opportunities

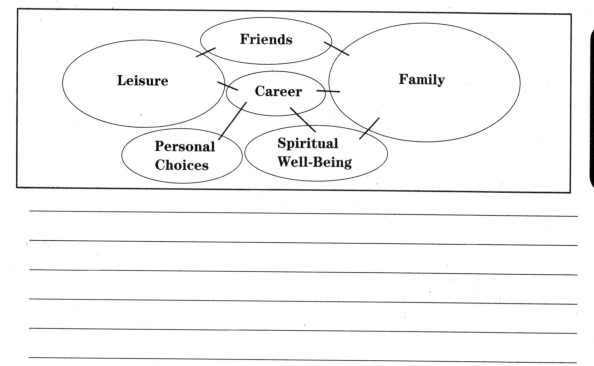

Real-World Application
Lifestyle Choices

Directions Study the lifestyle pattern below. On the lines following the diagram, describe a real or fictional person whose lifestyle fits this pattern.

_____

_____

_____

_____

_____

_____

Directions In the space below, draw a diagram of your own lifestyle either now or as you wish it to be ten years from now. On the lines below the box, provide a brief explanation of why you structured your lifestyle pattern the way you did.

_____

_____

Chapter 37

Chapter 37 Identifying Career Opportunities

 Real-World Application
Career Choices

Directions Select a career that interests you, and fill out the following questionnaire. Then decide if it might be a suitable career choice for you.

Career _____

A. Values

   1. Does this career match my values? Explain.

   _____

B. Salaries and Benefits

   1. What is the salary range from beginning to highest level in this career?

   _____

   2. Would my salary be adequate to support my lifestyle in 5, 10, or 20 years? Explain.

   _____

   3. Will this career provide the benefits I need? Explain.

   _____

C. Education/Training Required

   1. What requirements for pursuing this career have I already completed?

   _____

   2. What requirements must I complete before I can enter this career?

   _____

   3. How will I pay for this?

   _____

D. Skills and Aptitudes Required

   1. Do I have the skills and aptitudes needed to succeed in this career? Specify.

   _____

E. Work Environment and Relationships

   1. Is the working environment satisfactory? Explain.

   _____

F. Career Outlook

   1. Will there be a demand for this career when I am ready?

   _____

   2. Is this a possible career choice?

   _____

Chapter 37

Chapter 37 Identifying Career Opportunities

 DECA Connection
Marketing Manager

Role Play You are to assume the role of employee of a large advertising agency. Your agency has formed a partnership with a local high school to provide unpaid internships for high school students interested in advertising careers. Your supervisor (judge) has asked you to develop plans for four internships for presentation to the rest of the management team and the high school counselors. You are to present your ideas to your supervisor.

Directions Organize your thoughts around the performance indicators noted above. Use these performance indicators to jot down your ideas during the preparation period. Time your preparation period to last 15 minutes and your role-play presentation to last a maximum of ten minutes. After your role play, use the performance indicators to evaluate your efforts.

Assessment You will be evaluated on how well you meet the following performance indicators.

Score:

_____   Assess personal interests and skills needed for success in business.

_____   Describe techniques for obtaining work experience.

_____   Analyze employer expectations in the business environment.

_____   Explain employment opportunities in marketing.

_____   Make oral presentations.

Scoring Each performance indicator equals 20 points (20 × 5 = 100 points).
Excellent (16–20)   **Good** (10–15)   **Fair** (4–9)   **Poor** (0–3)

Chapter 37 Identifying Career Opportunities

 Study Skills
Improving Study Habits

Directions Use the following tips to help improve your study habits. Then review Chapter 37 using the tips as you answer the questions that follow. If the statement is true, circle **T**. If the statement is false, circle **F** and rewrite the statement so that it is true.

Study Habits
• Developing good study habits will help you become a better student. The first thing you need to do is take responsibility for your actions.
• Do not allow yourself to become distracted by friends and fellow students. Keep in mind the bigger picture. Know what you have to do and when it needs to be done.
• When you put your best effort in your work, then you have succeeded.

1. The *Occupational Outlook Handbook* describes what workers do on the job, working, conditions, the training and education needed, earnings, and expected job prospects in a wide range of occupations.   T   F

_____

2. An occupational area offers students direct work experience and exposure to various aspects of a career, either with or without pay.   T   F

_____

3. Your values are your natural ability or talent, or represent your potential to learn a certain skill.   T   F

_____

4. A specific goal is stated in exact terms and includes some details.   T   F

_____

5. The small steps you take to get from where you are now to where you want to be are called "realistic goals."   T   F

_____

_____

6. The kind of life you would like to live is called your "lifestyle."   T   F

_____

7. A realistic goal is one that you may not be able to reach.   T   F

_____

Chapter 37 Identifying Career Opportunities

 Study Skills
Test Preparation

Directions Study the Test-Prep Tips and think about how you can use them to improve your test scores. Then use what you have learned in Chapter 37 to answer the questions below.

Test-Prep Tips
• Make sure that you study for an open book test. You need to be able to locate the information you need in your textbook or notes quickly
• It is a good idea to have your materials organized before the test. It may help to list dates, data or formulas separately so the ideas can be retrieved quickly
• Be sure to read the questions on the test carefully. Do not waste your time. Answer the easier questions first then move on to the more difficult ones.

1. What are six steps in the decision making process that can help guide career choices?

_____

_____

_____

2. What are some things that will influence your lifestyle as an adult?

_____

_____

_____

3. How will having a progressive series of goals help you to reach your ultimate career goals? How could it lead to you changing your career goal?

_____

_____

_____

4. What information is included in a job description? What is its purpose?

_____

_____

_____

5. What are some of the benefits of a career in marketing? What are some drawbacks?

_____

_____

Chapter 37

Chapter 37 Identifying Career Opportunities

 **Test Taking**
Practice Test

Directions Complete the following statements by filling in the blanks using words or phrases from the chapter. Note: In some cases, there may be more than one correct answer.

1. Deciding whether you would prefer to live in the city or the country, or if you value leisure time over work, is part of setting _____.

2. When you make a survey of your values, interests, skills and aptitudes, personality, preferred work environment, and relationship preferences, you are doing a form of

   _____.

3. At the center of most people's lifestyle goals will probably be their _____.

4. In deciding which career is ideal for you, you should assess whether you relate best to data, _____, or _____.

5. Learning about a particular career by talking to someone who works in that career is known as an _____.

6. As you look at a career, it is important to ask whether it will provide the

   _____ support for the lifestyle you want.

7. More than anything else, jobs are distinguished by their _____ and

   _____.

8. Trying a job to help you learn about it is called _____.

9. A personal career profile allows you to compare your self-assessment side by side with a particular _____.

10. In order to avoid being locked into an unsuitable career, you should make your decisions

   _____.

Chapter 37

Chapter 38 Finding and Applying for a Job

 Note Taking
Main Ideas and Supporting Details

Directions As you read, write key words and short phrases in the Cues column.
Write notes, facts, and main ideas in the Note Taking column. Then summarize
the section in the Summary box.

Cues	Note Taking
• Finding a Job	• Finding a Job
• Applying for a Job	• Applying for a Job

Summary

Chapter 38

Chapter 38 Finding and Applying for a Job

Academic Integration: English Language Arts
Word Processing Application

Applying for a Job Imagine that you have just graduated from high school and are looking for a job. You see the following help wanted ad in the local newspaper, and decide to write a letter of application.

Marketing/Sales Trainee

Advertising specialty and promotional products company seeks a motivated, customer-minded person for inside sales trainee position. Must be outgoing, organized, a team player, and have good communication skills. Salary, full benefits, and a sales territory position in 1–3 years. Send résumé to: Karen Salo, Director of Human Resources, The Daily News, 28 N. First Street, Springfield, IL 60702.

To help you get started writing your letter, the correct form to use in addressing your letter is shown below:

Month Day, Year

Ms. Karen Salo
Director of Human Resources
The Daily News
28 N. First Street
Springfield, IL 60702

Dear Ms. Salo:

Directions Follow these steps to complete the letter. Then answer the questions that follow.
- Open your word processing software program on your computer.
- Write a letter expressing interest in this position and describing why your skills fit the needs of the job. When you are finished, proofread your work and make any corrections.
- Save your letter.
- Print out a copy of your work if your teacher has instructed you to do so.

Chapter 38 Finding and Applying for a Job

 Academic Integration: English Language Arts
Word Processing Application *(continued)*

1. Compare the skills mentioned in your finished letter with the skills described in the ad. How does your letter highlight the skills that are needed for the job?

_____

_____

_____

_____

_____

_____

2. Does your opening paragraph grab the attention of a reader? Is your letter accurate in spelling and grammar? Could your letter actually be sent to a prospective employer? Why or why not?

_____

_____

_____

_____

_____

_____

3. Some newspaper ads give only a post office box number for replies. In such a case, whom should you address in the salutation?

_____

_____

_____

_____

_____

_____

Chapter 38

Chapter 38 Finding and Applying for a Job

Real-World Application
Following Up on Job Leads

Directions The classified ads below describe two jobs in marketing. In each ad, the information about the job is incomplete. Answer the questions below to help you develop a plan to follow up on these job leads. If the information is not given, state that it is not given.

A. ABC Marketing
Part-time customer help. Contact Bonnie 555-8617. Call for appointment 8-10 a.m.

B. Marketing
CAREER MINDED?
Ecologically sound product brokerage seeks career-oriented individuals to help fill entry-level positions with potential for management. Attitude more important than experience. 818-555-0331

1. What is the name of the company that is advertising?

   A. _____

   B. _____

2. How would knowing the name of the company help you in preparing to submit an application for the job?

   _____

   _____

   _____

3. Does the job involve dealing with a product or a service?

   A. _____

   B. _____

4. Both of the ads list telephone numbers for contact. Make a list of four or more questions that you would ask over the phone to help you in preparing to apply for these positions.

   _____

   _____

   _____

   _____

   _____

Chapter 38 Finding and Applying for a Job

Real-World Application
Preparing for an Interview

Directions Preparing for an interview is an important step in the process of getting a job. In many interviews, the interviewer will say something like "Tell me about yourself." This can present an awkward moment unless you are prepared to answer in a way that will make the interviewer want to hire you. Think about how you would respond to such a request and write your response on the lines below.

_____

_____

_____

_____

_____

_____

_____

_____

_____

_____

_____

_____

_____

_____

_____

_____

_____

_____

_____

_____

_____

_____

_____

Chapter 38

Chapter 38 Finding and Applying for a Job

 **DECA Connection**
Career Counselor

Role Play Imagine you are an employee at a career-counseling firm. Your supervisor (judge) has asked you to prepare an oral presentation on using the Internet for gathering career information as well as for job searching. Your presentation should include an explanation of how to use online government career resources as well as how to search for specific jobs using search engines and online career sites.

Directions Organize your thoughts around the performance indicators noted below. Use these indicators to jot down your ideas during the preparation period. Time your preparation period to last 15 minutes and your role-play presentation to last a maximum of 10 minutes. After your role play, use the performance indicators to evaluate your efforts.

Assessment You will be evaluated on how well you meet the following performance indicators:
- Utilize job-search strategies.
- Demonstrate basic search skills on the Web.
- Explain employment opportunities in business.
- Identify sources of career information.
- Make oral presentations.

_____

_____

_____

_____

_____

_____

_____

_____

_____

_____

_____

_____

_____

_____

_____

_____

Chapter 38 Finding and Applying for a Job

 **DECA Connection**
Career Counselor (continued)

Scoring Each performance indicator equals 20 points (20 × 5 = 100 points).
Excellent (16–20)   **Good** (10–15)   **Fair** (4–9)   **Poor** (0–3)

Utilize job-search strategies.   **Score** _____

_____

_____

_____

Demonstrate basic search skills on the Web Score.   **Score** _____

_____

_____

_____

Explain employment opportunities in business.   **Score** _____

_____

_____

_____

_____

Identify sources of career information.   **Score** _____

_____

_____

_____

_____

Make oral presentations.   **Score** _____

_____

_____

_____

_____

Chapter 38

Chapter 38 Finding and Applying for a Job

Study Skills
Learning New Vocabulary

Directions Use the following tips to help you learn new vocabulary. Then, study the lists below and the Magic Square puzzle block. Notice that each lettered vocabulary term has a matching lettered cell in the magic square. To solve the puzzle, select a definition for each term from the numbered list. Then write each definition's number in the appropriately labeled puzzle cell. If you have correctly matched all the terms and definitions, the total of the numbers will be the same across each row and down each column.

Learning New Vocabulary
• Forgetting vocabulary already learned is one of the biggest problems students have.
• Use games and activities to review new words, and strengthen your vocabulary.

A. public employment agencies

B. standard English

C. cover letter

D. job lead

E. private employment agencies

F. staffing/temporary agencies

G. résumé

H. references

I. networking

1. Document that summarizes your personal information, education, and experience.

2. The formal style of writing and speaking you have learned in school.

3. Staffing services that hire you and assign you to a company.

4. These charge a fee to help you find a job.

5. The art of building alliances.

6. Tax supported places where you can find job hunting help and leads.

7. A letter of application without information on education and experience.

8. Information about a job opening.

9. People who know your work habits and will recommend you.

A	B	C
D	E	F
G	H	I

Magic number: All rows and columns add up to _____.

Chapter 38

Chapter 38 Finding and Applying for a Job

 Study Skills
Test Preparation

Directions Study the Test-Prep Tips and think about how you can use them to improve your test scores. Then complete the following statements by filling in the blanks using words or phrases from Chapter 38.

Test-Prep Tips
• Have a nutritious snack before a test. Having food in your stomach will give you energy.
• Stay away from heavy foods which can make you sleepy.

1. Before you can legally work, you may need a _____.

2. When obvious sources of job leads have dried up, _____ is a way of finding more leads on your own.

3. _____ is finding and using contacts among all the people you know.

4. When speaking with prospective employers, it is expected that you will use

 _____.

5. In the employment history section of a job application form, you should list your employment in _____.

6. Frank thought of several adults who would vouch for his honesty and willingness to work and who could be _____ for him.

7. When you write a _____ to a prospective employer, you are essentially writing a sales pitch.

8. A _____ helps an employer during an interview by organizing all the facts about you that relate to the job you want.

9. The decision to hire an applicant is often based on the _____.

10. During an interview, grooming, body language, and speech all combine to make a

 _____.

Chapter 38

Chapter 38 Finding and Applying for a Job

Test Taking
Practice Test

Directions Circle the letter of the word or phrase that best answers the question.

1. Which is another term for building alliances?
   - **a.** cooperative education
   - **b.** staffing
   - **c.** direct marketing
   - **d.** networking

2. Which is a good thing to do before writing a letter of inquiry about a job opening?
   - **a.** mail in a résumé
   - **b.** conduct research about the company
   - **c.** phone for an appointment
   - **d.** complete an application

3. Which would be the best place to apply if you wanted a job for a few weeks?
   - **a.** staffing/temporary agency
   - **b.** public employment agency
   - **c.** private employment agency
   - **d.** company personnel office

4. Which is NOT usually a reason for hiring a job candidate?
   - **a.** How well the candidate can do the job.
   - **b.** How willing the candidate is to do the job.
   - **c.** How many other jobs the candidate has had.
   - **d.** How well the candidate will fit in.

5. Which should you do in a cover letter?
   - **a.** Write on colored paper so your letter stands out in a stack.
   - **b.** Describe any special qualifications you have for the job.
   - **c.** Avoid discussing experience so you can explain it better in the interview.
   - **d.** Describe both your strengths and weaknesses.

6. Which is probably not a good way to do research about a company you are thinking of contacting about a job opening?
   - **a.** Read company brochures or catalogs.
   - **b.** Ask others in your network about the company.
   - **c.** Visit the company's Web site.
   - **d.** Call with questions for someone in the Human Resources Department.

NOTES

NOTES